PEOPLE AND COMPUTERS:
How to Evaluate Your
Company's New Technology

ELLIS HORWOOD BOOKS IN INFORMATION TECHNOLOGY
General Editor: Dr JOHN M. M. PINKERTON, Principal, J. & H. Pinkerton Associates, Surrey (Consultants in Information Technology), and formerly Manager of Strategic Requirements, ICL

EXPERT SYSTEMS IN BUSINESS: A Practical Approach
M. BARRETT, Expertech Limited, Slough, and A. C. BEEREL, Lysia Limited, London
ELECTRONIC DATA PROCESSING, Vols. 1 and 2*
M. BECKER, R. HABERFELLNER and G. LIEBETRAU, Zurich, Switzerland
EXPERT SYSTEMS: Strategic Implications and Applications
A. C. BEEREL, Lysia Limited, London
APPLICATIONS OF OPTICAL STORAGE*
A. BRADLEY, Ind. Adv. Congleton, Cheshire
SOFTWARE ENGINEERING ENVIRONMENTS
P. BRERETON, Department of Computer Science, University of Keele
SMART CARDS: Their Principles, Practice and Applications*
R. BRIGHT, Information Technology Strategies International Limited, Orpington, Kent
PRACTICAL MACHINE TRANSLATION*
D. CLARKE and U. MAGNUSSON-MURRAY, Department of Applied Computing and Mathematics, Cranfield Institute of Technology, Bedford
ENCYCLOPAEDIA OF IT*
V. CLAUS and A. SCHWILL, FRG
KNOWLEDGE-BASED SYSTEMS: Implications for Human–Computer Interfaces
D. CLEAL, PA Computers and Telecommunications, London, and N. HEATON, Central Computer and Telecommunications Agency, London
DISTRUBITED CONTROL IN A BLACKBOARD SYSTEM*
I. CRAIG, Dept. of Computer Science, University of Warwick, Coventry
KNOWLEDGE ELICITATION: Principles, Techniques, Applications*
D. DIAPER, Section of Psychology, Liverpool Polytechnic
KNOWLEDGE-BASED MANAGEMENT SUPPORT SYSTEMS*
G. I. DOUKIDIS, F. LAND and G. MILLER, Department of Information Management, London Business School, London
KNOWLEDGE-BASED SYSTEMS: Applications in Administrative Government
P. DUFFIN, CCTA, HM Treasury, Riverwalk, London
MULTI-LINGUAL SPEECH ASSESSMENT*
A. FOURCIN, Dept. of Phonetics and Linguistics, University College London
KNOWLEDGE ENGINEERING FOR EXPERT SYSTEMS
M. GREENWELL, Expert Systems International, Oxford
EXPERT SYSTEMS: Safety and Risks*
E. HOLLNAGEL, Computer Resources International, Denmark
KNOWLEDGE-BASED EXPERT SYSTEMS IN INDUSTRY
J. KRIZ, Head of AI Group, Brown Boveri Research Systems, Switzerland
ARTIFICIAL INTELLIGENCE: Current Applications*
A. MATTHEWS and J. RODDY, Aregon International Ltd, London
INFORMATION TECHNOLOGY: An Overview*
J. M. M. PINKERTON, J & H Pinkerton Associates, Esher, Surrey
PRACTICAL TOOLS IN HUMAN–COMPUTER INTERFACES*
S. RAVDEN and G. JOHNSON, MRC/ESRC Social and Applied Psychology Unit, University of Sheffield
EXPERT SYSTEMS IN THE ORGANIZATION: An Introduction for Decision-makers
S. SAVORY, Nixdorf Computer AG, FRG
ARTIFICAL INTELLIGENCE AND EXPERT SYSTEMS
S. SAVORY, Nixdorf Computer AG, FRG
COMPUTING: The Next Generation
P. SALENIEKS, Dept. of Mathematics and Computer Science, University College of Swansea, Swansea
BUILDING EXPERT SYSTEMS: Cognitive Emulation
P. E. SLATTER, Telecomputing plc, Oxford
SOFTWARE MANAGEMENT*
H. M. SNEED, FRG
SPEECH AND LANGUAGE-BASED COMMUNICATION WITH MACHINES:
Towards the Conversational Computer
J. A. WATERWORTH and M. TALBOT, Human Factors Division, British Telecom Research Laboratories, Ipswich
THE IMPLEMENTATION OF COMPUTER SYSTEMS
R. J. WHIDDETT, Dept. of Computing, University of Lancaster

* In preparation

PEOPLE AND COMPUTERS:

How to Evaluate Your Company's New Technology

CHRIS CLEGG, PETER WARR, THOMAS GREEN, ANDREW MONK,
NIGEL KEMP, GORDON ALLISON and MARK LANSDALE
in collaboration with
COLIN POTTS, REG SELL and IAN COLE

ELLIS HORWOOD LIMITED
Publishers · Chichester

Halsted Press: a division of
JOHN WILEY & SONS
New York · Chichester · Brisbane · Toronto

First published in 1988 by
ELLIS HORWOOD LIMITED
Market Cross House, Cooper Street,
Chichester, West Sussex, PO19 1EB, England
*The publisher's colophon is reproduced from James Gillison's drawing of the ancient
Market Cross, Chichester.*

Distributors:

Australia and New Zealand:
JACARANDA WILEY LIMITED
GPO Box 859, Brisbane, Queensland 4001, Australia

Canada:
JOHN WILEY & SONS CANADA LIMITED
22 Worcester Road, Rexdale, Ontario, Canada

Europe and Africa:
JOHN WILEY & SONS LIMITED
Baffins Lane, Chichester, West Sussex, England

North and South America and the rest of the world:
Halsted Press: a division of
JOHN WILEY & SONS
605 Third Avenue, New York, NY 10158, USA

South-East Asia
JOHN WILEY & SONS (SEA) PTE LIMITED
37 Jalan Pemimpin # 05–04
Block B, Union Industrial Building, Singapore 2057

Indian Subcontinent
WILEY EASTERN LIMITED
4835/24 Ansari Road
Daryaganj, New Delhi 110002, India

© **1988 C. Clegg/Ellis Horwood Limited**

British Library Cataloguing in Publication Data
Clegg, Chris, *1948–*
People and computers.
1. Companies. Technological innovation. Management
I. Title
658.4′063

Library of Congress Card No. 88–21954

ISBN 0–7458–0419–5 (Ellis Horwood Limited)
ISBN 0–470–21207–1 (Halsted Press)

Printed in Great Britain by Unwin Bros., Woking

Table of contents

Preface   ix

1. Looking behind the initial problems   1
   Some typical problems   2
   Case study: The engineering factory   2
   Underlying issues   7
   The principles of evaluation   12
   The structure of the book   16

Introducing Chapters 2 to 7   **19**

2. Equipment and working conditions   21
   2.1 Meeting essential requirements   21
   2.2 Compatibility between components   26
   2.3 Reliability and repairs   28
   2.4 Maturity and obsolescence   31
   2.5 System security   34
   2.6 Working conditions   36

3. Usability   41
   3.1 Ease of learning   41
   3.2 Being in control   48
   3.3 Degree of effort   51
   3.4 System speed   54
   3.5 Getting information in and out   57
   3.6 Errors and error correction   59
   3.7 Avoiding serious errors   62

4. Job quality and operator performance   64

   4.1 Users' control over their work   65
   4.2 Skills required   69
   4.3 Variety in the job   73
   4.4 Work demands   75
   4.5 Uncertainty   77
   4.6 Pay   79
   4.7 Communications and social contact   81
   4.8 Health and safety   83
   4.9 Users' performance and attitudes   84

5. The wider organization and overall effectiveness   87
   5.1 Organizational structure   88
   5.2 Bureaucracy and decision-making   92
   5.3 Communications   94
   5.4 Selection and training   97
   5.5 Industrial relations   100
   5.6 Pay and career progression   102
   5.7 Job losses   105
   5.8 Organizational performance and morale   107

6. How to carry out evaluation   110
   Managing evaluation   110
   Basic methods of evaluation   114
   1. Interviews   115
   2. Meetings   116
   3. Working parties   116
   Initial diagnoses   117

7. Managing change   135
   7.1 Developing a strategy for change   136
   7.2 Specifying your requirements   139
   7.3 Assessing financial costs and benefits   142
   7.4 Gaining commitment and managing conflict   146
   7.5 Providing organizational support   150
   7.6 Changing over from old to new   152
   7.7 Reviewing progress against plans   154
   Concluding advice about the management of change   154

Introducing Chapters 8 to 12   **157**

8. Specialist methods of information-gathering   158
   1. Questionnaires   158
   2. System walk-through   162
   3. Formal observation   164
   4. User diaries   166
   5. System logging   167
   6. Task analysis   168
   7. Comparative testing   170

8. Company records   172
Overview   173

9. More detailed questions about equipment and working conditions   174
A checklist about system security (2.5)   174
Four checklists about working conditions (2.6)   175
Two questionnaires about equipment (2.6)   187

10. More detailed questions about usability   189
Three checklists about ease of learning (3.1)   189
A checklist about being in control (3.2)   192
A checklist about degree of effort (3.3)   193
A checklist about getting information in and out (3.5)   194
A checklist about errors and error correction (3.6)   197

11. More detailed questions about job quality and performance   199
A questionnaire about users' control over their work (4.1) 200
A questionnaire about skills required (4.2)   202
A questionnaire about variety in the job (4.3)   202
A questionnaire about work demands (4.4)   203
A questionnaire about uncertainty (4.5)   205
A questionnaire about pay (4.6)   206
A questionnaire about communications and social contact (4.7)   207
Three questionnaires about health and safety (4.8)   208
A checklist about users' performance (4.9)   210
Three questionnaires about users' attitudes (4.9)   211

12. More detailed questions about organizational aspects and overall
effectiveness   215
A questionnaire about organizational structure (5.1)   216
A questionnaire about bureaucracy and decision-making (5.2)   217
A questionnaire about communications (5.3)   218
Two checklists about communications (5.3)   219
A checklist about selection and training (5.4)   221
A questionnaire about industrial relations (5.5)   223
A questionnaire about pay and career progression (5.6)   225
A checklist about job evaluation (5.6)   226
A checklist about job losses (5.7)   227
A checklist about organizational performance (5.8)   228
Questionnaires about employee morale (5.8)   230

Additional reading   231

Some sources of information   237

Subject index   241

Preface

Computers offer exciting opportunities to companies of all kinds. Yet problems often arise from inadequate attention to their human aspects.

This book aims to redress the balance, taking a positive approach to the human and organizational features of computer systems. How can problems in those areas be defined and tackled, and how can improvements most effectively be made? How can purchasers anticipate possible difficulties and take steps to avoid them?

The book is primarily intended for two sorts of reader: those whose company uses one or more computer systems, and who are experiencing problems; and those who are considering an investment, for the first time or as an extension to their present equipment. We have classified and described the causes of typical human and organizational problems, listed key evaluation questions, and suggested a variety of possible improvements. For potential purchasers, our goal is to help in the identification of features to be checked before an investment is made, and to describe procedures to be followed in the management of change.

The book does not set out to answer the broader question of whether or not a company should invest in new technology at all. That depends upon the special circumstances of each company and its market. Rather, we seek to help people to solve problems with their current computer systems, and to assist in choices between possible purchases.

Two smaller groups of readers might also benefit from the book. Consultants working in the field will be familiar with much of the material, but the systematic listing of issues and the provision of checklists and other aids to evaluation might help some of this group in their work. Similarly, designers of new systems may find parts of the book helpful, to remind them of important human issues to be considered at the design and development stages.

Whatever your initial motivation, the book can be used in three ways. It can be read from cover to cover, following through the themes as they are developed. Or you might prefer merely to dip into a range of sections to discover if their content interests you.

The third type of use is the one we would most like to see. The book can serve as a tool in its own right, to be applied throughout an evaluation exercise. You can draw upon it in thinking about how to start, in gathering information, and in creating change. We believe that the material which follows is unique in several respects: in its broad perspective, its identification and description of thirty major evaluation issues, its presentation of several hundred questions which might be asked during evaluation, its advice about the management of change, and its coverage of specialist procedures for readers who wish to examine their systems in particular depth. We have also included a brief guide to the research literature, for those who wish to pursue further the methods outlined here.

As a group, we have been very fortunate whilst undertaking this work. The United Kingdom Alvey Directorate funded a substantial part of our endeavour under their programme of research and development into the human-computer interface. The support of our various employers has also been invaluable, since writing the book has been a collaborative effort lasting three years. Thanks are also due to the people and organizations who have helped us by discussing and trying out our ideas and materials, by suggesting illustrations, and by reading earlier versions of the chapters. We would especially like to thank Digital Equipment Company in Reading for the considerable help given in researching this book. Finally, we are indebted to June Staniland of the MRC/ESRC Social and Applied Psychology Unit, who has administered and supported us so effectively. We are extremely grateful to all those people.

1

Looking behind the initial problems

Is your company's computer-based equipment working at its full business potential? Is it effective in meeting your objectives? Is the investment providing a good financial return? Unfortunately, many companies are disappointed with the contribution made by their new technology, and are seeking to understand what lies behind their relative failure. This book seeks to help in those cases, examining computer technology through the process of 'evaluation', and emphasizing human and organizational issues.

Evaluation can have several purposes, but its main function is to make *improvements*, either in the face of problems or when taking advantage of opportunities. The approach described here will assist you in gathering and interpreting information, identifying areas of possible improvement, and introducing change to increase effectiveness.

The approach is also appropriate for companies intending to purchase computer-based equipment, whether on a small or a large scale. You may be considering one or more systems and wish to identify key performance criteria. The evaluation procedures described in this book may be applied to make a more informed and rational choice, avoiding problems when the system is later implemented. The 'people' issues that should be examined by potential purchasers are very much the same as those facing the evaluators of current equipment, and we will link them together in the chapters which follow.

Our aim is to help companies to carry out evaluation through asking the questions which are important in their own case. Internal resources and skills can be harnessed through the procedures outlined, and improvements will be possible in most settings. However, evaluating a computer-based system will raise technical, psychological and organizational issues, which may benefit from additional expertise. If specialist staff are not available from within your own company, you should when necessary seek advice from suppliers, consultants or other knowledgeable people. Nevertheless, if you first work through the framework we offer, your need for additional expertise will be reduced, and you will be better able to devise questions for those experts who are required.

SOME TYPICAL PROBLEMS

Employees in many companies can readily describe difficulties they experience with new technology. Statements of the following kind are very common.

(1) We have spent a great deal of money investing in the most modern computerized manufacturing technology, but a year later there is no way we have got it operating effectively. We were aiming for better productivity, better quality and faster throughput times, but we haven't achieved any of these.

(2) Since we got the computer, staff turnover has gone completely out of hand. People are not happy with the job, so they leave.

(3) Every time the computer breaks down, everything grinds to a halt. I never thought it could cause so much trouble.

(4) We have spent a great deal of money on this system, and yet people are still using the old technology whenever they get a chance.

(5) The system we introduced some years ago works well, and now we want to upgrade it. The problem is how to choose from all those alternatives.

(6) We changed the computer last year. It's certainly an improvement, but introducing it was a real headache. We must learn how to reduce the disruption next time.

(7) The people who use it complain that it's tiring. Some of them are even worried about their health.

(8) The equipment works, but it seems to need an enormous amount of support. We are spending much more on supervision, maintenance and planning than we ever expected.

(9) It has completely changed my job. I used to feel responsible. Now the work is so simple they could replace me with a machine.

(10) I can get it to do what I want, but I am sure there must be easier ways.

(11) The work I have been doing since they introduced the computer is much more skilled. I think I should be paid more.

(12) I like using it, but you have to keep your wits about you. You think you understand how it works and then it does something quite unexpected.

These statements are unfortunately quite typical, and each one can be viewed as a symptom of deeper-seated issues. Let us take a closer look at one of them.

CASE STUDY: THE ENGINEERING FACTORY

The first statement came from the Production Director of a light engineering factory, in discussion with one of the authors of this book. In order to identify the underlying issues, several other members of the company were interviewed. The picture that emerged is quite a common one, with parallels in many other settings. You might recognize similarities in your own office or factory.

Here are some excerpts from the interviews, starting with the original statement.

Tony Barrett, Production Director
'We have spent a great deal of money investing in the most modern computerized manufacturing technology, but a year later there is no way we have got it operating effectively. We were aiming for better productivity, better quality and faster throughput times, but we haven't achieved any of these.'
   Tony's statement continues:
'Privately, I must say that, if I had put the actual performance we are achieving into my original capital expenditure submission, we would never have got the funding—there just isn't the return on investment. My board were right behind me, and were keen that I should specify our goals and exactly what the investment could do to help our business. I really believed that we would reduce manufacturing costs, defects and throughput times, all of which would have generated higher sales and a better image.'

Chris Stopwood, Department Manager
'I gather Tony has told you how disappointed we have been with our new computer-controlled machines. We bought four of them and they cost a small fortune. Perhaps we got off on the wrong foot from the start. Because people in the department were nervous about the new technology, I asked for volunteers to work the machines, and eight of our existing machinists came forward to be trained up. The suppliers seemed to do a reasonable training job, but the operators now say it was little help to them in solving the problems we have with breakdowns and machine downtime. I think perhaps we recruited the wrong people and then made it worse by giving them inadequate training. I must say our productivity for this first year has been awful, and I've had a lot of hammer from our quality people. They say too many defects are getting through, more than when we were a basic manual operation.'

Doreen Manning, Trade Union Representative
'Yes, our performance has been poor. There have been lots of problems, but not all of them have been the operators' fault. Chris decided they should monitor the machines and call on the engineers if there were any problems. "Let the experts sort it out", he said. But at first the operators didn't know who to call—they didn't know if it was a mechanical problem or something wrong in the software. So they often called the wrong engineer. Pretty soon everyone got fed up, because the engineers often said it was somebody else's work, and even when it was their job they didn't always know what to do. Their training had been no better than ours. Very quickly the machinists could solve most of the problems anyway, but they weren't allowed to.'

Peter Plant, Machine Operator
'Yes, we have become machine-minders. But another problem is that the suppliers fitted safety glass on the tops of the machines. It turns out that this reflects the ceiling light back at us, so that we can hardly see into the machine.

We certainly can't keep pace with the speed it is working at. In any case, the main part of the machine is so far off the ground that we have to stand on stools and steps to look into it. It's exhausting and ridiculous. You should remember that all of us are semi-skilled operators and we are fed up with machine-minding all day. But what we really resent is getting the blame for poor quality when we don't think it's our fault.'

Sam Taylor, Engineering Supervisor
'Really, we got it wrong from the beginning. My section spends enormous amounts of time on call to these machines. We repeatedly go into that department for quite trivial problems, ones that the operators could easily solve themselves. The machine downtime and productivity have been awful, and we get blamed. So much so that my boss is thinking of allocating a team of engineers just to look after this equipment. It seems mad to me, because we're chronically short of staff, and we can't afford to have mechanical and electronic engineers on call for just one set of machines. They might have been expensive, but the attention they are getting is out of all proportion.'

Tony Barrett, again
'The rest of the Board are very critical. And yet the technology really is very good. I know for a fact that our competitors are heavy investors in the same machines, and their quality and throughput are better than ours. I'm sure it is not a technology problem.'

So what happened? Clearly something had to be done. Tony decided to set up a working party, with the remit of evaluating the causes of poor performance and low morale in the department and of recommending actions for improvement. He ensured that this group represented a range of different opinions by including two machinists, one of their supervisors, an engineering supervisor, the local trade union representative, and a member of the quality control department, all under the chairmanship of the Department Manager, Chris Stopwood.

Chris set about the task with a mix of enthusiasm and trepidation, recognizing the political importance of getting the problems sorted out. First, the working party held a short meeting, at which their objectives were discussed. This lasted longer than intended, partly because people were keen to volunteer suggestions for change. However, it proved very useful. One item which emerged was that they were all happy for the quality control representative (Jane Green) to play an important role in the evaluation exercise, in part because she was relatively independent but also because she was well respected.

During the next fortnight Jane interviewed all the machinists and engineering staff about the difficulties in the department, aiming to draw up a list of the main problems which needed addressing. At this stage she deliberately avoided considering any actions that might be taken—they could wait till later.

Jane then suggested to the working party that she should collect more detailed information on the problems she had identified. She decided to use three more specialist techniques for that purpose. First she analysed the performance data from company records, with particular focus on productivity, machine utilization, quality statistics, and throughput times. That proved quite straightforward, given her experience in quality control. In fact, the data substantiated Tony Barrett's worst fears. The performance of the new machines was awful, well below that initially expected, and the rate of defects getting through to the test area was worse than before the new technology.

Jane also asked the machine operators to complete 'user diaries' for two weeks, in which they recorded all the problems they experienced with their machines, including difficulties in setting up, equipment breakdowns, software problems, periods waiting for materials, time waiting for engineers, and so on. As a result of this, she was able to identify the principal causes of machine downtime. Many of these turned out to concern relatively minor and routine adjustments to the machines and the software.

Finally, Jane administered a short confidential questionnaire which investigated how the operators felt about their jobs, what aspects they were dissatisfied about, and what changes to their work would make them more effective as well as more satisfied. She looked for consistent patterns in the data, and quickly saw that most of the machine operators felt deskilled by the new technology, felt frustrated by their lack of control over it, and wanted to be able to take more responsibility for solving production problems as they occurred. They did not like the role of machine-minding, could not see why they always had to refer to engineers, and wanted more training. They also wanted to replace the reflecting glass on the machines, so they could see what was happening, and to have walkways which allowed better access.

At this stage, Jane carried out additional interviews with the four engineers who serviced the machines, as well as their supervisor, Sam Taylor. She learned again that they were frustrated at having to spend time on minor issues, especially as their work-load was building up in other departments. However, they were reluctant to allow the production employees to carry out repairs, because they feared that the need for their own skills might be diminished, and because their union had previously shown opposition to that kind of move. Nevertheless, Jane formed the opinion that the engineers would probably be willing to move some way in that direction, in part because they knew this was happening among the company's competitors.

Jane fed back her findings to the working party, who discussed them at some length, particularly regarding the respective roles of engineers and machine operators. Chris, the Department Manager, was nervous about this, given the potential repercussions elsewhere in the factory, and felt it was now time once more to involve Tony, the Production Director. The latter was delighted with progress, and immediately spoke to the Engineering Director. As a result Chris and the working party were asked to make a presentation to the two directors, at which the following recommendations were made.

(1) The machinists' jobs should be extended to include responsibility for running the machines, for solving everyday problems as they occur, and for improving the quality of their output.
(2) The engineers should train the machinists to take on these responsibilities,

whilst retaining responsibility for a defined set of more substantial problems.

(3) Discussions should be initiated to consider a programme of multi-skilling, so that in time the distinction between mechanical and electronic engineers would be reduced. This would require the involvement of other managers, several shop stewards and the regional trade union official.

(4) Arrangements should be made to improve operators' access to the machines, remedying the initial design faults.

In due course it all happened. There were some difficulties over the engineers' roles, but they and their union were persuaded it was not an attempt to undermine their status or to reduce the company's need for their skills. There was also a problem replacing the reflecting glass. For a variety of reasons it proved extremely expensive to change that, and in the end Chris gave up, reasoning that it was less important now the machinists were no longer restricted to machine-minding.

Returning to Tony six months later:
'The exercise was well worthwhile. Chris and his staff did an excellent job, and our follow-up data show that morale and performance have improved considerably. Productivity is significantly better, and quality is improving steadily. We are beginning to achieve our original business goals, and I can now see a way forward throughout the department, so that we can capitalize on what we've done.'

That 'way forward' involved a change in how the department worked, so that operators each took responsibility for a greater number of activities and for their own product testing. To describe those ideas would take us beyond our present focus on evaluation, but they serve to illustrate how inquiries of the kind described in this book can create new opportunities by generating resources and suggestions which extend beyond an initial project.

The case itself illustrates how investments in new technology can fail to meet their goals, even in otherwise well-managed companies. Unfortunately, those failures are not unusual, in work settings of all kinds. The equipment can be technically superb, but unless the human and organizational aspects are also right, then it will perform below expectations. The case also shows that there may be several causes for poor performance and for a poor return on investment. In this instance a number of suggestions were made, for example: that the wrong staff were recruited for the machines; that the training was inadequate for both machinists and engineers; that the engineers were not providing a good enough service, and that they needed reorganizing; that the equipment was poorly designed; and that operators were given inappropriate and uninteresting jobs. To tease these out, some systematic evaluation was required which enabled the company to identify and introduce changes, and thereby make significant improvements to productivity. The financial return on this investment would have been very poor without this study.

Of course not all evaluation exercises are done on this scale. A small office, for example, may be experiencing difficulties with its computerized word-processing and accounts systems. Staff may complain that the system is difficult to learn and use, or perhaps that it does not really do what they want it to. Symptoms of that kind can be investigated in less formal and briefer projects, supported by advice given later in the book.

UNDERLYING ISSUES

It is helpful to think of human and organizational themes in terms of four sets of issues. First are questions to do with the equipment and physical working conditions, which are the subject of Chapter 2. Next are issues concerning the operation of the system: is it easy to learn and easy to use? This we term 'usability', and it will be covered in Chapter 3.

The other two groups of issues have a less obvious connection with hardware and software. They concern the content of jobs, and the effects of new technology on the organization more widely. How jobs can be designed to provide satisfaction, motivation and high levels of performance is the subject of Chapter 4; and Chapter 5 deals with questions about a department as a whole or about the organization more widely.

Each chapter identifies a set of issues to be examined when evaluating a particular system. Some of those issues can be introduced by illustrating their links with the 12 quotations set out earlier in the chapter. Recall that these referred to systems which were already in use.

Four of the quotations are in the centre of Box 1A. Each is a complaint about low productivity, and possible underlying causes are summarized in the corners of the diagram. These are grouped according to the four chapters introduced above, and are framed as questions which might be asked. The bracketed numbers indicate a section in the book which covers that question. For example, '(2.1)' refers to Chapter 2, section 1.

You can use Box 1A to identify which sections are most likely to be of concern if you have problems of low productivity. Box 1B is laid out in a similar manner, and can provide a launch pad for inquiries into poor morale.

You will notice that many of the issues listed in the corners of that second box also appear as possible underlying causes in Box 1A. For example, a system which is unreliable (section 2.3, in the top-left corner) will impair productivity, but also make the user's job frustrating and unsatisfactory. Inappropriate staff selection and training (section 5.4, in the bottom-right corner) will similarly affect both productivity and morale.

The two problems in the centre of Box 1C are concerned with how to operate the system. Accordingly, issues arise particularly from Chapter 3, on usability, but again there are important questions to be considered in all other chapters.

Finally, Box 1D covers some problems in introducing or extending a computer-based system. Most of the issues described in the book need to be addressed when you make a purchase, so that a large number of items have to be included in this diagram.

The four diagrams are not exhaustive; they provide illustrative pointers to

Box 1A   Problems with low productivity and some possible underlying causes

Technology (Chapter 2)

Is the system capable of doing all
of the job? (2.1)
Are certain important components
incompatible? (2.2)
Could maintenance and repaire
procedures be improved? (2.3)
Are back-up procedures inadequate?
(2.5)
Are working conditions all satisfactory? (2.6)

Usability (Chapter 3)

Is the system hard to learn? (3.1)
Does it sometimes respond too
slowly? (3.4)
Is there a problem getting certain
information in or out? (3.5)
Can mistakes easily be corrected?
(3.6)
Is the system prone to serious
errors? (3.7)

Problems

(1) 'We have spent a great deal of money investing in the
most modern computerized manufacturing
technology, but a year later there is no way we have
got it operating effectively. We were aiming for better
productivity, better quality and faster throughput
times, but we haven't achieved any of these.'

(3) 'Every time the computer breaks down, everything
grinds to a halt. I never thought it could cause so
much trouble.'

(4) 'We have spent a great deal of money on this system,
and yet people are still using the old technology
whenever they get a chance.'

(8) 'The equipment works, but it seems to need an
enormous amount of support. We are spending much
more on supervision, maintenance and planning than
we ever expected.'

The job (Chapter 4)

Do operators have an appropriate
amount of discretion? (4.1)
Are the operators adequately
trained? (4.2)
Is the work too demanding? (4.4)

The organization (Chapter 5)

Is the organization structure
appropriate to support the
system? (5.1)
Has the organization become too
bureaucratic? (5.2)
Have communications been
adversely affected? (5.3)
Are the right people being recruited
and adequately trained? (5.4)

Box 1B   Problems of poor morale and some possible underlying causes

Technology (Chapter 2)	Usability (Chapter 3)
Is the system frustratingly unreliable? (2.3) Are working conditions poor? (2.6)	Is the system hard to learn? (3.1) Do users feel they are in control of the system? (3.2) Is the system unnecessarily hard to operate? (3.3) Is it too easy to make serious errors? (3.7)

Problems

(2) 'Since we got the computer, staff turnover has gone completely out of hand. People are not happy with the job, so they leave.'

(7) 'The people who use it complain that it's tiring. Some of them are even worried about their health.'

(9) 'It has completely changed my job. I used to feel responsible. Now the work is so simple that they could replace me with a machine.'

(11) 'The work I have been doing since they introduced the computer is much more skilled. I think I should be paid more.'

The job (Chapter 4)	The organization (Chapter 5)
Do the operators feel in control of the work? (4.1) Is there enough variety in the job? (4.3) Is the job sufficiently demanding? (4.4) Do operators get enough feedback about how they are doing? (4.5) Are the operators paid appropriately? (4.6) Is there sufficient face-to-face communication? (4.7) Do users find the system unsafe? (4.8)	Has the organization become too bureaucratic? (5.2) Are procedures for selection and training appropriate? (5.4) Can industrial relations be improved? (5.5) Are there problems with pay relativities? (5.6) Are there fears about job losses? (5.7)

Box 1C   Problems when operating the system and some possible underlying causes

---

Technology (Chapter 2)

Was the system designed to do the
  job you are using it for? (2.1)
Are different parts of the software
  truly compatible? (2.2)
Is the technology well tried and
  tested? (2.4)
Is there an undue emphasis on
  security? (2.5)

Usability (Chapter 3)

Does the user have the required
  degree of control? (3.2)
Is there too much to remember?
  (3.3)
Is the system too slow at critical
  points? (3.4)
Could it be easier to get information
  in and out? (3.5)
Does the system encourage errors?
  (3.6)
Is it easy to avoid catastrophic
  errors? (3.7)

Problems

(10) 'I can get it to do what I want, but I am sure there
      must be easier ways.'
(12) 'I like using it but you have to keep your wits about
      you. You think you understand how it works and then
      it does something quite unexpected.'

The job (Chapter 4)

Do operators have the skills
  required? (4.2)

The organization (Chapter 5)

Has personnel selection and training
  been adequate? (5.4)

Box 1D   Problems of implementation and some possible underlying causes

---

Technology (Chapter 2)

Will the system do the job you want it for? (2.1)

Will it be compatible with existing equipment and data? (2.2)

Can you get competent and rapid maintenance? (2.3)

Is the technology either too new or too old? (2.4)

Are there appropriate and effective back-up procedures? (2.5)

Will there be an adverse change in working conditions? (2.6)

Usability (Chapter 3)

Is the new system going to be easy to learn? (3.1)

Is it clear what the user should do at all points? (3.2)

Does the style of operation suit the task, or is unnecessary effort required? (3.3)

Is it difficult to get information in and out? (3.5)

Will the new system be prone to errors? (3.6)

Problems

(5) 'The system we introduced some years ago works well, and now we want to upgrade it. The problem is to choose from all those alternatives.'

(6) 'We changed the computer last year. It's certainly an improvement, but introducing it was a real headache. We must learn how to reduce the disruption next time.'

The job (Chapter 4)

Are the new jobs designed to be varied and satisfying? (4.1, 4.3, 4.7)

Will the work be more demanding or less demanding? (4.4)

Will the new system require changes in pay? (4.6)

Will there be any problems of health and safety? (4.8)

The organization (Chapter 5)

Will the organization structure need changing? (5.1)

What effect will the new system have on communications within the organization? (5.3).

How will you select and train operators for the new system? (5.4)

What are the implications for pay and career progression? (5.6)

Will there be job losses? (5.7)

issues which might need investigation in your organization. But you will almost always need to look beyond a single theme, picking up issues from more than one box, and tracing them through several of the chapters which follow.

THE PRINCIPLES OF EVALUATION

The book will help you to evaluate your new technology in each of the four main topic-areas: equipment, usability, job quality and organizational factors. This will be achieved through identification of principal issues in each area, and the presentation of key questions to be asked. Issues, questions and detailed advice will be set out in later chapters. At this stage, however, the approach can be introduced in terms of broad principles. Successful evaluation work is based upon the following seven propositions.

(1) *Evaluation should concern tasks to be done, not merely the computerized system*
This fundamental principle emphasizes that evaluation should be focused upon the objectives of a department or company, not simply upon the efficiency of a piece of computer-based technology which supports those objectives. The primary concern is with business goals and their attainment, not merely with a particular computer system.

There is a tendency to look only at the efficiency with which the system is being operated, without broader consideration of whether that system is appropriate or needed to meet current business objectives. Yet it may be the case that merely amending the current system would miss the fundamental point, because increased effectiveness now requires quite radical changes to equipment and/or procedures. In rare cases, the business goals themselves may need to be modified, leading to quite different technological requirements.

This distinction, between increased efficiency and increased effectiveness, is an important one, and the first principle of evaluation is to aim for the latter. However, the principle can lead to practical difficulties, since investigations might thereby expand into many disparate areas, sometimes where company objectives are ill-defined or subject to disagreement. The evaluators in those cases might need to spend considerable time in discussions about policies and overall strategy. There is clearly a need for that in some circumstances, but evaluation of new technology does not always require such a wide-ranging approach.

At the other extreme, by looking only at the efficiency of equipment use, evaluators may develop tunnel vision, missing the important wider issues of objectives and their attainment. Some compromise needs to be found between these two extremes, and it is desirable to identify the boundaries of an evaluation study at an early stage. That will often require a decision by senior management about the scope of an inquiry.

(2) *Evaluation should be oriented to action*
It will already be clear that detailed evaluation of large systems can take a

considerable time. That is only justified if the exercise is aimed at improved performance, and this should be made explicit to everyone involved. In practice, the expectation of change is likely to sustain interest in the evaluation and provide the necessary motivation to see it through to completion.

(3) *Evaluation should be systematic*
A big danger in all evaluation work is that an unsystematic approach will result in conclusions being dominated by informal impressions, untested assumptions and the views of a small number of individuals. It is therefore important to devise and follow a plan for the collection and use of information. That plan, and its associated timetable, may of course be amended as you get going, but without it you are liable to overlook important issues and may miss out on certain key decisions.

(4) *Evaluation should look beyond obvious problems*
As stressed in the previous section, it is a mistake to focus on a set of symptoms without careful consideration of what may lie behind them. For example, word-processing operators may exhibit symptoms of muscular fatigue that initially suggest a problem of equipment design or layout. But wider investigation may reveal that the problems arise instead because operators have to perform the same, unchanging set of tasks without any variety.

Try not to make up your mind about the nature of problems and about preferred solutions until you have gathered information of several kinds. And always seek to look beyond the obvious, perhaps using this book to remind you of additional possibilities.

(5) *Evaluation should be participative*
Evaluation is sometimes carried out by a single manager who has knowledge of the system. When problems are reasonably circumscribed and their nature is broadly agreed, that one-person approach may be effective. But in many cases problems are not clear-cut, they may extend widely throughout the company, and people's views can differ depending on the nature of their job. It can then be a mistake if the evaluation is based only upon a single view. In these instances the opinions of people who use, support, or are affected by the technology should also be sought; their experience can shed quite different light on the issues.

Such a participative approach will almost certainly take longer than leaving everything to a single person. But the solutions are likely to be better, because of the wider expertise and knowledge that have been tapped. Although the views of many people can be considered, that is quite compatible with managers' retaining responsibility for the final set of decisions; participation does not mean that decisions must be taken by majority vote.

However, application of this principle can depend on other features of an evaluation. In the majority of cases the aim will be modification of current equipment and procedures; staff participation in information-gathering and interpretation is then very desirable. Rather less frequent will be assessments of broad-ranging goals (see principle (1)), which result in recommendations to make radical changes in policy and practice. In those cases of fundamental shift within an entire organization, it will be essential for senior management to identify and press through changes. Top-down leadership will in those cases take priority over extended participation, at least in the early stages.

(6) *Evaluation should be comparative*
Sometimes the results of an evaluation activity are straightforward: the system is obviously inadequate and certain specific changes would remedy the deficiencies. In other cases the data might be ambiguous, and benchmark information might be required, against which your own situation can be compared. For example: is the system performing as well as published standard performance? Or as well as the suppliers said it would? Or as well as it is in other departments, or other companies? This is not always straight-forward, since published performance figures may not be appropriate for your situation, or it may be difficult to find the system being used in directly comparable circumstances. However, the attempt is always worthwhile in clarifying your thinking, and benchmarks are important elements in evalu-ation. In some cases you can also make comparisons over time; is the system doing better or worse than it was previously?

As a purchaser you also need to be comparative. Use this book to draw up a list of factors which are important in your situation, and then try to evaluate not one but a range of possible purchases against those requirements. You can then ask whether version X or Y will achieve your needs better. Or you can assess whether your new model will be an improvement on the old one against these criteria.

(7) *Evaluation should be tailor-made to meet local needs*
Finally, there is no single way to evaluate computer-based systems. You should certainly aim to be systematic and comparative, and follow the other principles outlined here. But choices within those principles will need to be made, taking into account a range of factors. Among those are the nature of your system, the presenting problems, the size of your company, the resources available, the time before a decision is required, and the number of other systems you have previously evaluated.

For example, a small company which is profitably providing a routine service may sometimes need to focus upon a limited aspect of its computer equipment, perhaps usability or compatibility between functions. The appro-ach may be quite informal, participative and short-term, leaving aside the fundamental issues of business goals raised in the first principle. However, a more wide-ranging and radical exercise might be appropriate for a larger company in a rapidly changing market. Overall strategy could need examina-tion, with technological investments dependent on the outcome of that process. Evaluation in this case would probably be more systematic, through the establishment of relatively formal structures, and it would almost certainly be the job of senior management.

The seven principles of evaluation are summarized in Box 1E. They can provide a good starting-point for your own evaluation work.

In all cases the goal is to improve the performance of a company or part of it. Certain aspects of 'performance' can be measured in customary terms, and data may already be available in the company. For example, return on particular investments, market share, time taken to meet customer queries, frequency of customer complaints, scrap levels, cost per item produced, machine utilization rate or product lead times may be known or could be measured.

In addition, however, we will introduce criteria in terms of the behaviour of employees and the functioning of the organization. These contribute to performance in the above terms, but are less often measured. Particularly important are the frequency and type of errors made by people operating the system. Research has shown that attention to features considered in this book can reduce operating errors by up to 50 per cent, with consequent saving of time and direct expenditure and a reduction in repair costs. Systematic selection and training of staff can also have strong beneficial impacts upon productivity. Reorganizing work to use skills in new ways and to handle problems at source can markedly improve financial return on investment (as in the true case study described above). And profitability is directly linked to a matching of new technology with explicit business goals. Using evaluation in the ways suggested here will contribute to better performance in all those ways.

THE STRUCTURE OF THE BOOK

This book introduces thirty different issues which need to be considered in evaluating computer-based technology. For each one we identify the questions you should ask and indicate some of the steps to take if changes appear to be needed.

Box 1E   Summary principles of evaluation

(1) Look at the primary work objectives, not merely the computer-based system
(2) Don't start unless you are prepared to change things
(3) Be systematic
(4) Go beyond the immediately obvious
(5) Ask the people involved
(6) Make comparisons
(7) Do it your own way to meet your own needs (but don't forget the previous six points)

Several hundred questions are presented, to guide your evaluation. These are at two levels of detail. In the next four chapters we describe the thirty main issues for examination, and present the key questions about each one. Most readers will need only that degree of complexity.

However, Chapters 9 to 12 contain additional questions which are more detailed, for readers with special needs and the extra resources which might be required in posing them. Those more detailed questions are in two forms: checklists to be applied in making complex inquiries, and questionnaires to be completed by staff who use or are associated with the technology. Those more detailed approaches will be described later in the book.

Chapter 2 examines computerized equipment in relation to company goals. Key issues concern hardware aspects of the computer and its associated equipment, and the conditions in which work is carried out. Chapter 3 looks at the system's usability in practice: how easy is it to understand and to avoid errors? Chapter 4 explores the impact of the computer on the quality of the jobs of the people concerned, including their attitudes. And Chapter 5 examines wider aspects of the organization, considering the impact of technology on industrial relations, communications and organizational structure.

In each of those four chapters we present the principal questions to be asked when evaluating a computer-based system. The core procedures for asking and answering those questions are interviews, meetings and working parties, and we refer to those as the *basic evaluation methods*. Chapter 6 covers how-to-do-it aspects of those basic methods, illustrating how you can use the book to make improvements in the areas covered by Chapters 2 to 5.

Next, we turn to the management of change. Chapter 7 examines issues of strategy, financial assessment and the provision of organizational support, identifying issues to be considered as you turn your evaluation findings into practical improvements.

Those seven chapters will be sufficient to meet the needs of most readers. They cover the key issues, the principal questions to ask, the basic evaluation methods and the management of change. Readers can extract material as required, and apply it within their own setting. Different sections will particularly concern different groups. For example, senior managers might be more interested in job and organizational issues and in the introduction of change, whereas technical staff will concentrate more on issues of equipment and usability.

Although the first seven chapters contain enough detail for most readers to make progress in their evaluation, a small number of people will have additional specialist needs. They may wish to carry out detailed investigations of particular issues, applying procedures which are more demanding of time and expertise. For them, Chapter 8 describes *specialist evaluation methods*, such as questionnaires, system walk-through, user diaries, and system logging. These will be used only rarely, and suggestions about particular applications are made in advance in Chapters 2 to 5.

Chapters 9 to 12 are intended for the minority of readers who wish to undertake more complex investigations. Those chapters set out specialist checklists and questionnaires for many of the issues introduced previously. The checklists contain additional questions to supplement an evaluation, and in some cases should be used alongside a specialist method, such as a system walk-through. We recommend that all readers glance at Chapters 8 to 12, but expect most people to pay greatest attention to the earlier material.

Finally, the book contains details of other books which you might find useful, and a list of places from which specialist help may be obtained.

Introducing Chapters 2 to 7

The following four chapters introduce the thirty central issues to be examined when evaluating a computer-based system. Each is presented in a standard form, using four main headings. First is 'Importance', when we describe the issue and the ways in which it can influence effectiveness. Second, we present some 'Questions you should ask', covering the initial points to be explored during evaluation.

The third standard heading is 'Things you can do' if improvement appears to be needed. Practical suggestions are offered, describing changes which have been found useful in other settings. Then comes a section with the heading 'Conflicts and trade-offs'. This points to ways in which individual pieces of advice, equally good on their own, may in practice conflict with each other. For example, one recommendation may enhance the security of your system against intruders, but this could slow down working procedures to an unacceptable degree.

In addition to those main sections, we have in some cases included forward-references to later parts of the book. These cover specialist procedures and detailed forms of questioning for use in a minority of cases. Their advantages and disadvantages are described in Chapter 8, and at this stage you need merely note that they are available later.

Each of Chapters 2 to 5 begins with a list of the issues to be covered. Together those define the subject-matter for evaluating computer-based technology in human and organizational terms. We move on in Chapter 6 to describe how to set up and manage an evaluation exercise. Three basic evaluation methods are introduced: interviews, meetings and working parties; and advice is given about each. Suggestions are made about initial screening enquiries, which can be followed by more detailed types of information-gathering.

Recognizing that the primary aim of evaluation is to make improvements, Chapter 7 gives advice about managing change. The introduction of new or modified computer-based equipment is considered in terms of the development of strategy, the specification of requirements, the assessment of financial costs and benefits, and processes of change, organizational support and conflict management.

2

Equipment and working conditions

The issues dealt with in this chapter are:

2.1 Meeting essential requirements   21
2.2 Compatibility between components   26
2.3 Reliability and repairs   28
2.4 Maturity and obsolescence   31
2.5 System security   34
2.6 Working conditions   36

This chapter describes what to look for when evaluating computer-based equipment and the working conditions in which that is operated. The chapter is primarily written for members of companies who wish to evaluate systems already in use, but the suggestions which follow can also be applied by readers who are contemplating new purchases.

Issues 2.2 to 2.6 will be of greatest interest to line managers, technical staff and users themselves. However, issue 2.1 raises basic questions of how well your technology contributes to company or departmental goals. To evaluate equipment in those terms will require the attention of senior management, and members of that group should be included when questions from the first section are examined.

2.1 MEETING ESSENTIAL REQUIREMENTS

Importance

The key question in evaluation is whether a computer-based system does what it is required to do. A surprisingly large number of systems are lacking in this respect: the hardware and/or the software is not right for the job. An example from one organization is given in Box 2A.

There is usually no need to become involved in technical discussions about particular hardware or software features on their own: the focus should be on the goals of your company and what the system is required to do. Can it meet your current and anticipated needs?

You should concentrate on identifying your operational requirements, and leave the hardware and software issues to computer specialists. In practice, this may be best achieved through a cycle of discussions, raising with the specialists

---

Box 2A   Getting it right—eventually

An administrative department which is spread across several sites wanted to extend its computerized information and control systems. It decided to buy 12 personal computers, each costing over £2000, to be connected to the already-operating mainframe system.

After a decision had been taken about which hardware to purchase, a choice was made between alternative software systems. Three packages were available, but two were quickly eliminated, because they did not have enough functions or could not undertake other administrative tasks that were required. So the remaining package was chosen, out of necessity.

The system proved to be far from ideal. It was very complex, and users and their supervisors could not really understand it. Certain important functions could not be made to work, and the keyboard layout produced regular problems and staff frustration. These arose because the shift keys on either side were slightly unbalanced in their layout. When working rapidly, users frequently tried to type 'shift plus u' in order to type a capital U, but in practice pressed 'ESC plus u'. That had the effect of deleting all work since the last 'save' command, in some cases several hours previously.

After some months, new software became available, which was less complex and could handle the functions absent from the previous version. However, it turned out that this software would not run on the earlier equipment.

That was the last straw. So replacement hardware was purchased from another supplier. Only after installation did it become apparent that this system was too slow to meet the department's requirements. It simply would not do the job.

So the department tried again. At the third attempt, they bought equipment which operates the new software and meets their needs. But it took them over a year, a lot of money, and a great deal of wasted energy.

The lessons? Define your needs explicitly in terms of departmental objectives. Analyse possible solutions. Then approach specialists and demand practical work-outs to check that your needs can be met.

general issues at an early stage and gaining outline ideas about what is technically possible. However, the emphasis throughout should be on your own requirements and how to meet your business goals.

It is important to include future developments in your thinking about this issue. New technology makes possible many different achievements, and your requirements could soon change if you grasp the opportunities it provides. For example, one company we know has become a new market leader by integrating data-bases from different parts of its existing business; its technology requirements are now quite different from those it had only a few years ago.

Although lack of important functions is quite common, many companies have purchased a system which offers *too many* possibilities. It can perform a wide range of tasks which are not required, and some facilities are therefore not used. The problem is that 'functionality' or 'facilities offered' sells systems. If a buyer is confronted by two pieces of equipment or two software packages which are broadly similar but one offers 20 facilities and the other 50 facilities, he or she may be tempted to choose the one offering the greater number, thinking that this is better value for money. That might sometimes be the case, but the extra facilities can result in greater confusion, by presenting too many options simultaneously or by making procedures slow and unwieldy.

Questions you should ask

In evaluating a current application or considering possible future systems, the following questions should be asked about this first topic. They can be pursued through one or more of the basic methods of information-gathering: interviews, meetings or working parties.

What are the business goals you are seeking to meet in the department or company in question?

Have the tasks been defined which the system must undertake to meet those business goals? What are those tasks?

Do separate groups have different views about those essential requirements? What are those views?

Can the system undertake the essential tasks cost-effectively?

Would a modified or new system help the company better to meet its business goals?

What new requirements are expected in the next few years?

Can the system meet those anticipated requirements cost-effectively?

Does the system have facilities which are at present not utilized, and which could be helpful to the company?

Should changes be made in order to use those facilities?

Things you can do

You may find that the system you are evaluating falls short of the ideal in terms of essential requirements. However, most systems, especially large ones, can be

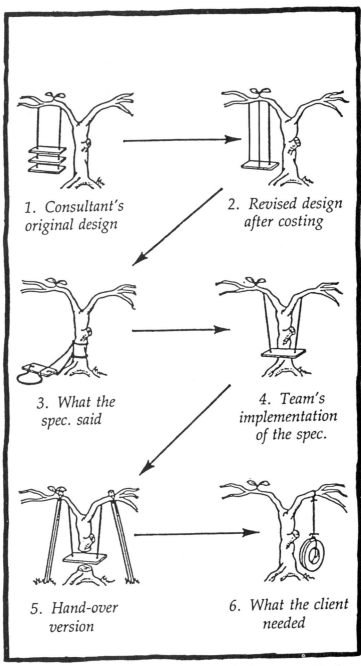

1. Consultant's original design

2. Revised design after costing

3. What the spec. said

4. Team's implementation of the spec.

5. Hand-over version

6. What the client needed

This joke has appeared in one form or another in hundreds of computer publications. It is a problem that any computer professional will recognize instantly, usually when it is too late to do anything about. What the machine does is not what its users want it to do. This is the issue described in section 2.1.

modified somehow. It might be appropriate to keep the existing hardware and buy new software, or to alter the work procedures to fit the constraints imposed by the system. In all cases, you should resist the temptation to blame all your problems on 'computers', as though all computer systems were the same and equally troublesome. There are good and bad systems for your job, and it would be wrong to conclude that no improvements were possible.

Positive changes usually come about through more detailed application of the above questions. After specifying the business goals, you must identify the key individuals who have a stake in the system, and get them to analyse and write down their requirements. Draw up lists of 'must do' items, others which the system 'can do', and those which would be 'optionally helpful'. Bear in mind the strategy and objectives of the company or the department, and identify where the technology makes its contribution. Try also to anticipate future changes in those areas. Once the specification is becoming clear, you can discuss requirements with suppliers: tell them what you need to do, not the kind of technology you want.

These themes are developed further in sections 7.1 and 7.2, where we cover suggestions for the effective management of change. Financial appraisals are examined in section 7.3.

Conflicts and trade-offs

The obvious conflict here is between equipment characteristics and cost. There will often be a range of equipment at different prices that can do the same jobs to varying degrees of adequacy and cost. Some compromise will always be needed, depending in part on anticipated as well as current requirements, and on expected financial costs and benefits.

Another trade-off may be between alternative systems, all of which are less than ideal. You are likely to find that one set of equipment copes very well with certain essential functions, but is less good with others. A rival system may have a different profile of success and failure, but overall be about as good as the first one. Choosing between alternatives here will require further discussion about priorities. Which functions are *really* the most important ones in this setting? Which system will provide a better financial return? Which is preferable in other respects?

This first issue, meeting essential requirements, should usually be paramount in evaluation decisions. However, the objective can sometimes conflict with other targets identified elsewhere in the book. For example, compatibility between components is examined in the next section. Some systems which are functionally ideal can prove quite incompatible with hardware or software in use elsewhere within the company. And systems which appear attractive through having many desirable functions may turn out to be difficult to use, being unsatisfactory in terms of the usability criteria described in Chapter 3.

A emphasis on equipment function can also conflict with requirements in Chapter 4, concerned with job quality. Extending the automation of functions may well reduce the options for designing interesting jobs. For example, if you computerize decisions about production scheduling within a manufacturing system, the operators' sense of control may be reduced to a harmful degree. It can sometimes be sensible to forsake additional functionality in order to gain greater job quality and enhanced employee commitment. In cases where advanced technology is deemed to be essential, the design of jobs should always be examined: can a different mix of tasks, with and without the computer, help to enhance the quality of users' jobs?

Finally, the future may of course be different from the present. It is essential to make some prediction about future needs, examining possible changes in products or services, markets, employees or equipment over the next few years. It might be that your current requirements conflict in some respects with likely future needs, so that both of those cannot be met through the same system. By making those conflicts explicit, you can think through the options more systematically, taking business decisions on the basis of assessed probabilities.

Specialist procedures for minority use

If you have the need and resources for a more complex investigation of this issue, consider the specialist procedures of system walk-through and comparative testing in conjunction with task analysis (see pages 162, 170 and 168).

2.2   COMPATIBILITY BETWEEN COMPONENTS

Importance

The rapid pace of development and the proliferation of new equipment and software mean that incompatibility between components is a major problem. For example, a recent survey of office automation projects in the United Kingdom reported that inability to link new facilities to current systems was the main obstacle to expansion.

Compatibility may be viewed at three levels. First is *equipment compatibility*, in respect of interconnections between pieces of hardware: different computers, printers, plotters, etc. Second is *software compatibility*, in terms of interactions between different data-sets within a particular system. 'Islands of information' are quite common, with data held in different software structures, between which intercommunication is extremely difficult. For example, in one company we know, warehouse and invoice staff both have to type in the same information about orders, since there is no way to transfer data between them. Third is *compatibility between software and hardware*, whether or not particular programs can run on the equipment available.

Compatibility is clearly important from the outset, but it becomes crucial when new software is envisaged (will it work on the current system?) and when other hardware is to be linked into the installation (can it handle our data and the current software?). These issues are central to an assessment of your system, and need to be considered in terms of the future as well as the present. Expert advice, from within the company or from external specialists, may become needed if major difficulties are foreseen.

Evaluation will often focus upon local issues of hardware and software, within the framework of this chapter's concern for equipment. However, there is also a need sometimes to consider broader organizational questions under this heading. Would the company's objectives be better attained if it aimed for greater integration between departments, or with external suppliers? If so, what are the current and anticipated problems of incompatibility? Questions of that kind will be examined in section 5.3.

Questions you should ask

In gathering information to evaluate this aspect of your equipment, you should start with these questions:

Are there any current problems resulting from incompatibility?

Can these problems be resolved cost-effectively?

Is there useful new equipment which cannot be used because of incompatibility?

Are there useful new programs or data which cannot be used because of incompatibility?

Can you envisage additional problems of incompatibility arising in the next few years?

Would enhanced compatibility create new business opportunities?

Things you can do

If there are difficulties in this area, a first step is to work out how much compatibility is really essential in your company. You should not strive for greater intercommunication just for the sake of it. If your approach is to treat different departments as separate (for example, design and manufacturing), it may not be essential to have equipment and software compatibility on a large scale. However, information-sharing between departments is in general becoming more important, and increased compatibility may be desirable to reduce costs and improve quality.

An obvious (and often expensive) strategy is to continue to rely on one manufacturer's equipment. However, even a single company may be unable to guarantee true compatibility. For example, currently adequate software may no longer work when a hardware system is upgraded; or a manufacturer might completely alter the primary specification, to keep up with changes in the market. In general, you should identify the points where you require better compatibility, and discuss those with a number of suppliers. Particular forms of compatibility should in this way be included within the 'essential requirements' specification described in the previous section. As mentioned at that point, a cycle of discussions with hardware and software experts will often be helpful in developing your thoughts about what is possible as well as what is required.

Eventually, it then falls to the specialist suppliers to work out ways to meet your needs. For example, some manufacturers sell general-purpose visual display units, that can 'impersonate' different makes of terminal at the flick of a switch. Other software 'translators' are available to allow different programs and data-sets to interact with each other. And a number of agencies provide a specific service, enhancing software compatibility to meet individual needs.

Conflicts and trade-offs

As with other essential requirements, compatibility can usually be bought, but sometimes at a very high price. In deciding what should be aimed for, a compromise in financial terms will therefore usually be required.

You may also have to sacrifice some flexibility or power. For example, you might be able to send a word-processed document between two different types of computer, but only if it is reduced to a 'text file' (a file that contains only the text, all the formatting commands having been removed). This means that the user will have to check the text and renew all formatting, such as underlining, emboldening, centring of text, and so on. Incomplete compatibility of this kind creates plenty of scope for small mistakes and ineffective working.

If greater compatibility leads to increased integration across departments, you need to look out for possible organizational implications. Connecting together different operations can alter the power structure within a company, or even remove the need for a particular group of employees. Wider issues of that kind are discussed in Chapter 5 and should be examined whenever greater integration is being considered.

2.3   RELIABILITY AND REPAIRS

Importance

Computers, like all other equipment, will undoubtedly fail to work properly from time to time. This likelihood, and the impact of malfunction on performance, need to be examined within an evaluation exercise. The importance of the issue varies according to the work undertaken. If you are producing material to a tight deadline, an entire order might be lost through unreliability. On the other hand, if only a part of the process is affected and deadlines are not pressing, you might suffer little inconvenience while you wait for the equipment to be repaired. In general, however, the more central the role played by the technology in meeting your business goals, the greater is the importance of high reliability. Furthermore, since maintenance can make up a substantial proportion of total operating costs, there is a general need to reduce expenditure incurred through unreliability.

Possible problems extend beyond the performance of hardware alone, into the associated software. 'Bugs' in a program can lead to unexpected problems, as a specific but unrecognized set of factors combine to thwart a user's intention. Many systems 'save' work automatically as you proceed, placing it into a long-term store. However, people have often lost a whole session's work through no fault of their own, because of some unknown quirk. Office microcomputers can sometimes be subject to temporary distortion through brief changes to electricity supply deriving from other equipment, or even through static electricity from staff walking on carpet fibres of certain types.

Other problems arise because the system is not sufficiently protected against user errors. Substantial expenditure can be incurred through poor design of that kind: downtime is increased, delays become more common, customers are inconvenienced, repair costs have to be met, and work has to be repeated once the system is again running. Software features which can encourage or discourage errors are described in Chapter 3. Those need to be considered in conjunction with the hardware problems which are the main focus of this chapter.

Associated with hardware and software reliability are questions of repairs and maintenance. How effectively and cheaply can faults be remedied? In some cases you will have a maintenance contract with a local company, calling out their engineer when needed. Larger organizations may have their own repair and maintenance staff, whereas some smaller firms may call in technical assistance for individual repairs as they arise. The effectiveness of this process needs to be examined as part of your evaluation.

A related topic concerns the impact of unreliability on the morale and confidence of staff. Breakdowns do not only result in interrupted work schedules, they also carry hidden costs in terms of frustrated and irritated employees.

Questions you should ask

Is your system as reliable as is needed?

Is the system designed to be fault-tolerant, anticipating and automatically coping with principal faults?

Are there bugs in the software? How serious are they?

What other faults are most common? How serious are they?

Is the time lost through faults increasing, decreasing, or remaining stable?

How effective are your repair and preventive maintenance procedures?

Would alternative arrangements provide better support?

Is the cost of equipment repair reasonable relative to the overall capital cost?

Do you have enough replacement equipment and software available for immediate use?

Are there alternative procedures to carry out critical activities during a period of breakdown?

If you are considering purchase of new equipment, do you have information on its anticipated reliability and probable maintenance costs?

Things you can do

If near-100 per cent reliability is crucial to your operations, then a reserve system must be installed, since you can assume that no single system is absolutely perfect. Fault-tolerant designs are also essential. In other cases you may additionally need to consider 'back-up', or archive, copy procedures. On a heavily used system it may be worthwhile making an hourly or a daily copy.

If this is too time-consuming, and the cost of losing several days' data is not prohibitive, you may choose instead to back-up only parts of the data daily, and take a complete copy every week or every month.

If software bugs are a problem, an essential first step is to create some type of 'bug report form'. Operators should record each system error, identifying precisely what actions had preceded it and what were the consequences. Analysis of a number of completed report forms will make it easier to locate needed changes. This is especially important in early stages of implementation of a system (see section 7.6, 'Changing over from old to new').

Problems of unreliability may point to unrecognized training needs. It is often the case that inexpert users compound their difficulties by piling one small error on top of another. Poor system reliability can thus be a sign of inadequate user expertise. That can often be improved quite quickly, by getting a number of users to share their experience and the procedures they have themselves developed to get around difficulties. For example, it is not uncommon for particular individuals to acquire special knowledge but to keep it to themselves. Their expertise could be passed on more widely, with

---

Box 2B   Robot reliability

A recent investigation into robots in British industry reported as follows:

Altogether 26 per cent of current robot users experienced problems with reliability and maintenance. Many firms have had more unintended downtime than they expected, and 24 per cent have had 'frequent' or 'very frequent' downtime due to problems with the robot itself.

These problems are often associated with the firm's lack of specialist expertise, a difficulty experienced by 27 per cent of users. They are compounded by difficulties resulting from inadequate after-sales support, experienced by no less than 33 per cent of users. This latter appears to be a particularly intractable problem for plants in remote locations far from the supplier's base and often an insoluble one when the supplier firm has gone out of business or lost a robot franchise.

The prospect of breakdowns in complex and ill-understood equipment is a nightmare for production managers. The obvious solutions are to foresee the potential problems and provide for them, either by acquiring the necessary expertise in-house, or by making very firm arrangements with the supplier, but in practice either solution can be difficult to achieve completely. Clearly the development of as much in-house skill as possible in maintenance is a prudent course for any robot user to take.

improved reliability as a result. Some large companies have found it useful to introduce a 'suggestions scheme', with financial incentives to speed up this process.

If your repair procedures seem inadequate, it is obviously important to consider alternative maintenance arrangements. In addition, you might consider whether your in-house repair facilities could usefully be strengthened. Minor repairs might be carried out by users on the spot; or call-out procedures for maintenance engineers might be improved. Also check whether your programmes of preventive maintenance could be improved. Issues in that area have been examined in a recent report on robots (see Box 2B). Finally, it may be appropriate to consider buying new equipment, if one benefit is a reduction in maintenance charges.

Conflicts and trade-offs

The fundamental link between effectiveness and cost cannot be avoided here. Greater financial investment can provide a more reliable system, better reserve facilities, and prompt and efficient repair services. But a compromise has to be made, depending on the needs of your business and the financial resources which are available. For example, if a reserve computer is likely almost never to be used, would it be better to spend the money in other ways?

There may be conflicts between the guidelines above and the elements of job design set out in Chapter 4. At that point we describe how opportunity for personal control and raised skill level are particularly important to ensure high-quality operator jobs. In many settings, job quality can be raised through permitting operators to have some influence over preventive maintenance and basic repairs. Such a decentralized approach, often desirable in itself, can clash with more formalized procedures devised and implemented by a central engineering group. The latter may be very effective in the terms of this section, but harmful in respect of several issues described in Chapter 4.

Specialist procedures for minority use

If you have the need and resources for a more complex investigation of this issue, consider the specialist procedures of user diaries or system logging (see pages 166 and 167).

2.4 MATURITY AND OBSOLESCENCE

Importance

We turn next to the age and performance characteristics of a computer-based system: very new and very old systems (both equipment and software) can each present problems of their own kind.

The issues with a very new application are clear. Not being tried and tested, it may be especially unreliable; unforeseen programming faults may come to light; the system may even be withdrawn from the market after quite a short time. Against that, its novel characteristics might give you a competitive edge just when you need it.

The older system can have two disadvantages. Its design may lack 'state of the art' characteristics, and long-term use might have led to unreliability, as mechanical components lose their initial precision. Obsolescence has another drawback in many cases: your data, programs or ancillary equipment may turn out to be unusable on any replacement machine. The ability to transfer in this way (sometimes known as 'upward compatibility') is clearly something to be sought. (See also section 2.2)

The degree of maturity or obsolescence of a system is likely to be of particular concern to the potential purchaser. But this issue should also be considered within a company evaluating its current system. Remember that it is not age on its own that matters; older systems might be fine if the field has not advanced very far and if the work is still being done in an efficient manner.

Questions you should ask

Is the system you plan to buy well established with a good track record?

Are more recent models likely to meet your requirements substantially better?

Could input and output be much faster with more modern equipment?

Can you make some prediction of the life-span of the system? Is that adequate for current business goals?

Is the system extremely new? If so, do its advantages give you a substantial competitive edge?

Are updated versions expected?

Is leasing or rental more cost-effective than purchase in coping with potentially rapid obsolescence?

If you are purchasing software, will the supplier provide updated versions at low cost?

Does your supplier have a good reputation in the trade?

Things you can do

If your system is obsolescent, you will of course have to assess the costs and benefits of replacement. Suppliers or manufacturers might be able to provide information about the expected life-span of your hardware or software and about future developments. It may prove possible to introduce new items of equipment singly, or to transfer to more advanced software with the same equipment. Options may be available to exchange your current equipment for new products.

In reviewing off-the-shelf software, find out what rights you have for free or discounted updates. These are later versions of the same program that incorporate certain improvements. For example, known 'bugs' may have been removed; or an update may run faster, be able to use a wider range of equipment, and generally be easier to operate as a result of feedback from users.

Investment in computer-based equipment should be discussed at the time when annual budgets are being prepared. It is prudent to make advance plans for the continuing replacement or updating of obsolescent equipment, setting aside money over a period of years. You should also consider whether it might be appropriate to lease equipment, rather than buying it. Leasing has important cash-flow advantages, and can increase your flexibility (see Box 2C). If you decide that purchase is the preferred option, then depreciate the equipment over the shortest time acceptable to your company's financial plan. Other factors to be included in your financial assessment are described in section 7.3.

If you are considering a very new application, try to assess the manufacturer's or supplier's place in the market: is the company likely to remain solvent and continue to provide replacement parts or updated software? Include within the estimated cost of untried systems the expense of teething troubles and initial failure. (Could you revert to the old system in an emergency? Could you afford quickly to provide an alternative?) Also try to define precisely the probable competitive gains. (Will this very advanced system place us at a commercial advantage? Will it remove the need for additional capital expenditure in the next three years?).

Box 2C   Leasing and renting

'Leasing' involves making payments over a number of years for the use of an item of equipment. This may be through an 'operating lease' or through a 'finance lease'.

A finance lease is rather like a hire-purchase agreement, usually through a finance company or a bank, with the user company typically acquiring ownership at the end of the period of lease.

In an operating lease, the user company never becomes the owner, and the leasing company will aim later to sell the equipment on the second-hand market. This frees the user to invest in new equipment.

Both methods help to spread the financial demands and make future expenditure more predictable. The operating lease also protects against obsolescence, especially if it contains clauses permitting review of the agreement after, say, three years. Similar possibilities arise with a finance lease, but in that case you will have to sell the original equipment yourself (and its second-hand value is usually depressingly low).

In both cases, there can be problems if the leasing company becomes bankrupt, or sells your lease to another company. And some leases can be for *too long* a period, if your business is changing rapidly or if newly designed equipment is substantially better than your own.

Shorter-term arrangements can be made through a rental agreement, perhaps only for a few months. This is similar to an operating lease, but usually requires a substantial down-payment at the outset. The cash-flow advantage is thus reduced.

Conflicts and trade-offs

As already noted, a basic trade-off is between performance and system reliability (section 2.3). 'Middle-aged' systems may be more reliable than those which are very new or old, but they may be less able to undertake important tasks than their innovative counterparts. Immature technologies or new applications are more risky; but they could hit the jack-pot.

Up-dated systems can sometimes be rendered ineffective through unexpected and specific forms of incompatibility (see section 2.2). Even when you can afford new equipment, it may turn out to require additional technical input before it meets your needs.

2.5　SYSTEM SECURITY

Importance

Security of information can be lost either through fraud or carelessness. *Computer fraud* in the United States has been estimated to run at several hundred million dollars each year. In addition to possible breaches of privacy, in respect of someone's health record or personal data, there are *three main commercial risks*: disclosure of confidential information to rival companies; unrecognized changes to information you are using; and the wiping out of crucial data. Security can be breached by telephone lines from outside the company (and ex-employees might find that quite easy), or from within, as current staff take advantage of their direct access. The problem is growing, as more information is stored and processed by computer, and as multi-user systems become diffused throughout a company.

Central data-processing departments are often quite secure, but what about the personal computers which have been installed elsewhere in the company, perhaps with their own access to the mainframe or wider network? Opportunities for fraud or insecure use have been increased enormously by this widespread development.

In evaluating your current or prospective system, you should therefore include examination of its degree of security in these several respects. It may be appropriate to consider separately the areas of personnel (staff records, individual documents, etc.), finance (materials costs, monthly performance figures, future projections), sales and marketing (selling prices, advertising plans, new products), production and purchasing (schedules and suppliers' discounts), and design and development (future plans and possible innovations). Threats from both inside and outside the company need to be considered, and the risk of entry by former employees should be assessed.

Other questions about security concern safeguards against *unintentional loss of data* rather than fraudulent interventions. Insecurity of that kind arises from system unreliability and from certain types of user error; those are considered in section 2.3 and in several parts of Chapter 3.

In many countries there is legislation to protect personal information. For example, in the United Kingdom computer users who handle data referring to any living individual are required to register under the Data Protection Act of

1984. Any automatic processing of information, even sorting through a list of individuals for a mailshot, is an application which comes under the scope of the Act. Registered data users must ensure that personal material is protected against unauthorized access or alteration, and individuals must be allowed to see information relating to themselves. If the information in incorrect, it has to be amended or deleted from the system. Parallel legislation in the USA is included in the Privacy Act of 1974 and the Right to Financial Privacy Act of 1978.

Questions you should ask

Is your computer system adequately secure against fraud, in respect of information about personnel, finance, sales and marketing, production and purchasing, and design and development?

Do threats to data security come from inside the company, outside the company, or both?

Does access need to be further restricted within the company?

Does the system need modification to exclude access from outside the company?

Can former employees enter your system?

Is the computer system secure against unintentional loss of data?

Are employees sufficiently careful and adequately trained in respect of security?

Is the company meeting legislative requirements (for example, in the United Kingdom the Data Protection Act)?

Things you can do

Security in very large systems is best tackled by experts, and advice should be sought if you think there are problems in this regard. Design changes to software and/or hardware might be required. In smaller installations, it may be possible and desirable to restrict the number of individuals who can use the system. This is usually done by having a personalized 'log-on' procedure, containing a password unique to the individual, which must be recognized by the system.

Sometimes you will need a more sophisticated procedure, where certain files are 'locked', or where the system is programmed to recognize different classes of user. For example, staff in the finance department require access to information about current and projected costs, which should not be available to other employees entering the system. Alternatively, while a document might need to be *read* by a number of people, it might be appropriate to restrict who is authorized to *change* it. Profiles of access can be designated for each user, with individuals' use of the system controlled through commercially-available security cards or other devices.

If you transmit confidential data down public telephone lines, you should consider the use of 'cryptographic' (or 'encryption') techniques. These code the message at the sending computer, transmitting it down the telephone line as a jumble of characters. It is then decoded by a similar piece of software at the receiving end. Although this is a very specialized procedure, you can buy quite effective programs to make it work.

It is easy to consider security of information as a technical issue and to think that the existence of passwords, security cards and different levels of access will solve the problem. However, security depends on people, and the success of any measures introduced will stand or fall according to the diligence of the staff. For example, it is disturbing that people store disks containing important data in cardboard boxes, and that these are left lying around the office. Security passwords are sometimes written down in obvious places, and they may have a rational sequence which can increase the chances of unauthorized access. In addition to paying attention to issues of that kind, some companies have found it helpful to obtain written undertakings from staff that they will follow established security procedures.

Conflicts and trade-offs

Elaborate security procedures can sometimes slow down normal working, cause distrust among employees, and reduce overall performance. Estimates of risk have to be balanced against possible detriment to performance and raised irritation among staff. There is always a danger that people will find ways around complex precautions, simply because they consider them too much of a hassle.

Aspects of job quality and the wider organization (considered in Chapters 4 and 5) can have knock-on effects to system security. If a job is badly designed from the employees' point of view and if organizational aspects have been ill-considered, there may be little staff identification with the system or the company. Resentment, alienation and even sabotage may then sometimes occur.

More detailed questions for minority use

A checklist of supplementary questions about system security is provided on page 174.

2.6 WORKING CONDITIONS

Importance

Human beings excel in their adaptability, and can cope to some degree in a wide range of environmental conditions. However, if they are to work really efficiently, their optimum range of conditions is very much narrower. For example, to ensure that seated operators remain comfortable indoors, temperatures between 19° C and 23° C should be maintained.

Employers in most countries are required by law to provide certain standards of working conditions. For example, in the United Kingdom employers are bound by the regulations of the Offices, Shops and Railway

Premises Act, 1963, and the Health and Safety at Work Act, 1975. In the United States, regulations derive from the Fair Labor Standards Act of 1938 and the Occupational Safety and Health Act of 1970. These legally required conditions should always be regarded as the minimum, and evaluation enquiries should extend more widely. In doing that, it is helpful to think in terms of *three separate headings*: the working environment, equipment and its siting, and physical hazards.

The *working environment* comprises the layout and structure of an office or shopfloor work-place, and the lighting, temperature, humidity, air quality and noise levels experienced by the user. Introducing computer equipment can have a significant effect on these environmental conditions. For example, a work-station of the kind used for computer-aided design can give off as much energy as a fan-heater. Even a standard visual display unit emits the same amount of heat as a 100-watt bulb. And computer terminals may have a drying effect on the atmosphere, lowering the amount of water vapour in the air and making operators feel uncomfortable.

In respect of *equipment and its siting*, the system and its user should be considered as a unit, with displays and controls easily accessible and effective. Yet many problems occur. In offices, for example, keyboards may merely be placed on previously installed furniture, without any thought being given to optimum position and the new operational requirements. More generally, ergonomic criteria are not always given due weight in the design of controls and displays.

Possible *physical hazards* include electrical shock, explosion, collision and unsafe walkways. These are widely recognized in principle, but in practice they are frequently ignored. For example, cables have recently proliferated in many offices, with clear dangers from tripping and electrocution.

The visual display unit (VDU) has itself been the object of much concern. There have been suggestions that VDUs can cause facial rashes, cataracts of the eyes, abnormal pregnancies, muscular injuries and eye strain.

Box 2D   Radiation and visual display units

The Health and Safety Executive in Britain has examined the possible health consequences of VDU working. Among their conclusions are the following:

(1) Some electromagnetic radiation is emitted from any piece of apparatus like a VDU. However, exposure to VDUs during the working day does not subject a person to levels approaching international limits of radiation. In most cases, measured levels are very substantially below existing limits.

(2) Electromagnetic radiation in the general environment is, by and large, several orders greater than that obtaining in the vicinity of a VDU.

The first three of these have been attributed to radiation or static electricity. However, research suggests that VDUs do not themselves particularly give rise to those effects, and that radiation and static electricity are not usually present in troublesome quantities. (Box 2D summarizes the conclusions.) But eye strain and muscular problems can occur widely, if screens and keyboards are badly sited and/or poorly designed, and if lengthy periods of concentration and fixed posture are required. These issues clearly deserve scrutiny within your evaluation.

Questions you should ask

Are there problems in respect of the working environment, for example regarding lighting, temperature, humidity, air quality or noise levels?

Are there problems in the layout of work-spaces?

Is the equipment and associated furniture designed and located in ways which fit the abilities and requirements of users?

Can equipment, furniture and work layout be adjusted by users to meet their needs?

Does the equipment conform to relevant safety standards?

Does the company carry out appropriate safety inspections and hazard audits?

Should more safety training be introduced?

Additional questions related to this issue are presented in section 4.8, when the possible impact of poor working conditions on users' health and safety is considered.

Things you can do

Specific problems will clearly need their own individual solutions. However, in general you should aim for maximum flexibility: chairs that adjust, detachable keyboards that can be placed where individual operators wish them to be, and visual display units that can be moved, tilted or swivelled, to achieve the best viewing position and to avoid unwanted reflections on the screen. A person required to work for long periods at a keyboard should be able to sit with feet flat on the floor or on a footrest, and with forearms approximately level. However, continuous sitting throughout the day should be avoided; some movement is necessary for both physiological and psychological reasons.

Office lighting is particularly important when considering VDU installation. Most lighting systems have been designed to illuminate the horizontal plane of a work desk, and they can cause problems for the near vertical screen of a VDU. Furthermore, the ideal amount of light required for reading a sheet of paper is greater than the illumination level best suited to VDU work. A number of companies have introduced local task lighting from desk lamps or hidden strip-lights that bounce light off the ceiling. In general, VDU screens should be placed at right angles to windows or other sources of strong light, and windows should themselves have adjustable screening. Anti-glare treatments for screens are available, and should be considered when there are problems.

Particular characteristics of VDUs have been subject to many investigations, and desirable features can now be specified. Detailed sets of evaluation questions are provided in Chapter 9, but at the very least you should expect stable, non-flickering characters and a consistent quality of presentation right up to the edges of the screen. Incidentally, the 'raw material' used by an employee responsible for data-input should also be examined: is the written source material adequately clear and suitably illuminated?

If an office has many VDUs and other items of equipment, the air may become excessively dry. That is especially likely when ventilation systems do not draw in sufficient air from outside the building. In those cases, the use of humidifiers should be considered. Other difficulties can arise from the generation of static electricity; anti-static carpets are sometimes desirable.

Noisy impact printers can be another problem, and acoustic shields should be considered where appropriate. Trailing power cables must at the very least be fastened together, preferably covered, and wherever possible they should be routed out of harm's way under the floor, in the ceiling cavity, or in ducts attached to the wall. Additional power sockets should be installed where necessary. Modular furniture can be bought which features special conduits to take cables. Employees should frequently be reminded of hazards. In that respect, notices drawing attention to safety on the shopfloor are commonplace, but education in office safety is less often provided.

More generally, capital equipment budgets should be reviewed in the light of information produced through this part of an evaluation project. It is common to find that companies set aside money for computers and other items of technology, but that they make no provision at all for the setting into which these will be placed and the furniture which will house them and their users. Yet small additional investment could yield major benefits.

Finally, it should be stressed that many complaints about equipment and working conditions have multiple sources. There may indeed be equipment problems of the kind illustrated in this section, but those can be compounded by the nature of users' jobs. For example, very limited variety in a VDU operator's job, or very long periods of continuous work, can magnify any problems in the equipment. So the issues of this section should be viewed in conjunction with themes introduced in Chapter 4, when job quality and user attitudes will be examined. Section 4.8 specifically takes up health and safety issues which are related to the present section.

Conflicts and trade-offs

A major conflict is once again between the desirable and the affordable. Operators and managers may have somewhat different views about that: managers may think they can afford less than operators desire. Nevertheless, if an equipment feature has been agreed to be unhealthy or unsafe, no compromise should be considered.

Conflicts of another kind can arise as equipment or its siting are modified to meet the problems illustrated here. Technically ideal solutions can sometimes run counter to the job quality principles described in Chapter 4. For example, procedures to reduce glare may lead to social isolation, with employees cut off from contact with others. And, as work-stations come closer to being technically faultless, there is a temptation for management to expect long continuous periods of work and to raise task demands beyond psychologically appropriate levels.

More detailed questions for minority use

Four checklists of detailed questions about equipment and working conditions are provided on pages 175 to 187.

Questionnaires for minority use

Two specialist questionnaires about VDU and keyboard use are provided on page 187.

3

Usability

The issues dealt with in this chapter are:

3.1 Ease of learning   41
3.2 Being in control   48
3.3 Degree of effort   51
3.4 System speed   54
3.5 Getting information in and out   57
3.6 Errors and error correction   59
3.7 Avoiding serious errors   62

This chapter will help you to evaluate the usability of your computer-based equipment. The focus is upon an individual user and the ways in which the system supports effective working or encourages errors. As in Chapter 2, we will present the basic evaluation questions to be asked through interviews, meetings and working parties. Practical recommendations about how to use these procedures will be given in Chapter 6. In Chapter 8, we will describe some more complex data-gathering approaches for use by a minority of readers, and forward references to possible applications will be made throughout the present chapter.

3.1 EASE OF LEARNING

Importance

It is very desirable that a computer-based system can be easily learned. That will speed up its effective use, reduce errors and other sources of disruption, allow flexible movement between jobs, help the induction of new staff, and encourage motivation rather than feelings of resentment and personal inadequacy.

Nevertheless, in some circumstances it may initially appear that ease of learning is not particularly important. When use is restricted to specialist programmers or engineers, their expertise can more often be taken for granted, and complexity may cause fewer problems. However, in accepting difficult software you have limited the options for organizing work.

For example, in the case of computer-controlled machine tools, programs which are difficult to understand and edit might be usable only by specialist engineers and never by machine operators. The alternative approach, insisting on programs that can be learned by less qualified users, permits enhancement of the quality of operators' jobs (see Chapter 4), and can improve machine utilization. It will also free programmers and engineers for more skilled and specialized work.

The general message here is that, although greater computing power may sometimes be available through difficult systems, those which are easy to learn provide greater organizational flexibility. That can be a major benefit, both for the company and for its employees.

In assessing ease of learning, *three separate themes* should be explored: the range and nature of available commands, the comprehensibility of concepts, and the adequacy of documentary and training support.

In respect of the *commands employed by the system*, the following are important: absence of arbitrariness, sensible grouping and appropriate number.

To reduce arbitrariness, it is desirable for individual commands to suggest by their nature what is intended. Thus within a word-processing package, it would seem natural that pressing the control key with 'P' will display the 'print' menu. There is in practice an inevitable limit to the number of simple commands which can be non-arbitrary in this sense, but you should look for naturalness in at least the very important ones.

Sensible grouping requires the bringing together of related instructions; an example in terms of keyboard layout is in Box 3A. This principle also involves the separation of commands which are unrelated. Learning is sometimes made more difficult by the fact that quite different activities are initiated by very similar instructions. For example, the keys for lower-case d, upper-case D, and control-d can within a single system have entirely different meanings. That results in learners becoming uncertain about the three instructions, with 'confusion errors' creeping in at unfortunate moments.

The actual number of commands is important, but on its own is ambiguous as an index of this form of usability. People do not need to learn all the instructions at once, and many specialized commands are never used at all. The crucial factor is not number alone but whether the set of commands seems to be excessive for the task in hand.

Command structures can sometimes be very rigid, with no flexibility or with very limited optional procedures. That is often intended to increase ease of learning and use, but the intention can be taken too far. For example, many systems rely extensively on 'menus' (lists of possible things you can do) and

---

Box 3A   Grouping of commands

Within the WordStar package for word processing, the following editing commands (preceded by the 'control' key) have the meanings as indicated:

A: move to the left one word
D: move to the right one character
E: move upwards one line
F: move to the right one word
S: move to the left one character
X: move downwards one line

That allocation of letters to commands may seem very unnatural, until you notice that part of the keyboard, very familiar to users, is laid out like this:

Q   W   E   R   T
A   S   D   F   G
Z   X   C   V   B

From a starting point between 'S' and 'D', the group of six commands is thus very sensible, with magnitude and direction of each move being indicated by the position of its key.

'prompts' (requesting you to type something), so that there is less need to learn a special language of commands. These types of system are easy to grasp, but they are often rigid in operation, requiring a user to move through each pre-specified step on every occasion. In considering learnability, therefore, we must recognize that programs which have been made more easy to learn will thereby sometimes be less flexible in operation. (See also section 3.2, on controlling the software.) Some flexibility in menu-based programs can be introduced by providing 'jump-ahead' facilities; these are described in Box 3B.

The second general factor to be considered when assessing ease of learning is the degree to which the system's *core concepts are readily understood*. Ideally, an employee should be using ideas or terms which are generally familiar or which are part of everyday work for the company. You need, therefore, to watch out for concepts which are strange or which are specific to a particular make of system. Furthermore, the conceptual framework should be as obvious as possible, and used consistently throughout. For instance, the system should not refer to a 'mail-box' at one point and an 'in-tray' at another. It is difficult to learn how to operate an overall system, if different concepts are required at different stages.

There should be a good fit between the concepts normally used in a person's work, and the concepts around which the system is built. This is one of the reasons for the popularity of 'spreadsheet' programs. These provide a display which consists of rows and columns of figures, with text where needed, for

---

Box 3B   Jump-ahead procedures in menu-based systems

It is easy to understand a menu-selection system, but expert users can become frustrated by its slowness. They have to go through each step of successive displays, waiting for every transition, even when they know in advance which options they intend to choose. A solution is to provide a jump-ahead facility, allowing people to skip several levels of the menu tree and to omit a lengthy series of menu displays. Two kinds of jump-ahead procedure are the 'type-ahead' method and the 'direct-access' facility.

In the type-ahead method, the user who can remember a string of choices he or she wishes to make can type all of these in at once. The number of pre-chosen steps is at the discretion of the user at any point, and the system then moves on as far as it is requested.

The direct-access method relies on each point in the menu having its own unique name. The user is able to jump directly to that point by typing in the name. He or she is likely to learn the names of particularly frequent routes, and short-cuts can be taken in one single jump.

Both procedures have been found to be effective for experienced users. The direct-access method is particularly helpful if the menu structure is complex and difficult to understand, and when the menu points have easy-to-learn names which cannot be mixed up with each other. However, if the organization of the menu system is familiar and if clear and easily distinguishable labels cannot be found, then the type-ahead facility can provide a possible alternative.

---

example along the top and down the left-hand column. Each cell (the intersection between a row and a column) can receive a figure or a formula (for multiplication, division, calculating a monthly average, or whatever). As new figures are inserted, calculations are made automatically, without the need to learn a detailed language of accounting instructions. The concepts and procedures fit well with people's usual way of thinking. See Box 3C for an example.

Some systems allow you to act directly on visual representations ('icons') of relevant objects. For example, in a computer-based process-control system the user might be able to set the desired operating temperature, control flows, etc. by directly adjusting pictures of thermometers and opening taps on the VDU screen. The Macintosh office system works in a similar manner: pictures of documents can be placed into pictures of folders or into the 'trash can' if they are no longer required. An example of this approach can be seen in Box 3D. Systems of that kind are quite easy to learn, and users benefit from having immediate feedback about the results of any action.

Third in assessing ease of learning, you should examine the provision of *documentary and training support*. In part this is a question of equipment design, where on-line training programs and facilities to provide help should

Box 3C   Example of a company spreadsheet

Company details of all kinds can be stored and updated as illustrated below. Cells can hold numerical data as inserted (for example, in rows 4, 5, 6, 9, 13 and 14), but they can also hold formulae. It is the results of applying these formulae which appear in the spreadsheet (e.g. in rows 8, 10, 15 and 17).

Running totals or averages can be requested, or monthly progress against targets. When you change any one number, all the cells holding formulae referring to that number will display an updated value.

	1	2	3	4	5
1					
2		January	February	March	April
3	EXPENDITURE				
4	Wages	81050	83010	82950	86170
5	Materials	77450	79620	79870	82690
6	Overheads	31270	32110	36060	37230
7					
8	Total	189770	194740	198880	206090
9	Last year	182610	181620	186520	190370
10	% difference	4	7	7	8
11					
12	INCOME				
13	Sales	271490	203130	252170	263410
14	Last year	233130	199080	222380	236980
15	% difference	16	2	13	11
16					
17	GROSS PROFIT	81720	8390	53290	57320

be envisaged. The quality of those facilities, and of associated manuals and other documents, should be assessed within your evaluation. People rarely read a manual from cover to cover, but use it when they have special needs. So there should be a clear layout, with a good index which allows users to enter the text at appropriate points. Descriptive headings and sub-headings should be employed, with examples and diagrams when required. It is particularly important that you can obtain the specific information you need when you are having difficulties, and good 'trouble-shooting' sections should be provided for all principal problems.

Ease of learning is of course also influenced by the training provided to novice users. The characteristics of your company's training should be assessed within your evaluation, and training issues are discussed at several points in the book. Relevant sections include 4.2, 'Skills required'; 5.4,

Box 3D   Example of a graphics-based system

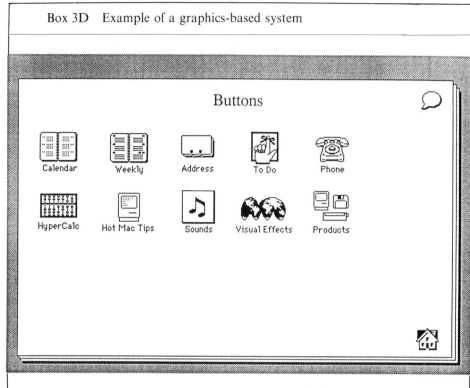

A screen from the Apple Macintosh HyperCard™ system. Each small picture or 'icon' represents a collection of information which can be accessed by selecting that icon with a pointing device called a 'mouse'.

'Selection and training'; and 7.5, 'Providing organizational support'. (See also pages 48, 61 and 63 in the present chapter.)

For the beginner, it is much easier to learn a large system bit by bit than as a whole. So a system in which the learner can start with just a part is much less demanding and less likely to cause despondency. If possible, avoid systems where an inadvertent move by a confused person might suddenly bring to light new aspects that the learner is not yet ready to meet.

Questions you should ask

In order to evaluate this first aspect of usability, the following questions should prove useful:

Do the required actions or commands appear to be arbitrary, or can reasons for them easily be seen?
Are the commands organized into sensible and understandable groups?
Are the operating procedures over-elaborate and excessively rigid, in an attempt to increase learnability?

Does the system use understandable concepts, or are there many difficult new ideas to be learnt?

Are any of the system's messages ambiguous?

Are there effective on-line help screens?

Can on-line help be accessed from any part of the system?

Does the system behave consistently throughout? And are users required to operate in consistent ways?

Are training procedures adequate, both for novices and experienced users?

Does the system have an on-line training facility? If so, is it a good one?

Is it easy or difficult to get information which you need from the manual provided?

Is the documentation well indexed to help people get out of current difficulties?

Do manuals and documents present information in a language appropriate for users?

Can learners be 'insulated' from wider aspects of the system, so that they can safely learn separate parts?

Things you can do

Potential purchasers ought to enquire about these aspects when choosing between systems. If you have equipment already installed in your company, ease of learning can still be influenced, through local documents or through tailor-made training.

For example, when the manufacturer's manuals are large and forbidding, try making up your own two-page document on 'How to get started with...'. It may also be worth writing short descriptions of how to do particular jobs which are common in your organization and how to solve frequently-occurring problems. Charts of main command sequences or options can be drawn up. These local documents might be in loose-leaf folders, for subsequent additions, and can be extremely valuable to novice users. In other cases, additional 'help' files might be set up within the computer itself.

Besides documenting how-to-do-it, some kinds of system might also benefit from an overall picture of how things work. This need not be in any way an engineering or technical description; indeed it need not be strictly accurate, and an analogy might suffice. Go for something on the lines of 'You can think of it like this...', and describe in simple terms what happens at each stage of the system's activity. Giving new users this kind of map of the system is particularly important when concepts are unfamiliar and complex.

Remember that opportunities to acquire skills and knowledge occur frequently in any job setting; learning does not occur only on a training course. It is desirable to encourage colleagues to assist each other, and to make notes about useful procedures which can be shared around. Such informal training is especially important for new employees, but it should also be fostered among established work-groups. Gains in effectiveness will often be matched by increased feelings of personal commitment and group cohesiveness.

More generally, a substantial investment in training is required if your company wishes to move to really advanced equipment. (The fact that such a move is not always appropriate for every company was emphasized in section 2.4.) 'State of the art' technology requires very high levels of operator skill, and this cannot be acquired without the expenditure of considerable effort, time and money. Whereas the thrust of this section remains true for equipment at all levels of sophistication, that ease of learning is a desirable attribute, there are occasions when even a relatively easily learned system of an advanced kind presents a substantial challenge. If that system is judged essential for your company's effectiveness, there is no way to by-pass the provision of quite sophisticated training.

More detailed questions for minority use

Checklists about the three aspects of ease of learning are provided on pages 189 to 192.

Specialist procedures for minority use

If you have the need and resources for a more complex investigation of this issue, consider the specialist procedures of system walk-through and comparative testing in conjunction with task analysis (see pages 162, 170 and 168).

3.2 BEING IN CONTROL

Importance

A common complaint about computer systems is that users feel they are not 'in control'. They will describe how there are times when the system behaves unpredictably, 'does its own thing', refuses to do what they want, or simply goes dead on them. In these cases, the users' problem is that they do not know why it is behaving in this way or what they can do to regain control. Loss of control interrupts work, causes frustration, makes the system hard to learn, undermines morale, and might mean the loss of valuable information.

There can be problems of 'modes', or operational subsystems. These make the meaning or the validity of a particular command depend upon the current state of the system. For example, a word-processing system may have an 'insert' mode and a 'replace' mode. In the former, typed characters are inserted into the text, whereas in the latter mode they overwrite and replace the current text. It is easy to think you are in 'insert' mode, when in fact you have forgotten your earlier shift to 'replace'. As a result you can inadvertently delete previously typed material.

It is generally believed that systems with fewer modes are easier to control, because there is less likelihood of confusion about which mode you are in. However, there is a limit to this, and 'modeless' systems, in which the meaning of each command always stays the same, present software designers with particularly difficult problems.

In the typical system which does have modes, you should make sure that each one is labelled in a distinctive and obvious way on the screen, so that confusions are avoided wherever possible. You should also examine the users' tasks. Do changes in mode fit naturally with changes of task, or do they occur at apparently arbitrary points? What would happen at each point if the user forgot to change mode? If the system would reject the next command (or if the user could undo it easily), the problem may not be serious. But if the system would obey it, and if the user could not reverse the consequences quickly, this aspect deserves a low mark in your evaluation.

What about ease of movement in a complex program? Some systems consist of a lot of 'menus' (lists of options, from which a choice is to be made), arranged in a tree-like organization. When the user selects one option in a menu, another menu is presented, and then another (see also section 3.1, 'Ease of learning'). Having reached the end of a sequence of menus, users can find themselves in the wrong place, needing to go somewhere else to get what they want done. Or they may simply be lost. In either case, time is wasted and irritation increased as users have to return to previous menus and go down other branches. It is most important that the form and content of a menu system is such that users can easily find their way around.

Good systems have clearly labelled options to 'go back one step' or 'go back to the beginning'. In addition, material which has been deleted by accident should easily be retrievable. Even if users have successfully done what they wanted, they may still have to work hard to extricate themselves from one part of the system in order to do something else. This process can be assisted if the system has kept a log or a history of what has happened, allowing you to 'replay' your activities and locate previous stages for reworking. The presence or absence of that facility should be checked in your evaluation. An effective on-line 'help' facility is also desirable.

Any system has of course to set some constraints on the user. The point is that these constraints can sometimes remove options in a way which users find unreasonable and counterproductive. Data-entry programs can require fixed sequences and refuse to move on until a blank field has been filled. Data-bases may prohibit enquiries which seem sensible to the user. To control the system, users need at any point to have clear bearings in terms of modes, menus, etc. (the points raised above), but they also need to be provided with options which are appropriate for getting the work done.

Questions you should ask

Do users report that they frequently do not feel in control of the system?
Do users complain that the system is often unpredictable?
Is it clear what are the possible user actions at any stage?
Does the system clearly acknowledge all entries by the user?
Does the screen indicate the state of the system at each stage of a task?
Is it possible easily to go back to earlier stages?
Does the system contain an on-line 'help' facility? If so, is that adequate?

If the system contains different modes, are they easily distinguished on
screen, and do they naturally fit the structure of the task?

If the system contains menus, are they effective for the tasks in hand?

Does the system automatically keep a log of modifications which have been
made during this session of work?

Do users frequently find it necessary to experiment, because they are not
certain where they are?

Things you can do

Once again, locally prepared documentation may be useful. This is particularly the case for menu-based systems, where a diagram of each set of options can
increase people's feelings of control. However, merely showing the names of
optional commands is often not enough. Also required are notes about how
each one should be used and about how it should be formatted. Details about
the consequences of use should also be given, with information about
procedures which can undo any changes and which can provide help in case of
extreme difficulty.

If there are any particularly common tasks which regularly cause users to
lose control, it might help to include detailed step-by-step information on how
to perform them, rather than leave people to struggle through the manual or to
experiment with whatever seems a good idea at the time.

If errors are frequent, you should identify the more common ones and
provide notes on how to recover from them. That is less satisfactory than
avoiding mistakes in the first place, but it is cheap and can be very effective. In
other cases, specialist staff may be available to modify programs through
inserted reminders and warnings about possible mistakes. (It is of course
preferable to amend programs more substantially, to exclude the possibility of
errors, but that is usually less practicable.)

If you are considering a new system, you should set up procedures to
examine themes of the kind described here. For a microcomputer or small of-
the-shelf system, you should work on it yourself or get the suppliers to
demonstrate tasks needed in your own company. Look to see whether, and
under what circumstances, you or they lose control of the software. For larger
systems, or those specifically designed for your own needs, the same questions
should be asked through use of interim prototypes or mock-ups of early
versions.

More detailed questions for minority use

A checklist of detailed questions about this issue is provided on page 192.

Specialist procedure for minority use

If you have the need and resources for a more complex investigation of this
issue, consider the specialist procedure of system walk-through (see page 162).

3.3 DEGREE OF EFFORT

Importance

Another aspect of usability is the degree of effort which has to be put into each task. Some effort is of course essential to get any job done, and moderate demands are psychologically desirable (see section 4.4, 'Work demands'). However, some systems require excessive and unnecessary effort.

Four aspects need to be considered. First is the *physical effort* involved. In manufacturing or assembly applications of new technology, this may be a question of lifting components or finished products and stretching to operate equipment, perhaps for sustained periods. In office settings, the question may be how long are periods of continuous data-input work or how many keystrokes are needed to undertake a task.

Reducing the number of keystrokes is in principle desirable, and this has sometimes been attempted through use of a 'macro-language'. That form of 'customization' permits a set of actions to be grouped together, perhaps with their own descriptive name, so that a small number of keystrokes can initiate a longer sequence of work. Parcelling up frequently-used sequences in this way can be helpful in reducing keystrokes, and a variety of applications are possible.

In practice, however, there are often difficulties. The procedures for building up macro-commands are often hard to master, and problems are not easy to anticipate without considerable experience of the system. Macro-languages should therefore be viewed with caution in the majority of work settings.

A second type of effort comes from the level of *demand on a user's memory*, for example in remembering what one is doing, where one has got to, or what one was doing before an interruption. Moving material from one place in a document to another is a typical problem where memory demands can be too great. Some systems do not show visually, before the operation, exactly what material is to be transferred to where. Sometimes the operation is in two stages, moving the material first into a hidden store (a 'register', 'buffer' or 'clipboard'). If this hidden store cannot readily be checked, the user has to rely on his or her memory, increasing the probability that mistakes will be made. This type of memory-load problem can occur in many other settings (see for example Box 3E).

Perhaps the worst type of memory load occurs when dealing with material which contains cross-references. These can be of many sorts, such as forward references in the text, or references to other tables or to other entries in spreadsheets or data-bases. Keeping track of all these interdependencies can be very difficult, and a well-designed system should be sufficiently integrated and explicit that it takes this memory load off the user. It is thus desirable if interdependencies can be displayed visually on request.

Third is *effort which comes from 'knock-on' effects*, when a small modification to part of the text or data demands a search through the rest of the material in order to make compensatory adjustments. For instance, changing the position of a component in a drawing may mean that all other components need to be

Box 3E   How poor visibility can cause mistakes

Suppose that the department manager, Maggie Neale, wants to send a message by electronic mail to two colleagues, and to send a copy of the message to all persons who might be affected by it. The message gives the two individuals permission to use a certain room, and Maggie's first thought is to notify other users of that room. So she heads her message thus:

To: Arnold Bartram, Cathy Davies
Copy to: Elizabeth Forster, Graham Hancock, Ian Josephson

Now she must close the address list, and move on to her message:

You can use Room 213 to store your video equipment. It will have to be kept locked, of course. Other users please note.

Here, Maggie remembers that besides the other users, she needs to inform the security staff. Unfortunately, on this particular system, the address list is not visible or editable at the same time as the message itself. She could store the message, re-open the address list, add the name of the security officer to the list, close the list, and re-open the message. However that would require a lot of effort, and by then she might have lost track of what else she wanted to say; so Maggie decides to finish the message and add the additional name to the address list afterwards.

··· Keys will be available from my secretary tomorrow.

Now Maggie makes a mental note that she must ask her secretary to obtain keys for all users. She realizes that she must copy this message to her secretary, but judges it better to continue with the text and fix the address list later.

··· You can ask the chief porter to arrange help with moving the gear to Room 213.

The chief porter is yet another person who needs a copy. At this point Maggie has three additional people to notify. It is quite possible that she will overlook one of them. This apparent carelessness would not be Maggie's fault, but a by-product of the system design. The cost of it is organizational confusion and bad feeling.

In a better electronic mail system, the whole message, including the header part (here containing the 'copy to' information) would be visible and editable continuously. Systems should always let you act on something you have just remembered, rather than requiring you to retain it in memory until you are allowed to use it.

adjusted; inserting a new figure in a document means that all other figures need to be updated; even inserting a new sentence may mean that all page breaks have to be inspected, to see that they occur in the intended places.

Taking time out to deal with these details may mean that users lose track of what they were doing. If there are four or five modifications and each one creates a wave of knock-on effects, users are likely to forget one of the planned modifications. The better systems give some help in protecting you against unfortunate consequences of small changes, by automatically excluding potential mistakes. A good word-processing package, for instance, includes a 'conditional page throw' command, which can ensure that a table does not become split over two pages.

Finally, we should consider the amount of *effort required in making decisions.* These occur, for example, in classifying documents, deciding how to lay out information, choosing sub-headings, and organizing where each piece of information should go in the finished product. The need for this type of effort has increased substantially as software has become more powerful. Options are offered in terms of style and layout, with users having themselves to decide what is most desirable. (Needing to anticipate the preferences of colleagues and bosses can sometimes add to the decision-making load.).

Extreme cases of decision-making effort are seen in desktop publishing systems, where, in the words of one advertisement, you are offered 'power bounded only by your own imagination'. Such flexibility is excellent for some purposes, but it is often bought at the price of excessive load on the user, who may be uneasy at the increased responsibility which has to be borne. Systems for computer-aided design also require particular decision-making effort, for example in planning where to start a 'drawing', where to locate it on the screen, and what scale to use. Many of these decisions are unavoidable, but their impact on the effort required of the user can be minimized by good design. For example, a good system will remember what decision was made last time, and present that as the first option, but with the possibility of amending the earlier choice if you wish.

Questions you should ask

Do experienced users report that it is hard work to operate the system?

Does the number of keystrokes or other physical actions seem excessive?

Is there a macro-language for customizing the system? Does it do what it is claimed to do? Is it easy to use? Could it be simplified in any way? Could you take better advantage of it?

Are there points where the user has too much to remember?

Are there some actions that deflect the user away from the main chain of actions, such as dealing with knock-on effects?

Does the system offer many different ways of doing the work? If so, is adequate guidance or structure provided? Is the decision-making load frequently too great?

Things you can do

If there are points where the users have a lot to remember or where they have to transfer complex material from one part of the system to another, try to devise and write down a systematic procedure for them to follow. If knock-on effects are unavoidable and the system has a macro-language, it may be possible to devise extra commands in the macro-language to make the job easier. However, this will require some programming expertise, either within the company or from an outside agency.

Several suggestions in other parts of this chapter may prove helpful. For example, systems which assist the user to retain control (section 3.2) also reduce the required effort, as do locally produced documents to describe procedures and to assist in tasks with a high memory load.

As with other issues in the chapter, evaluation must be in relation to the sophistication and complexity of the system being examined. With 'state of the art' technology which is considered necessary for company success, required effort tends to be greater than with simpler equipment. The point to stress is that, at all levels of complexity, a well-designed system is one that minimizes effort in the ways described here.

More detailed questions for minority use

A checklist about degree of effort is provided on page 193.

Specialist procedures for minority use

If you have the need and resources for a more complex investigation of this issue, consider the specialist procedures of system walk-through, formal observation, user diaries, system logging, task analysis, or comparative testing (see pages 162 to 172).

3.4 SYSTEM SPEED

Importance

Almost all current systems require you to wait at some point while information is processed. The issue for evaluation is whether these periods of waiting interfere with the task in hand.

Requirements vary between situations. For example, system response times must be extremely short for a tele-sales operator entering information into a terminal while a caller is on the line. Requests for a new menu or for the movement of text should also be handled quickly. However, searchers in a large database may be prepared to accept delay as the price for achieving results. In general, delays can be very annoying if they interrupt the rhythm of the task or distract you from a current line of thought. This is often a major problem with multi-user systems, when other people's work can slow down your own activities. On the other hand, if you have in any case to stop and think about what to do next, it is quite acceptable for the machine to be dealing with your last command while you work out the next step.

When users need to carry out a series of intermediate operations (see the 'knock-on' problems described in section 3.3), long response times may have particularly serious consequences. People forced to wait for what they consider an excessive time can often be forgetful. Long pauses which occur at unpredictable moments can cause particular irritation, especially when high levels of mental effort are required or when tasks seem to be of minor importance.

In evaluating this aspect of usability, it is therefore important to examine not only the frequency and duration of enforced pauses. The key questions are whether the pauses are predictable and where they occur in relation to the task.

Another aspect of system speed concerns processes occurring after a user has made an input. He or she might have moved on to other work, assuming that consequential changes have been made in the relevant database, whereas that process may be delayed through priority allocations of time to other functions within the system. As a result of such a delay, other people accessing the database may receive false information. An example of this is shown in Box 3F.

Box 3F   Delayed updates to a stock control database

A wholesaling company known to one of the authors installed a computer system to handle business in its depots and also to manage company accounts and personnel records in head office. Its designers used a shared processing system which prioritized particular activities, especially changes to the company ledgers. When priority tasks were being undertaken, other inputs were held in store for later processing.

Check-out operators in the depots were required to key in all items as they were sold, as a result of which recorded stock levels were adjusted and (when required) replacements were ordered. Managers had separate access to the current levels of stock, in part so they could answer enquiries from customers.

Serious problems arose because the prioritizing system delayed the incorporation of check-out information for varying, and unknown, durations. Although the operators received feedback that their input had been received, changes to the central database followed erratically, in a few minutes or up to two days later. As a result, the depot managers had no confidence in their information about stock levels. Worried that they might lose business owing to stock-outs, they played safe by ordering additional quantities of the most popular lines. As a result of computerization, stock levels were thus increased, rather than decreased as intended.

Questions you should ask

Do people often complain that the system is slow?

Are there certain times of the day or other occasions when this happens? Could work be re-scheduled to avoid those delays?

Are there certain operations after which users have to wait before they can take the next important step?

Is the system's response time short enough when users are carrying out mental calculations or holding information in mind; or do they have to remember too much while they wait for the machine?

If the system requires users to investigate knock-on effects (or any other repetitive operation), can they do it quickly? If not, does it matter seriously if users choose to save time by not checking?

In multi-user systems, is the method for selecting priority work appropriate for meeting business goals?

In multi-user systems, do all users understand the method for selecting priority work?

Do long response times sometimes surprise the users?

Generally, are response times appropriate to the task?

Are databases updated either promptly or with known delays?

Things you can do

Suppliers can advise you about devices and software packages which can speed up processing and the transfer of data between components. Make sure that changes you make are compatible with your current (and anticipated) software and data (see section 2.2).

Rather than buying new hardware, it may be possible to change your work practices so that they better suit the processing limitations of the system. Indeed, departmental objectives, work practices and possible alternatives should always be examined before hardware investments are made. For example, systems which are used by several people simultaneously tend to be very slow at particular peak times of the day. You should examine usage and needs, attempting to even out the load and thus reduce delays. Sometimes merely forewarning other users of predicted high workload can permit them to schedule tasks to everyone's advantage. With prospective purchases, it may be worthwhile simulating typical peak-time loads to assess response time and throughput in a similar way.

In making changes of those kinds, you should bear in mind the issues of job quality raised in Chapter 4. It may be possible both to cope with low system speed and to improve the quality of users' jobs through the same set of changes.

However, delays in multi-user systems may be unavoidable. In those cases it is particularly important to check that priority is accorded through decision rules which are explicitly geared to business goals. It would be unwise to operate on the basis of a 'first come, first served' principle, if certain tasks have clear business priority. In all cases the decision rules which are applied in determining priority should be clear to all users, so that they can plan their work within a known framework.

In the last resort, then, if speed cannot be increased at desirable points, users need to accept unavoidable pauses as an opportunity for brief respite or for completing other tasks. This can be helped if the system gives some indication that appropriate processing is underway. Better still, it may communicate to the user how much time remains before the operation is complete. Some systems provide a clock face and moving finger, or a decreasing row of symbols, for that purpose. A statement of how many other users are currently working on a multi-user system can also give a general rule-of-thumb guide to likely response times.

Specialist procedure for minority use

If you have the need and resources for a more complex investigation of this issue, consider the specialist procedure of user diaries (see page 166).

3.5   GETTING INFORMATION IN AND OUT

Despite the processing speed of computers, it can sometimes be difficult to get the necessary information into or out of them. Well-designed keyboards, high-resolution displays and effective printers are essential, but the issue is not merely one of hardware. Problems often stem from a mismatch between the way the system works and the task being undertaken by the user.

Input difficulties can arise when a system requests information in a sequence or format incompatible with the user's source of information. For example, when entering data from invoices, problems arise if information is required by the computer in a different sequence from that laid out on the hard copy. Deviations from a standard input procedure can also cause problems, for example when the same customer address covers several successive invoices but the system requires repeated typing of those details in each case.

Visual representations of the structure of information to be entered are particularly desirable. In addition, it should be clear what inputs are valid. 'Visual templates' can sometimes be appropriate, to help users remember what information the system expects. Examples include 'on-screen forms', which look like conventional paper forms with spaces for direct entry of data. Another useful type of template, for a different application, is the outline which is provided for spreadsheet calculations (see section 3.1).

When getting information out of the system, many problems also stem from system—task mismatches. It is common to find software which prints out enormous quantities of material, when the amount required is in fact very limited. Superficially, comprehensive output might appear desirable, to cope with all possible needs, but in practice it often wastes time and energy. Template-based methods are again often helpful. For example, instead of having to learn the vocabulary and grammar of a command language, a user might simply fill in a form displayed on the screen, specifying directly the information to be retrieved.

More generally, users need to be able to extract information quickly from a screen or printout. All required information should be available to view, and there must be as little extraneous material as possible. The structure of information displayed should match the user's thinking and current needs. Colour or other forms of coding should assist visual scanning and reduce possible ambiguities. Items of information should be grouped in sensible ways relative to the task in hand.

Questions you should ask

Do people complain that entering data is unnecessarily tedious?

Do they make a large number of errors when entering data?

Do the data characteristics or required concepts make it difficult to enter material in a straightforward way?

Can users suggest simple short cuts which should save a lot of time?

Do users complain that displays are confusing?

Is everything users need to see available easily?

How much of each printout is actually relevant to the job in hand?

Can users print out everything they would like to, and in the format they want?

Does the printed form of information correspond to the version displayed on screen, or does it contain unexpected changes?

Does the way information is presented fit in with the user's own way of viewing the task? Is it easy to misinterpret the information?

Things you can do

You may be able to reorganize work to fit the system more closely. For example, perhaps you could redesign the paper forms on which the information is received, so that they have the same layout as is presented on the VDU screen.

It may also be sensible to consider specialized input devices, to speed transmission into the system. An optical character reader or a barcode reader might be useful when input information refers to a single object. Voice input devices are rapidly becoming more sophisticated and effective. In some circumstances, you may benefit from a screen that is sensitive to touch, so that users can point directly at the options displayed to obtain information. That is particularly useful in environments where there is a limited space or where conventional keyboards could be damaged. Light-pens and mouse input devices may also be worth considering. Output will typically be printed in alpha-numeric form, but graph plotters should occasionally be considered; and some companies might find microfiche output useful for certain purposes.

Changes to input or output procedures should always be considered in terms of their influence upon the content of jobs more generally. Data entry, for example, is sometimes the largest part of a job and can be extremely tedious. Modifications here can have good or bad, but not always anticipated, consequences for job quality. Issues described in Chapters 4 and 5 are thus also important under the present heading.

If you are intending to buy new equipment, arrange for a trial which covers your own kind of work, and make sure that future users are given a chance to comment. With systems tailor-made for your own needs, prototypes and mock-ups are essential. (See also section 7.4.) As mentioned in other sections, it is highly desirable to undertake some typical work tasks, checking that all is well. Look for cases where users have difficulty finding what they need to know, and where input procedures appear to be unnecessarily complicated.

More detailed questions for minority use

A checklist of detailed questions about this issue is provided on page 194.

Specialist procedures for minority use

If you have the need and resources for a more complex investigation, consider the specialist procedure of system walk-through in conjunction with task analysis (see pages 162 and 168).

3.6   ERRORS AND ERROR CORRECTION

Importance

Everyone makes mistakes from time to time. This is particularly likely when people are under pressure, tired or subject to frequent interruption, or when they do not adequately understand the system.

However, some systems have characteristics which appear to encourage mistakes. (Here we are thinking of relatively small problems; particularly serious errors will be considered in the next section.) You should assess this feature as part of your evaluation of usability, and also examine whether or not errors can be corrected easily once they have been made; 'unforgiving' systems in the latter respect are particularly undesirable.

Several important classes of errors have been introduced in earlier sections. Confusion errors, where the user mixes up different instructions, and problems in switching between modes, were examined in sections 3.1 and 3.2 respectively, and errors arising from excessive memory or decision-making load were described in section 3.3. Four additional sources of error are as follows.

Inconsistency.   If the system requires users to carry out the same activity differently in different circumstances, then errors will be encouraged. A person is likely to fail to recognize the circumstance in question or to forget that there is a need to change behaviour between the settings.

Ambiguity of instructions.   The instructions presesented through the screen or other display should be unambiguous. That is not always so. (See Box 3G for an example.)

Encouragement of 'capture' errors. Other mistakes arise when a particular sequence of actions becomes highly practised and inappropriately draws in

---

Box 3G   An ambiguous instruction

One system with which we are familiar gives the following message when
you press 'quit'.

Changes made. Quit anyway? (Yes/No)

That seems straightforward. You might think the computer is telling you
that it has made the requested changes. But actually it is giving you a
warning that you have made changes which *have not been saved*. If you
quit the program by indicating Yes, you would lose everything you did
during that session. A better message would be of this kind:

Changes not yet saved. Quit will lose them.
Do you still want to quit? (Yes/No)

---

other actions. For example, if two files or two commands have similar names,
commencing with the same first letters, you are likely to run into difficulty. The
more common name may sometimes 'capture' the other one, so that you type
in the wrong item after starting the sequence of letters. That may only be a
minor inconvenience (irritating if you are under time pressure), but it can
sometimes lead to the loss of important data.

'Setting-up' demands.   Errors can occur when a separate and additional
action is required to initiate the events on which a person is primarily
concentrating. For example you may have to take time out to specify the size of
paper on which a document is to be printed. When in a hurry, you may forget
to do that, so the document is printed on the previously-requested basis.
Layout, page breaks, etc. will therefore be incorrect. Setting-up activities often
give rise to mistakes of that kind, especially when details are difficult to
remember or when changes are infrequent and unfamiliar.

It is clear that systems should be designed to discourage errors of these kinds.
In addition, you should examine the ease with which each type of mistake can
be corrected. Information might be provided on the screen to assist recovery,
for example, and 'undo' or 'go back' commands should be available. Many
systems make it surprisingly difficult to recover from mistakes, despite the
obvious importance of that process.

Some errors cannot be immediately corrected because the user does not
understand what has gone wrong. In those cases there will often be a need to
consult the trouble-shooting sections of documents supplied with the
equipment. Possible weaknesses in documentation have been considered in
section 3.1, 'Ease of learning', and you will need to include those aspects in
evaluating ease of error correction.

Questions you should ask

Do people seem overly cautious in the way they use the system?
Do they use long-winded methods to avoid making errors?

Do users spend a lot of time correcting simple slips?

Do users have to do what ought to be the same thing in different ways?

Are all important instructions completely clear?

Are there frequent 'capture' errors in the system, in which well-practised sequences wrongly take over other, slightly different sequences?

Does the system insist on troublesome setting-up operations?

Do manuals and documents meet users' needs when errors have been made?

Generally, is it easy or difficult to correct errors?

Things you can do

If a system seems particularly to encourage troublesome errors, or makes it difficult to correct them, the purchase or creation of improved software is likely to be worthwhile. For example, you should avoid packages with action sequences that are very similar. At the very least, prompts should be provided, to warn the user about possible confusions. Frequent setting-up operations are in general undesirable, but, if they cannot be avoided, it may be possible to give users an automatic reminder through a 'macro-language' (see section 3.3 and Box 3H).

Box 3H   Using a macro-language for setting up an activity

One of the authors used to archive his data onto disks that were kept 'locked' (protected against being overwritten or changed), and which he kept forgetting to unlock. On this particular system, trying to start the archive process before unlocking the disk wasted several frustrating minutes. So he used a macro-language to make a new archiving command, consisting of the old instruction with a relevant message.

The first thing the new command did was to display the message: 'Unlock the disk, if you haven't already, and then press the Return key'. Then it waited for the Return key to be pressed, and the author would unlock the disk before the archiving process got under way. This macro-language reminder worked extremely well.

If improved software is unobtainable, you should systematically prepare notes for local use. Summarize the main kinds of errors which are likely, and specify in detail how each one can be corrected. Use of this self-teaching procedure is a form of training. However, there may be occasions when more explicit training activities are required. For example, new users should be given instruction about likely errors and their correction, with practice at avoiding and resolving problems. For that purpose you should devise some typical error-creating situations, putting together documents and a systematic training package, which can also be used with new learners at a later time.

More detailed questions for minority use

A checklist of questions about errors and error correction is provided on page 197.

Specialist procedures for minority use

If you have the need and resources for a more complex investigation of this issue, consider the specialist procedures of formal observation and system logging (see pages 164 and 167).

3.7 AVOIDING SERIOUS ERRORS

Importance

Given that everyone makes mistakes sometimes, it is important that the effects are not catastrophic. Systems should be designed to prevent mistaken actions giving rise to devastating outcomes. 'Fault-tolerance' of that kind is increasingly built into modern equipment, yet calamitous errors are not unknown.

In simple cases, a small slip, such as missing the right key, can result in important information being irretrievably lost. That is preventable at the design stage if, for example, deletions are made possible only after simultaneous key depressions which are unlikely to occur accidentally. 'Crashes' in multi-user systems, with widespread loss of data, can sometimes arise from particularly high levels of use. The main protection in practice is to 'back-up' the files, taking archive copies in the way described in section 2.3. That is always desirable, but frequent backing-up wastes time and causes problems of storing and indexing the copies. Some systems have better facilities than others in this respect, with automatic storage of certain specified material, for example. Large systems may need defences against disaster from explosion or fire, for instance through back-up installations which are physically separate from the primary equipment.

Serious errors can also arise from misunderstandings or inadequate links between people. Recent examples occurred in the power stations of Three Mile Island and Chernobyl, but many smaller systems now require interdependent working, where individual operators rely upon the prior actions of others. In some cases they may *assume* that these actions have occurred, without actually verifying their belief. Good operating procedures prevent this from happening, especially in cases where a sequence of unchecked assumptions by different employees could together combine into a catastrophe. Evaluation of any large system should pay particular attention to this possibility

Questions you should ask

Do serious errors occur which are difficult to avoid even with training?
Do people have to be excessively cautious at certain points in their work?
Can serious errors occur simply because users lack vital procedural information?

Are users confident that it is difficult to do any serious damage while using
   the system normally?
Does the system have an adequate back-up facility?
Could certain combinations of unusual decisions or unchecked assumptions
   by different people in a large system lead to disaster?

Things you can do

Make a list of all the serious errors that have occurred, and all the ones you can
think of that could occur. Make sure everyone understands what they are, and
the procedures that are available to limit the damage which they cause. In all
cases, back-up files should be encouraged when reasonable (see section 2.3,
'Reliability and repairs').

Company procedures to avoid serious errors should be explicit and
available in written form to all employees. Managers should check at
appropriate intervals that these procedures are understood and are being
carried out.

Intending purchasers should seek to ensure that potentially disastrous
actions can be reversed before they are completely executed. The sales
representative is unlikely to alert you to problems in this area, since he or she
will be emphasizing the positive features of a product. Instead, try to make
contact with a company which is already using the system, and ask about their
experience.

There are advantages in engaging in occasional 'what if?' examinations.
What if the power failed at a certain stage in the process? What if someone who
changes a stored document overwrites it and accidentally stores it in the same
file? Within a computer-based manufacturing setting, what happens if one part
of the system breaks down: does it damage other components before the
process can be stopped? And in all large systems with interdependent decision-
makers, what happens if each one makes the most dangerous assumption
without checking with the others: can certain combinations of decision lead to
disaster?

Specialist procedure for minority use

If you have the need and resources for a more complex investigation of this
issue, consider the specialist procedure of user diaries (see page 166).

4

Job quality and operator performance

The issues dealt with in this chapter are:

4.1	Users' control over their work	65
4.2	Skills required	69
4.3	Variety in the job	73
4.4	Work demands	75
4.5	Uncertainty	77
4.6	Pay	79
4.7	Communications and social contact	81
4.8	Health and safety	83
4.9	Users' performance and attitudes	84

In thinking about what makes up a 'good' or a 'bad' job, eight major aspects of quality have been identified, as summarized in Box 4A. Jobs which meet those criteria lead to higher levels of performance, both in terms of output and quality, as well as to greater satisfaction and personal commitment.

In evaluating your computer-based technology, or when considering what new systems to introduce, all eight issues should be examined. In addition, this chapter covers the general topic of user performance and attitudes, since problems in any of the eight areas may be reflected in poor performance or negative attitudes of several kinds.

Also included here are suggestions about how unsatisfactory jobs can be 'redesigned', to meet criteria of high job quality. The need for a systematic approach to job design is particularly strong when computers are involved; you should seek to use new technology to enhance job quality as well as to meet performance and financial objectives.

There are several effective procedures for job redesign, of which three will be

---

Box 4A   The bases of high job quality

'Good' jobs

— allow the employee some personal control and responsibility for his or her work
— involve the use of skills and provide opportunities for learning new skills
— provide some variety
— make reasonable mental and physical demands
— have clear goals and requirements, and give feedback about their achievement
— are fairly paid
— permit good communications and social contact
— are safe and do not harm health

---

introduced in section 4.1. The procedures are directly relevant there (covering users' control over their work), but they should also be considered in relation to some of the other job features. As will be apparent, several of those are interconnected, so that high (or low) levels of each tend to go together within particular jobs.

In evaluating the quality of computer-based jobs, you will often be concerned with staff who use the same technology continuously throughout a working day. In those cases, the issues and suggestions of this chapter deserve particular attention. However, in other cases a person may undertake a range of tasks, not all of which involve the system under investigation. In those cases, it is advisable to consider the job as a whole, addressing each issue in respect of both computer-based and non-computer tasks. The two kinds of activity influence each other in determining job quality and employee performance, and you should take the overall view before focusing upon possible needs for change in the new-technology work itself.

4.1   USERS' CONTROL OVER THEIR WORK

Importance

One of the key features of a computerized system is the impact it has on the amount of decision-making discretion available to the users. In some cases new systems are less effective than they might be because people feel they have almost no impact on what happens. For example, manufacturing employees cast merely in the role of machine-minders may resent the fact that outside experts, such as programmers or engineers, are in effective control of their machines. When this happens, errors are likely to increase and output and quality can decline.

A general benefit of shop-floor and office employees' having more discretion over their own activities is that problems can be solved near to their point of origin, by the job-holders themselves. Users are also more able to identify improvements and suggest changed ways of working. Enhanced local problem-solving sets managers free to spend time on more strategic issues, with less concern for immediate fire-fighting. In addition, they can use their computer technology to provide information that permits speedy and accurate decision-making. The combination of increased operator discretion and enhanced information transmission can be a powerful aid for management.

From the user's point of view, it is psychologically very important to have some influence over the job and over the technology being used. That may take a variety of forms, such as having responsibility for the method of working, the sequence in which tasks are done, the pace of work, and the quality of outputs. Benefits are likely to follow in terms of greater satisfaction, more positive attitudes towards the equipment, raised quality of output, better anticipation of possible problems, and higher overall productivity. An example of how not to manage this aspect of a job is shown in Box 4B.

User influence over the job is particularly important in settings which are variable or uncertain, and which require frequent changes between batches or different types of work. There is a paradox in this, since those complex situations appear to be specially in need of central control and planning.

Box 4B   The minimal operator

In a recent study of computer-controlled technology in an engineering company, one of the authors came across a particularly bad example of a zero-discretion job. Management recognized the problem, but made it worse by introducing a meaningless task.

The job had been allowed to evolve so that operators merely sat on stools watching the machines. They had no responsibility for machine-setting or tool-setting and had no access to the computer tapes which controlled the process. These tapes were produced, edited and loaded by a separate group of programmers. Furthermore, the tapes were locked into the machine, in order to ensure (said the management) that 'operators could not interfere with them'.

In this minimal role, operators soon became bored and inattentive. Management therefore installed a device to make sure that some attention was maintained: the machines were programmed to cut out unless the operator pressed a button every 20 minutes.

That was adding insult to injury: operators had no control over their work, but an artificial and pointless activity was now demanded. In productivity terms, the arrangement was a failure, since large mainten-ance costs had to be met, arising from frequent breakdowns because of operators' low motivation and skill. Associated with that, machine utilization was undesirably low.

However, their very complexity creates many sources of variance and error, which cannot be predicted and which require early local intervention. Employees on the spot should have discretion (and also skills and knowledge) to handle those variations and to maintain throughput as well as flexibility. That is effective in operational terms, but also is important in sustaining high levels of user involvement.

Questions you should ask

Do users of the system feel they have enough influence over how the job is done?

Do the users have any responsibility for issues such as: the setting of priorities; the methods that will be used in the job; the scheduling and pacing of the job; the standards and targets being pursued; or the preparatory tasks needed to set the job up?

Do people outside the department control all of the users' tasks?

Are there any technological reasons against increasing user control?

Have the users got areas of personal discretion which can affect the level of their performance?

Can the users' performance influence product or service quality?

Things you can do

In view of the enormous importance of users' having some sense of job control, discussions should consider whether changes are needed and (if so) how they might come about. Possible improvements are to give users explicit responsibility for decisions about work methods, the order and timing of work, quality standards and quality control, or routine maintenance of equipment. Jobs *can* be designed in that way, to everyone's benefit; the trouble is that managements rarely think it important enough to bother.

In certain cases it may be impossible to change a person's influence over primary work tasks, since these are entirely determined by the technology. However, even in those circumstances it is usually possible to build in greater discretion over aspects of the job not directly concerned with the computer-based equipment itself. For example, in a manufacturing setting employees may be given responsibility for routine maintenance, quality inspection, or liaison with stores.

In other cases, the operators of computerized systems may be asked to apply that human intelligence which machines lack. For instance, stores employees can be required to keep a watching brief over the entire stores operation, tapping into the information network and interrogating the data-base about the daily flow of items. They might also be asked to look out for, and identify in advance, potential problems which the computer would not recognize as needing action.

If you believe that some people in your organization would benefit from better designed jobs, there are a number of approaches that you can adopt. Some of these seek to increase the overall level of responsibility entrusted to users (as in this section), whereas others focus upon different issues such as variety or level of work demands (considered in later sections).

The three most frequently adopted approaches to job redesign are referred to as job rotation, job enrichment, and the creation of autonomous work groups. *Job rotation* involves the movement of employees between jobs, and is often a solution to problems associated with low task variety. It will be described further when we reach that specific issue, in section 4.3.

Central to the present section is *job enrichment*, which seeks to increase a person's opportunity to control and plan the work. Employees may be given responsibility for scheduling work, sequencing activities and organizing their own time. Tasks of different people might be combined, to produce some elements within a single job which are challenging and personally significant. As noted above, this often involves bringing in activities from outside the traditional domain of a job. For example, production staff may take more responsibility for quality control or local stock levels, and clerical staff might be brought more into contact with customers. These possibilities apply in jobs of all kinds, but they deserve particular attention in computer-based systems; the temptation there is to let jobs evolve entirely around the computer without giving much thought to the abilities and needs of the operators.

In *autonomous work groups*, discretion is given to a group to decide for itself aspects such as job allocation, work scheduling and work methods, how to meet targets, liaison with other groups or departments, and (more rarely) recruitment and selection into the group. Obviously, far-reaching changes cannot take place overnight, and they will require wider developments in organizational style and culture. In practical terms, groups of this kind need a large amount of support from management, especially with tasks such as setting performance goals and monitoring progress.

Not all work situations can support autonomous group working of this kind. It is likely to be most successful when:

(a) the tasks are interrelated (perhaps around a single piece of equipment or a single product), and there is collective responsibility for work outcomes;
(b) each individual has a variety of skills (or can develop them), and thus is able to do large parts of the group's work;
(c) evaluation of performance is on the basis of what the group does rather than in terms of individual employees' contribution.

Given the current trend for new technology systems to become more extended through a department or organization, it seems likely that these conditions will increasingly be met. It is worth pausing to reflect: is that the way your department is moving?

Conflicts and trade-offs

Issues of control are sensitive and difficult. Just as shopfloor and office staff feel the need for some personal work discretion, managers worry about losing control over their area of responsibility if staff should gain too much influence. The resolution of this conflict will depend in part upon the personalities involved, and the attitudes of senior management with overall responsibility for the department.

More specific difficulties can arise if one group's sense of control is enhanced by taking work away from other people. For example, responsibility for routine maintenance may be given to the users of the equipment, leaving more complex maintenance and repairs within the discretion of specialist engineers. However, as occurred in the case study described in Chapter 1, engineers will resent a transfer of their duties in this way, unless they can be convinced of advantages such as an exchange of trivial tasks for more responsible and interesting work. Wider issues of job demarcation and trade union concerns about erosion of power are also likely to slow down changes in responsibility. These are considered in section 5.5, 'Industrial relations'.

Similar problems can arise in cases where tasks are transferred to operators from their supervisors. The latter may need to move to a less directly controlling role, concentrating more on target-setting, liaising with other departments, and providing expertise and support when major problems arise. This re-allocation of responsibilities can lead to more effective attainment of departmental goals, but the transitional period may be difficult.

Questionnaire for minority use

A specialist questionnaire about users' control over their work is provided on page 200.

4.2 SKILLS REQUIRED

Importance

Since the purpose of computer technology is often to automate work which was previously done by humans, it is likely to require staff to employ a different mix of skills from those needed previously. In some cases, the *level* of skills required can remain about the same, but their *nature* can change. For example, Chapter 3 showed how computer-based work can require mental and decision-making skills which are new and sometimes quite complex. However, it is also the case that computer technology can give rise to jobs with very low skill requirements. As indicated at the beginning of this chapter, that is one way to impair the quality of a job.

By creating jobs in which technology carries out the more difficult and challenging tasks, users are left with the residual activities, those which cannot be computerized. In the present state of technical knowledge, such activities tend to be simple for humans but extremely expensive or beyond the power of computers: seeing or hearing changes in the environment, lifting up a fragile item without breaking it, moving pieces from one place to another, or even tidying up the workplace. Computer-based jobs can thus result in employees being required to contribute only at unskilled levels. In those situations, poor attention to detail, negative work attitudes and low job commitment are likely to be widespread.

Box 4C   Skill levels: A question of managerial choice

A recent study commissioned by the United Kingdom Department of Trade and Industry investigated the organization of offices which had installed computer-based equipment. Two contrasting examples were cited.

(A) Reducing skill levels
At one site some professionals and managers keyed in their own text, and others asked the secretaries to input their first draft which they then edited themselves. The secretaries felt their jobs were being deskilled, they had less to do, and they had no satisfaction from producing the final document. Many lost interest, became disillusioned, and left to take other jobs.

(B) Increasing skill levels
At another site, time freed by the system allowed the secretaries' jobs to be expanded, with significant skill and career improvements. For example, secretaries became involved in systems administration, data-base administration, applications development, and training. Through-put of work increased, and staff morale reached high levels.

Different companies have adopted quite different approaches to the introduction of new technology. The same items of equipment can be built into jobs in very different ways. There is a choice, and managers should make that choice explicitly rather than by default. Two options in respect of office automation are illustrated in Box 4C.

This issue can also be viewed in terms of people's need to learn new skills and to expand their achievements. Members of management usually take those needs for granted when considering their own jobs and careers, but they often prefer not to think in those terms about shop-floor and office employees. Yet those members of a company have very similar concerns, and respond positively to jobs in which they can learn and develop. The opportunity to acquire new skills should always be considered when evaluating new-technology work.

Questions you should ask

Are users of the system mainly required to carry out the 'left-over' tasks, those which cannot be automated?

Do the users feel deskilled by new technology?

Is there scope for a greater use of skills, through making changes to the technology?

Is there scope for a greater use of skills, by re-arranging responsibilities between staff or by other ways of redesigning jobs?

Can changes in job content be made to help people develop new skills as
they become more experienced?
Is the required skill level too high rather than too low?

Things you can do

The level of required skill is often linked to the user's degree of control (see
section 4.1, above). Job changes of the kind suggested in the previous pages
may thus also be helpful in raising the skill demands of over-simple work.
Especially relevant here are the techniques of job enrichment and creating
autonomous work groups.

In general terms, you should ask whether there are some tasks at present
done by machine which could be undertaken equally well, or better, by the
operators. The assumption that more automation is always desirable is
certainly wrong in both operational and psychological terms: the need is to get
the right balance, with the computer and the person each helping the other.
This ensures that employees feel some satisfaction about their achievements,
because they have put something of themselves into their work. If that is
prevented through a very low level of skill demands, apathy and low
commitment are to be expected. In some cases, people's natural creativity
becomes diverted into forms of sabotage or attempts to circumvent rules and
procedures.

There are of course also cases of the opposite kind: users do not have
sufficient skills to do the job properly. That often demoralizes them, as well as
having obvious negative effects on productivity.

The problem is that companies are extremely unwilling to make available
the necessary resources for skill acquisition. Many managers who spend vast
sums on the purchase of equipment see no need to spend more than a basic
minimum on training. This failure is particularly marked among British
companies. A recent investigation concluded that in Britain only 0.01 per cent
of sales revenue was spent on training; the corresponding figure in Japan was
found to be 5 per cent.

In examining this aspect of your system, you will need to identify specific
training needs and develop programmes which meet those needs. This will
often require input from line management or personnel specialists, but it is
worth examining how far users can help to train each other. That can have
wide-ranging benefits beyond merely the enhancement of skills, including
greater group cohesiveness and motivation. However, time must be made
available for this; training by colleagues cannot easily be fitted into an
already busy working day. Other aspects of training have been considered in
section 3.1, 'Ease of learning'; and additional recommendations will be made
in section 5.4, 'Selection and training', and section 7.5, 'Providing organizational support'.

Changes may also be required in your personnel selection procedures. As
information technology spreads throughout a company, the nature of jobs can
change in important ways. Although a job title and its principal function may
appear similar to what they had been previously, the required skills may have

---

Box 4D   Job titles may fail to reflect current skill needs

Insurance offices dealing in cover for cars, house contents, foreign travel and so on still widely define their staff requirements in terms of 'sales ability'. That leads them to search for and employ socially adept, verbally fluent individuals. Yet these people are now required to manipulate complex data rapidly via interactive computer systems, making sophisticated adjustments and detailed numerical comparisons, in order to achieve quotations which are competitive in a rapidly-changing market. The numerical skills and orderly approach needed for that work are not always present in people selected for their social skills.

---

become quite different (see Box 4D for an example). Skill requirements in computer-based jobs thus need to be re-examined from time to time, to ensure that skills and people are still correctly matched. Without that, both job quality and job performance will suffer.

Conflicts and trade-offs

A major conflict here is between a short-term and a long-term managerial perspective. Companies often aim for unrealistically brief pay-back periods, aiming to cover their investment in a very short time, perhaps two or three years. That leads to additional cost-cutting stringency, within which it may seem sensible to employ unskilled, and low-paid, staff. The result can be a progressive deterioration, and sometimes a vicious cycle, as shown in Box 4E.

Deskilling often works against business goals, for a number of reasons. Users lack the ability (and often the motivation) to detect faults as they are developing; errors and down-time can therefore be substantially increased. Difficulties also arise when the 'expert' is away, perhaps solving problems beyond the ability of low-skill workers elsewhere in the company. Flexibility is

---

Box 4E   A self-fulfilling prophecy

A company known to the authors was seeking to increase its competitiveness by progressively introducing advanced manufacturing technology. The management felt that progress was being impeded by lack of skills and motivation in the local workforce. The engineering manager described it like this:

> Workers don't care any more about their jobs and about quality. You just can't get good people nowadays. That's why for the last few years I've been systematically deskilling the jobs in our factory.

reduced, speed of response declines, and job problems cannot be tackled at source.

The more skills are diminished at lower levels in a company, the stronger is the need for a large and costly central resource to handle problems beyond the power of system users. Conversely, enhancement of user skills may lead to greater training and development costs at the user level. In each case, it is important to view policy and procedures within a general strategy: the solution adopted should be consistent with the company's overall structure (see section 5.1, 'Organizational structure', and section 7.1, 'Developing a strategy for change').

A similar conflict between short-term and long-term perspectives arises in respect of skill demands which are too high. Improved training and personnel selection cost money, and, faced with that, management regularly take a short-term view; they choose to save money by doing nothing. In the longer term that is almost always wasteful. A target figure of around 5 per cent of an overall investment cost should be set for development of systematic and effective training. In thinking about that, recall that your *overall* cost extends beyond the equipment itself; section 7.5 illustrates other types of expenditure which are incurred in support of a new system.

Questionnaire for minority use

A specialist questionnaire about skills required is provided on page 202.

4.3   VARIETY IN THE JOB

Importance

All jobs require the repetition of certain basic activities from time to time, but they differ in the degree to which those recur without variation. At one extreme are jobs requiring unchanging work on identical brief tasks, transferring data from invoices into a computer for example. Jobs at the other extreme, those which have considerable variety, involve a range of different tasks, and are also likely to permit movement between locations and provide the opportunity for conversation with a number of different people.

Computer systems are particularly likely to generate low-variety work. Their strong point is primarily the rapid and accurate repetition of tasks without becoming tired. However, that is usually possible only through the collaboration of a human being, and he or she is likely to be drawn into the same style of work: non-stop execution of an unchanging task.

Low-variety jobs lead to a reduction in motivation and interest, and they stifle initiative. Furthermore, workers in low-variety jobs might be very competent at their own work, but they have no opportunity to develop a wider range of skills. This is in itself harmful (see section 4.2, 'Skills required'), but it also means that operators lack versatility, and are less able to cope with operational problems or to move into different jobs should the need arise.

Another concern over low-variety work is that it may cause muscular strain and possibly longer-term injury. That is most obvious in jobs requiring continuous keyboard work carried out in a fixed body position. In severe cases those problems, sometimes referred to as 'repetition strain injury', have required keyboard staff to give up their work and move into other jobs. Continuous unvarying attention to a VDU screen may also cause visual discomfort and headaches, the effect of which can extend beyond the workplace to the home. (See also sections 2.6, 'Working conditions', and 4.8, 'Health and safety'.)

At the other extreme, some jobs contain too many different tasks, so that a worker cannot concentrate enough on any one to perform it effectively. This is especially the case when interruptions and required switches between tasks are outside the person's control. Excessive variety is also particularly problematic when the different tasks do not combine to create a 'complete' job. Very varied work is in general more acceptable when there is some coherence between the different tasks, providing a sense of the job's own 'identity'. (See also section 4.4, 'Work demands'.)

Questions you should ask

Are users required to do the same thing over and over again without respite?
Could the present set of tasks be combined with other necessary work in order to create more varied jobs?
How much variety is there for users, in respect of the speed, location or difficulty of their tasks?
Should jobs be redesigned to permit more variety in any of the above areas? Can that be done?
Have the users got *too much* variety, doing an excessive number of unrelated tasks?

Things you can do

It is usually possible to improve variety levels, both in current computer-based work and in cases where a new system is being planned. For example, as suggested in section 4.1, there may be merit in a process of job rotation, whereby staff move between roles on different days, or even within the same working period. This is unlikely to be helpful if the different jobs are equally narrow in their own ways, since employees merely swap one repetitive job for another. If you do introduce a job rotation scheme, make sure it brings together activities some of which are clearly desirable in the terms of this chapter. It is even better if employees can have some control over the rotation which takes place.

However, in order to avoid too big a range of activities, it is often preferable to aim for some form of enrichment within the single job on its own. By introducing extra tasks around a core activity it is possible to increase levels of personal control and to require more appropriate skill use (see sections 4.1 and 4.2 on these topics), while at the same time building in greater variety and retaining a sense of coherence (see section 4.4, 'Work demands'). Permitting the users of computer-based equipment to have access to other (not confidential) parts of the system can also enhance their understanding of the work as a whole. Many companies have found these to be particularly successful procedures; you should consider them within your evaluation programme.

Conflicts and trade-offs

It is impossible to avoid repetition of certain basic tasks, since they are essential to the company's business. Some repetition is thus inevitable, in computer jobs and elsewhere.

Procedures for job rotation, which can benefit workers in low-variety jobs, may however be to the detriment of other staff, who become required to move into low-variety work for some of the time. It is important to examine the overall pattern of job variety within a department, not merely the variety available to users of the system in question.

Jobs with moderate levels of variety can also increase training costs, as new staff have to acquire a wider range of skills. Companies sometimes seek to avoid such additional expenditure, but longer-term advantages in terms of increased flexibility are likely to more than compensate for the short-term outlay.

Questionnaire for minority use

A specialist questionnaire about job variety is provided on page 202.

4.4   WORK DEMANDS

Importance

The demands on operators of computer-based equipment can sometimes be too high, more than they can effectively handle. Three issues need to be considered here.

First, the *nature* of tasks may have changed. In part this is because computers often require different ways of thinking about the job. These 'cognitive' requirements have been illustrated throughout Chapter 3, where we showed how problems of attention and memory can be caused by poor software design.

Second is the question of *quantity*, how much work a person is required to do. Since many types of computer equipment are expensive, there is usually an expectation that they must be operated at high levels of throughput in order to recoup the cost; the general problem is then one of overload.

Very high demand levels may be beyond a person's capacity, giving rise to errors, anxiety, tension, inability to relax, sleeping problems, and irritability at work and at home. Many computer-based systems, in both office and manufacturing settings, can increase employee stress in those ways, especially when non-stop machine-pacing is involved.

The dividing line between demands which are manageable and those which are excessive is an unclear one, and it differs between people. Overload cannot be completely excluded at all times, so that the key issue here concerns extended periods of very high demands. These can produce unacceptable levels of tension and strain, and are often linked to poor work performance.

However, there are many computer-based jobs with the opposite problem: the level of demands is too low. Sections 4.1 to 4.3 have emphasized that people do not want to sit passively throughout their working day: they almost always need to be challenged in their job. Very low levels of demands are therefore harmful in their own way, giving rise to boredom, apathy, low motivation, and feelings of being 'switched off' and depressed.

A third feature should be included under this general heading. Work demands can be varied and bitty, or they can create an overall job which feels like *a whole activity*, one which has its own coherent 'identity'. In these cases, an employee can see his or her work through from beginning to end, with a feeling that it is a whole and identifiable task. In the opposite situation, a worker undertakes fragmented tasks, passing on the material or service to someone else to finish off, and never seeing the final fruits of the work. This second, fragmented type of job gives rise to dissatisfaction, reduced morale, and poor quality of work. It should be avoided whenever possible.

Questions you should ask

How has the nature of work demands changed as a result of the new technology?

Are the work demands at a continuously very high level?

Can users of the system cope with the difficulty of the job?

Could more rest pauses usefully be introduced?

If machine pacing is involved, is it excessive? Is it really needed?

Is more training required?

Are people allocated to the jobs to which they are most suited?

Is there evidence that high work demands are causing excessive stress among users?

Are the work demands too low? If so, can they be increased?

Can jobs be modified to give them a greater sense of coherence and identity?

Things you can do

The overall need here is to look at job demands and discuss whether changes in their quantity or nature would be desirable. In some cases, assessment of very low or very high demands can be made through records taken by the computer system itself, but discussions with employees are always required. In addition, you should examine the adequacy of your personnel selection procedures, the identification of training needs, and the allocation of individual employees to work for which they are most suited.

If changes need to be made to this aspect of computer-based jobs, consider them from the perspective of job design, as introduced on page 68. Procedures of job rotation or job enrichment are widely appropriate, and can lead to an average level of job demands across a working day which is attractive to an employee and also increases overall group or departmental performance.

Conflicts and trade-offs

There is a continuing conflict between managerial needs for greater output and employees' needs to be challenged but not overwhelmed by their work. Actions which reduce work demands might improve job quality, but at the expense of lower productivity. However, as indicated above, demands can often be modified without a reduction in overall output. This can be achieved through attention to the technical and personnel issues described throughout this book: very high work demands can be handled by competent people, who are operating well-designed equipment, within an overall policy of careful job design.

Questionnaire for minority use

A specialist questionnaire about work demands is provided on page 203.

4.5   UNCERTAINTY

Importance

Here we are concerned with four related issues concerning job uncertainty: how clearly operators understand what is required in their job; how well they understand the system with which they are working; how much feedback they get about how they are performing; and, in the longer term, how certain they are about their future within the company.

Whilst some people can cope with uncertainty better than others, and indeed some people actually like it, it is generally true that people find that high levels of uncertainty of these kinds are difficult and demotivating. In extreme cases they can also be dangerously stressful.

Each aspect of uncertainty can be affected by the introduction of new technology, especially in the early stages of implementation. New systems can make job requirements, work targets and performance standards ambiguous or unclear, as the nature of work alters in unexpected and sometimes unnoticed ways. Large complex systems can be difficult to understand, especially if training has been limited and if operator roles are restricted. People may be unclear what impact their actions have on the system and the work of other people. Opportunities for individual feedback may disappear, especially in the case of large integrated systems, where it can be difficult to identify any individual contribution. And there may be real fears that jobs will be lost or that valued skills will no longer be needed.

Questions you can ask

Are users clear about job requirements, the standards that are expected, and to whom they are immediately responsible?

Do users understand the computer-based system, how it works, and their role in operating it?

Do the users get enough prompt feedback about their own performance, either from the equipment or from management?

As a result of the new technology, do users get either less or more recognition for good work?

Can the users predict their likely future careers, or are future developments unclear?

Things you can do

Actions to remedy problems in any of these areas naturally depend upon the particular issue in question. In large systems it may be necessary for management to bring together the operators, supervisors, programmers and maintenance engineers, to clarify and agree who is responsible for what. Training will be required, so that operators understand the overall system and their role in it. Improved feedback may be sought through technological or organizational procedures, and team feedback can sometimes be provided based on the performance of the system, rather than individually. Managerial styles may have to change to encourage greater recognition for good performance, again perhaps as a team. Finally, management will have to spend time thinking through and discussing the longer-term impacts of new technologies on the demands for people and skills, and the ways in which future prospects and plans can best be communicated to staff.

The key point at this stage is that the problems created by uncertainty need to be included in an evaluation of computer-based systems. Once the issues needing attention have been defined, plans can be made and solutions can be sought.

Conflicts and trade-offs

Uncertainty cannot always be avoided. For example, immediate clarity about future developments in the company may be unattainable; and discussions about responsibilities within the system can lead into difficult issues of demarcation. In harsh economic times there may be continuing uncertainty about future staffing levels, the mix of skills required, or even about the overall viability of the company. There can also be commercial reasons for keeping some facts confidential. Often however, there will be scope for greater sharing of information than is initially envisaged.

Questionnaire for minority use

A specialist questionnaire about uncertainty is provided on page 205.

4.6 PAY

Importance

Money makes the world go round, and pay makes people go to work. In this chapter *three particular issues* need attention. First is the question of differentials between users of computer-based systems and their colleagues. Second is the possible need for monetary gains from information technology to be shared in some proportion among employees as well as employers. And third is the question of motivation and incentives.

The introduction of new technology systems can alter the skill requirements of jobs, and hence the *level of pay* which users think they deserve. Associated with that, a company might find it difficult to attract and keep good staff if wage levels are left unchanged. Sometimes the need to pay more for computer-based work is met by simply transferring on to the job staff already receiving that level of pay, whether or not they have appropriate skills and background. As illustrated in Box 4F, results may be unsatisfactory.

Second, introduction of computer technology is often justified by management for the cost savings it will generate; employee numbers might be reduced, or improved levels of service or output may be achieved by the same number of people. In such a situation operators are likely to think that they too, as well as the company, deserve some *additional financial return*. Shift-working may become necessary, in order to justify the cost of particularly expensive technology. Changes in wage rates will then have to be considered, especially if employees are strongly reluctant to move away from conventional day-work hours. (See also sections 5.5 and 5.6, for a wider consideration of job evaluation and industrial relations issues.)

Third, the introduction of new technology provides an occasion to review the *incentive value* of current payment systems. In most organizations pay is

---

Box 4F   The wrong way to fill new technology jobs

A British company installed a computerized cold store, which created new jobs requiring people to monitor the status of the store using visual display units, and to issue orders for moving and refilling pallets via a computer. The job was designated as manual work and given the highest wage grade in the factory. In order to minimize disruption to wage levels, the workers selected to carry out the work — which could involve sitting watching a VDU screen for up to eight hours — were those who previously were paid on the highest existing manual grades, *fork-lift truck drivers!*

This group had been excellent at their previous work, but experience soon proved that their skills and interests were not appropriate for sustained work with VDUs. A short-cut to avoid changing the wages system had led to dissatisfaction and low productivity.

determined in the same way as it has been for many years, even though work content and procedures may have changed considerably. This is not simply a question of equity in differentials, the first point above, but primarily concerns the method by which a particular level of pay is determined. Should there now be a shift from simple timework payments to some form of bonus or profit-related system? Another issue is whether payment on an individual basis is more or less appropriate than some form of group bonus scheme; decisions here depend in part on the degree of interdependence between users of the system.

Questions you should ask

Are some adjustments needed in wage or salary rates for staff operating the new-technology equipment?

How do current rates compare with others in the area?

Are special payments now required, for example for shift-working?

Is the incentive value of the present payment system about right?

Should you move from individual to group incentive payment, or vice versa?

Has the company got too many different grades of job, with associated small differences in payment rates, thus reducing flexibility of movement between roles?

Things you can do

Issues of this kind require examination by staff at different levels of the organization. A senior manager should be asked to carry out a review of payment issues associated with new-technology jobs, using the opportunity to ask whether the company's system has by now become outdated. Trade union officials will also wish to consider the questions raised above, and at some point negotiations may be required. Additional recommendations are made in section 5.6, 'Pay and career progression', where these issues are considered more widely.

Conflicts and trade-offs

An obvious form of conflict is to be found in the different views likely to be adopted by management and employee representatives. A divergence of opinion is often inevitable in discussions about pay.

Trade unions usually resist attempts to downgrade jobs as a result of computer technology, and they might object to increased flexibility of job allocations, unless a general increase in pay is agreed. It may sometimes be impossible to make local changes without negotiating extensive modifications to a current payment scheme.

A more specific difficulty arises from the knock-on effects of changing one group's wage level within an overall job evaluation scheme. Increased pay for users of computer-based equipment may be resisted by other employees working in the same department on older equipment. They may use different skills, but can object that they work as hard as the new-technology group or that their contribution to the company is just as great. Knock-on effects of that kind are also considered in section 5.6.

Questionnaire for minority use

A specialist questionnaire about pay is provided on page 206.

4.7   COMMUNICATIONS AND SOCIAL CONTACT

Importance

Good communication is essential for effective goal-setting and task performance, and also as a source of personal job commitment. The introduction of a computer-based system can affect communications in many ways, sometimes beneficially and sometimes harmfully. Changes in the wider organization will be considered in Chapter 5; here we will examine what can happen at the level of the system user.

Problems may arise for a number of reasons. A need to attend continuously to a computer system can prevent an operator talking with colleagues or being open to receive messages from them. Layout of working areas can have the same effect. Communication may increasingly be through the medium of written reports or via electronic transmissions, cutting out the possibility of face-to-face meetings, which are often seen as enjoyable and important parts of a job.

Most people like from time to time to discuss work or other issues with colleagues, and computer-based systems may prevent that contact. An example is shown in Box 4G, and the process can be especially demoralizing if the job itself is one of low variety (section 4.3) or with particularly high demands (section 4.4). 'Teleworking' in one's own home (for example, in programming or data-input jobs) can be a source of particular problems in this regard. Advantages in terms of flexible hours and reduced travel-time can be outweighed for some people by very restricted contact with colleagues.

Box 4G   Computers can cut out social contact

Staff in the commercial credit office of an American bank complained that new technology had led to them becoming isolated. All information was now channelled through the computer, and they worked individually with their own terminals. Even when clarification of an issue was needed, employees had to inquire into their visual display unit. Previously in those cases they had approached a colleague or supervisor, but now there was almost no contact of that kind.

Conversely, a computer-based system can have the effect of improving communication to and from users in various ways. For example, speed of transmission may be increased. Individual employees can sometimes gain access to a greater variety of information, to be selected at their own choice. Careful organization of work to operate the new system might lead to more careful definitions of information needs and the establishment of new communication channels to meet those needs. A mixture of both gains and losses is thus to be expected.

Questions you should ask

Does the job require users to interact with an acceptable number of colleagues or clients? Are these formal communications effective?

Is there opportunity for some informal interaction, the development of friendships, the sharing of information, and the provision of mutual support?

Have there been changes in *type* of communication to and from users? For example, fewer face-to-face meetings and more telephone or electronic messages? Are these effective? Should they be changed in any way?

More generally, can communication to and from the system users be improved?

Things you can do

The nature of required changes will naturally depend upon the situation, and specific recommendations cannot easily be made here. It can sometimes be helpful to have short regular meetings (perhaps once a fortnight) between members of a work-group and their boss, to discuss current issues and to exchange information. In cases where technology clearly prevents informal discussion among employees, it may be necessary to make changes in layout or to reorganize the work tasks so that people do not feel isolated for excessive lengths of time.

Conflicts and trade offs

Computer-based communication needs to fit within a company's overall managerial style; see section 5.1, 'Organizational structure', and section 5.2, 'Bureaucracy and decision-making'. If that style emphasizes the need to spread information widely between employees and groups, then parallel changes should be introduced within technology systems. However, conflicts sometimes arise because one group of senior managers has responsibility for computer applications and another is responsible for communication structures. These groups can be pulling in opposite directions, yielding an overall pattern of communications which is internally inconsistent and even contradictory.

Questionnaire for minority use

A specialist questionnaire about communications and social contact is provided on page 207.

4.8   HEALTH AND SAFETY

Importance

Section 2.6, 'Working conditions', has already drawn attention to important issues under three headings: the working environment, equipment and its siting, and physical hazards. Computer-based equipment can give rise to excessively high temperatures or have a drying effect on the atmosphere. Users of visual display units sometimes report eye tiredness and headache after long periods spent concentrating on the screen. From a safety perspective, automatic guided vehicles in manufacturing plants are usually unable to 'see' human obstructions; and offices may gradually acquire a network of cables and loose connections, with potential dangers of accidents and even electrocution.

The present section expands that earlier one to consider those issues from the point of view of the individual user. High-quality jobs contain the characteristics described in sections 4.1 to 4.7, but they are also safe and do not harm employees' health. Health and safety should therefore be included in any assessment of job quality.

Questions you should ask

Do users of the system complain of any symptoms such as headache, eyestrain or backache?

Do users frequently feel tiredness or discomfort?

Do very long periods of continuous work cause excessive stress?

Are there safety hazards?

Are operators protected from moving equipment?

Are safety procedures clearly specified and understood?

Are safety inspections carried out, and followed up by action when needed?

Does your company's health and safety policy explicitly cover VDUs and other forms of new technology?

Things you can do

Companies in many countries draw upon the expertise of health and safety representatives from their work-force. Those individuals have an important role to play in evaluating this aspect of computer technology.

Specific themes about equipment design and working conditions have been covered in section 2.6, and some of the points made there might be appropriate to your setting. More generally, it is important to view health and safety within the overall framework of job quality. Levels of stress can be too high in many computer-based jobs.

Specific physical symptoms, such as eye-strain or backache, do not arise solely from working conditions or equipment. They are also brought about by heavy job demands, low variety, and high machine-pacing. These factors may need attention, just as much as the physical conditions of work.

You should consider, and build upon, the central importance of opportunity for control (section 4.1). If operators have some discretion over their work and its organization, they can adjust their speed and effort to cope with factors which could give rise to unsafe practices or accidents. For example, brief rest pauses taken when a person needs them can be more than compensated for by increased productivity and fewer errors. Being able to move around can enhance variety and promote physical and mental alertness. To improve health and safety, you need to look at job content as well as at possible hazards in the environment.

Conflicts and trade-offs

Health and safety should take precedence in any trade-off against cost. Nevertheless, it is often the case that some hazards are perceived as more important by workers than by management; a conflict of interest is thus sometimes to be expected.

Questionnaires for minority use

Three specialist questionnaires about health and safety are provided on pages 208 to 209.

4.9   USERS' PERFORMANCE AND ATTITUDES

Importance

Here we are concerned with the effectiveness of the people using the computer-based system, and their feelings about that system and their job more generally. There is no simple and direct link between job attitudes and job performance, such that more satisfied people necessarily work better than less satisfied ones. Other factors enter into this equation, such as personal ability, managerial style, financial or other incentives, quality of equipment, pressure from colleagues, and so on.

Nevertheless, there are many circumstances in which strong dissatisfaction contributes to low effectiveness. A dissatisfied worker may produce work up to the required minimum, but have no concern beyond that. He or she is not interested in raising quality, introducing improvements in the way things are done, looking out for future problems and potential failures, or working specially hard on occasions when extra commitment is needed to meet a deadline. Dissatisfied staff are also more likely to leave the company (generating new costs of recruitment and induction), and they may take more time off through periods of absence.

Positive user motivation and attitudes are therefore widely desirable. This chapter has illustrated how poor job quality in computer-based work can suppress motivation and reduce system performance. Enhancing job quality should thus be a target for straightforward financial reasons, as well as for the improvement of the health and well-being of employees.

It cannot be emphasized too strongly that overall effectiveness in relation to business goals derives also from a correct assessment of your essential work requirements. That point was made initially in section 2.1, and needs to be considered again at this point. If you have computer-based equipment which lacks the capability to meet your principal needs, then maximum effectiveness is inevitably beyond your reach. This means that in evaluating performance you should ask not only about the users' skills and motivation but also about their equipment's ability to do the work required. It is a combination of those two factors which makes for effectiveness.

Questions you should ask

What are the system's crucial performance objectives?
Does the system meet those objectives?
Has the work output or service changed? For better or worse? At lower or higher cost?
Has user productivity improved, or declined?
Are users committed to high-quality work?
Are the users more, or less, flexible in taking on different responsibilities?
Are the users more, or less, responsive to customer needs?
Has labour turnover increased or decreased amongst users?
Has absenteeism increased or decreased amongst users?
Have users' work attitudes changed?
In general, are users highly motivated?
Do users feel that the job enhances their self-esteem?

Things you can do

If you have problems in any of the areas listed above, you should regard them as symptoms of underlying causes. These may derive from badly designed jobs (as discussed in this chapter), but they could also stem from problems with the equipment and its potential to meet your needs (Chapter 2), its usability (Chapter 3), or with wider organizational and industrial relations matters (see Chapter 5). As was stressed in Chapter 1, you should consider a range of possible causes, and Chapters 2 to 5 aim to help you do this.

In some cases, it may be useful to set up a representative working party, with a remit to identify the causes of poor performance and attitudes and to make recommendations for change. Chapter 6 contains a fuller description of this approach, and suggests some procedures which might be followed.

In all cases, there is a need to complement the focus upon system users (as in this chapter) with a broader strategic view (as in Chapters 5 and 7). The previous sections have dealt with important aspects at the level of the job and the job-holder, but new technology must also be assessed in terms of its contribution to wider company goals. Evaluation of performance from that broader perspective is covered in section 5.8.

More detailed questions for minority use

A checklist of detailed questions about user performance is provided on page 210.

Questionnaires for minority use

Three specialist questionnaires about users' job attitudes are provided on pages 211 to 214.

5

The wider organization and overall effectiveness

The issues dealt with in this chapter are:

5.1 Organizational structure		88
5.2 Bureaucracy and decision-making		92
5.3 Communications		94
5.4 Selection and training		97
5.5 Industrial relations		100
5.6 Pay and career progression		102
5.7 Job losses		105
5.8 Organizational performance and morale		107

Computer-based systems can have wide-ranging effects throughout an organization, and these need to be included in any evaluation. The 'organization' in question is sometimes an entire company. However, the points made in this chapter also apply to a section, a department or a division, and readers should adopt the perspective which meets their needs. Earlier chapters paid primary attention to issues of equipment and its use, and were thus of interest to technical and non-technical employees at several organizational levels. However, this chapter is likely to be of greatest concern to a smaller group of readers: senior departmental or company managers with wide-ranging responsibilities for several different functions.

It is important that such managers are not merely reactive in their assessment. To evaluate organizational aspects of new technology, you must go beyond merely recording what has happened after the event. You should also decide upon the type of structure which is desirable, and the kinds of communication, training and other processes which you require. Decisions about these features must be consistent within an overall strategy and business plan, and they will of course be influenced by your knowledge of current and future technological possibilities.

In Chapter 4 we were able to define the characteristics of a 'good' and a 'bad' job, having a clear idea about what should be aimed for at that level. In this chapter we cannot prescribe a single 'good' form of organizational structure (or ideal forms of the other issues listed above), but the underlying point remains as it was in Chapter 4: *you can choose* the way computers are used and the structures in which they are placed, and companies should make choices after explicitly reviewing the options.

The introduction of computer-based equipment can itself provide new opportunities for change. After deciding what type of organizational structure or processes you wish to aim for, you can bring in systems which are particularly suitable for promoting movement in those directions. Evaluation of your new technology in organizational terms should thus be proactive as well as reactive: first review the options and decide on your objectives; second, introduce the new technology in a manner consistent with those objectives, predicting the likely consequences; third, assess the degree to which the organizational results have been as intended.

In practice, you may already have by-passed the first of those steps. You might have introduced new systems without much thought for wider organizational objectives, or you may have made tentative changes to be reviewed on a pilot basis. If so, the book's framework can still be helpful, urging you now to look at things strategically as well as in terms of local consequences.

The need for this kind of strategic view will be taken up again in Chapter 7, when we consider the management of change. The present chapter will retain the form of the previous ones, identifying a number of key evaluation questions for each issue. These should form the basis of your inquiries about current and prospective systems. However, for simplicity of presentation, questions have usually been worded in respect of *current* equipment.

5.1 ORGANIZATIONAL STRUCTURE

Importance

All organizations need some structure to meet their objectives, but structures differ widely among themselves. The two key elements are differentiation and integration: first, any structure involves some division of activities into functions, departments and levels; and second, some mechanisms are required to co-ordinate and control those separate sets of activities.

When thinking about how companies differ in their structure, we should thus look first at their differentiation: how many distinct parts are there? The parts can be spread laterally, in different sections or specialist groups; or they can be ordered vertically, at different levels, creating hierarchies which are either tall or flat.

Second, we must look at the procedures or systems which are established to integrate the work of different parts. The simplest form of integration is through a single person with supervisory responsibility for two or more groups, but other co-ordinating structures are common. Lateral co-ordination may be through liaison groups, advisory committees, staff assistants and people in other cross-boundary roles. 'Matrix' structures can be introduced, with a network of responsibility links, or project managers may be appointed with authority to cut across functions as they carry forward a special project or task.

Computer technology may have an impact on both differentiation and integration. For example, the introduction of a flexible manufacturing system may reduce the need for supervision and first-line management, but increase the need for specialist expertise in the form of additional programmers and development and maintenance engineers. It may also reduce the need for progress chasers who previously co-ordinated the work between production and sales, since such co-ordination may now be achieved by computer-based scheduling and inventory control.

New technology is sometimes used as a vehicle for pushing organizations towards either a centralized or a decentralized form of operation. Four major issues need to be considered when discussing which direction is appropriate for your company. These are the extent to which the business wishes to

Box 5A Four aspects of centralization or decentralization		
	More centralized	More decentralized
(a) Locus of decision	Decisions mainly taken at the centre, by senior managers and/or at Head Office	Decisions spread vertically and laterally throughout the company
(b) Communication source and direction	Communications directed from the centre and from specialist departments (e.g. marketing or finance)	Matrix of communications, with multiple sources and directions
(c) Provision of services	Specialist functions provided from the centre (finance, distribution, etc.)	Services spread throughout the organization
(d) Availability of specialist expertise	Specialist staff employed at the centre, divorced from day-to-day operations	Specialists employed within operational teams across the organization

centralize or decentralize the following: (a) decision making, (b) the source and direction of principal communications, (c) the provision of services, and (d) the availability of specialist expertise. Box 5A illustrates those four aspects.

Decisions about centralization or decentralization should be consistent with the overall culture of a company and its business strategy. New technologies can often be used in either way. In principle, neither is 'right' or 'wrong', and choosing either more centralization or more decentralization will have its advantages and disadvantages. The key point is that choices exist, and you should make them explicitly, rather than drifting into them on the basis of previous custom and practice.

Questions you should ask

What is the company's policy about its structure in the area affected by the computer-based system under evaluation?

Is the system helping or hindering attainment of that policy?

Do technological developments offer the prospect of radical structural change?

Thinking about the number of vertical levels in your company, are these too few, about right, or too many?

Thinking about the number of functional groups laterally, are these too few, about right, or too many?

Is co-ordination between groups adequate, both vertically and laterally?

Could the computer-based system help in any of the above respects?

Should the company be more centralized or more decentralized in the area affected by the computer-based system?

Is the system helping or hindering in that respect?

Things you can do

You should form a view of your ideal company structure in relation to your objectives, bearing in mind the types of technology now available. If the current structure appears inadequate, you should be devising changes before additional computer-based equipment is introduced (see also section 7.1, 'Developing a strategy for change'). The technology itself may be used to assist movement in the desired direction, opening up possibilities which were previously closed.

Although there are no generally 'right' or 'wrong' structures, a number of experienced consultants and researchers have recently emphasized the benefits of using new technology to promote flat and flexible organizations. The characteristics of these are summarized in the left-hand column of Box 5B, and you may find it useful to set up discussions about those options within your company. It is also desirable to consider the ways in which computer-based systems might permit separate decentralized units, which can be monitored effectively through the technology itself.

Look out also for one particular sort of limited centralization. In some cases, power can become unreasonably concentrated in groups who have particular

Box 5B Two types of organizational structure		
	More flexible structure	Less flexible structure
Supervisory and managerial roles	Supervisors and managers provide support and control the boundaries between groups. Operating staff are self-supervising within their boundaries	Supervisors and managers maintain close control over day-to-day operations. Operating staff have low levels of discretion
Expert roles	Experts are viewed as supports, called on by line employees when required	Experts of several kinds are in day-to-day control with considerable direct authority
Specialization	There are relatively few specialist groups	There are many specialist groups
Co-ordination	There is an inter-linked or matrix pattern, with responsibility sometimes shared across functions and levels	There is a structural split according to function, with formal co-ordination primarily at senior management level
Hierarchy	There are few levels in the hierarchy	There are many levels in the hierarchy

technical knowledge. Those responsible for installing or managing new information systems often find that their positions of privileged knowledge lead to them becoming centrally involved in wider decision-making. That may often be inappropriate, both because the individuals gain influence in matters outside their competence, and because organizational structures become distorted to fit around these seemingly special people.

Conflicts and trade-offs

Any choice you make here will have advantages and disadvantages. For example, it is often the case with new investments in manufacturing technology that managers feel they achieve better control by creating specialist groups of programmers and maintenance engineers, who are given considerable authority over the technology. But this can conflict with the guidelines offered in Chapter 4 for improving operator effectiveness and motivation through enhancing job quality.

Decisions to decentralize communication processes of the kind summarized in Box 5A can run into problems of technical incompatibility. It may become necessary to spend unanticipated sums of money on changes to communications hardware and software, and on training and development, in order to achieve the desired changes to the organization.

Questionnaire for minority use

A specialist questionnaire about organizational structure is provided on page 216.

5.2 BUREAUCRACY AND DECISION-MAKING

Importance

There are five principal aspects of any bureaucracy. A highly bureaucratic organization is one which has clear demarcations about job responsibilities, highly standardized ways of doing things, a strict and clear hierarchy, defined and regulated channels of communication, and formal processes of decision-making. Whilst the term 'bureaucracy' often has perjorative connotations, all organizations must have these characteristics in some degree. Furthermore, many large and highly successful companies (in Japan in particular) operate purposely in a bureaucratic fashion. The problems arise when this becomes too rigid or too formalized in relation to the needs of the business.

For example, job descriptions can become so fixed that they prevent people from working in the way that is now required. It may take too long to reach decisions, if information always has to be passed to a pre-defined level in the hierarchy. The organization may become inflexible, losing its ability to respond to changing circumstances. In extreme cases, following the rules can become an end in itself, with people losing sight of the goals they should be pursuing. And too much formal bureaucracy may lead to people becoming frustrated and demoralized. In some cases this will result in them trying 'to beat the system' whenever they get the chance, seeking to win battles in what they see as a personal conflict between themselves and the system they so dislike.

In general, older and larger companies tend to become more bureaucratic, but the order and predictability that bureaucracy brings is no bad thing if your work is fairly routine. For example, if you manufacture the same products as last year, in large batches, for the same customers, using the same suppliers, then life may be predictable enough for you to operate successfully in a highly bureaucratic fashion. The problem comes if your work is unpredictable, when you need flexibility and the ability to respond quickly to changing circumstances. In these situations, working bureaucratically will often prove ineffective.

The introduction of new technology can influence all these aspects of bureaucracy, but again the key point is that companies have a choice. For example, the introduction of an office network can be used to promote more strongly demarcated responsibilities, more standardized procedures, clearer hierarchies, more regulated communication channels, and more formalized decision-making; or it can be used to promote the opposite changes. Your choice should depend on the needs of your business.

Questions you should ask

What is your company's policy about degree of formal bureaucracy in respect of its five components: job demarcation, standardized procedures, clear hierarchy, regulated communications, formalized decision-making?

Is your new technology helping or hindering attainment of that policy?

Do technical developments offer the prospect of radical changes to your company's level of bureaucracy?

Has there been any loss in flexibility as a result of computerization?

Things you can do

As with your organization structure (in section 5.1), you should make a choice about the appropriate levels of bureaucracy for particular departments or divisions, and for the organization as a whole. If the work is predictable and you are seeking order and control, then bureaucratic methods of working may well help you. If your work is less predictable and your emphasis is more on flexibility and responsiveness, then do not organize yourself in a bureaucratic manner.

Opinions will probably vary within your organization. For example, people responsible for office networking systems, such as office managers, will generally want more order and regularity than people using them; the latter will usually seek flexibility to let them do the job as easily as possible. One way forward is to identify areas where pre-defined rules and procedures are mandatory, for example to comply with legal requirements or industry standards, and also where they are actually helpful for the users. Then contrast these with areas where more flexibility would apparently be helpful. Discussion can then focus on this second group.

Whilst again there are no 'right' or 'wrong' choices in this area, we should offer some words of warning. The introduction of new and costly technologies is often accompanied by a desire for order and tighter control. Many managers hope this can be achieved, at least in the early stages, by closely defining who will do what, by standardizing the work, by defining clear authorities for various actions, and by trying to formalize and regulate communications and decision-making. This sometimes seems the way to get the most out of the investment. But strategic motives for the investment are often to become more flexible, and to be able to make rapid decisions in response to changing circumstances. In practice, there is a danger that the new technology can make you more bureaucratic, exactly at the time you are hoping to become less so.

Other companies have avoided that by viewing the power of new technology as so great that groups of managers and other staff should be given maximum freedom from organizational constraints. They have aimed to abandon demarcations, abolish standardized procedures and minimize hierarchical structures, and have sought to encourage separate entrepreneurial initiatives in order to gain market advantage. That approach may be most suitable in small companies, or small subsidiaries of large companies, and among professional or white-collar groups. Maximum freedom also tends to be most appropriate in relatively new companies, or new subsidiaries, since later developments encourage consolidation and formalization. In all cases, the advantages of a non-bureaucratic approach need to be set against the problems: co-ordination of goals and actions can become very difficult.

Conflicts and trade-offs

Since all organizations seek a blend of order and predictability, at the same time as flexibility and responsiveness, some conflicts in this area are inevitable. Choices here may also clash with otherwise desirable features in other respects. For example, the establishment of rigid job responsibilities in operating the new technology can conflict with attempts to provide more interesting work (see Chapter 4). And if you want to operate systems in flexible ways, you will need to include this in your specification of essential requirements (see section 2.1), since that decision can influence system design and choices of system architecture.

Questionnaire for minority use

A specialist questionnaire about high levels of bureaucracy is provided on page 217.

5.3 COMMUNICATIONS

Importance

Computer-based systems can alter the content, speed, accuracy, nature and pattern of communications. For example, an integrated management information system can mean that the area manager of a retail company can receive on-line information on stock levels held in each of the company's warehouses, on screen or in paper print-out from the local terminal, without having to make personal contact with any of the warehouse managers or stock controllers.

The advantages of such developments are plain; less obvious perhaps are some of the problems. People can become over-reliant on computerized systems, and have difficulty in spotting mistakes that were readily apparent when personal contact and discussion were required. Organizations can become impersonal, depending more on machines and software than on personal contact by telephone or face-to-face meeting. People working in such systems may be dissatisfied, because they have lost their friendly relationships, and because they feel they have no personal influence over the work.

Another problem is that decision-makers may receive too much information, simply because the computer can deliver so much so easily. Individuals can respond by ignoring the information they receive in this way, preferring to rely on their old sources (e.g. informal contacts with key individuals), in which case the system has become useless. Alternatively, they can waste hours sifting through irrelevant information, seeking out what they need, in which case the system is highly inefficient. Information should be structured for local needs, and the standard widespread distribution of raw data is usually unhelpful. Electronic mail systems raise particular problems in this regard, with the danger of ever-increasing lists of recipients and an accumulation of 'junk-mail'.

In addition to communication distortions of these kinds, some large companies are increasingly experiencing an additional problem. Downloading of files from a central system onto local microcomputers can initially distribute consistent information to several different departments. However, separate updating and amending to meet local needs can result in files taking on quite different contents in different places. Since this is usually uncontrolled and often unrecognized, later interactions can easily run into difficulties.

Access to the communications power of information technology is likely to be unevenly spread within a company. That uneven distribution can sometimes give rise to unexpected distortions which are clearly harmful. For example, the position of middle management can be undermined by the fact that people above them in the hierarchy have direct access through computer

This cartoon illustrates how quickly one can generate a 'paper explosion'. Computers encourage an equivalent 'information explosion'. Does your computer system aid or hinder communication within the organization? See section 5.3.

terminals to all the information entered by junior grades, sales or accounting staff for example. On the other hand, the power of some groups is enhanced if they possess scarce computing skills or if they are able to control access to system use and training.

Relationships sideways in the organization can also be troublesome, between different groups of employees each of which is responsible for different aspects of the new technology. It is quite common to hear users, programmers and engineers blaming the others for ineffective system performance. Communications between them can deteriorate to the extent that all groups guard their corner against the others, with more concern for defending their position than for finding solutions to mutual problems.

One further development should be considered. Different organizations are increasingly working more closely together through their shared computer network. For example, manufacturers or retailers might have direct electronic links with suppliers; designers and manufacturers might share the same database. Such links can certainly improve speed and efficiency, but they may require changes to communication and decision-making procedures. Greater organizational consistency may become required both within and between companies, with knock-on effects which are unanticipated and difficult to modify at a later stage.

Questions you should ask

Has computer technology altered your internal communication procedures? Are they more, or less, effective?

Has computer technology altered your communication procedures with suppliers and customers? Are they more, or less, effective?

Do people receive too much information? Or information of the wrong kind? Or information that is out of date?

Do people use the information they receive?

Have communications become more impersonal?

Has improved information flow made some groups very powerful? If so, is this a problem?

Has computer technology led to any groups being by-passed or excluded? If so, is this a problem?

Are there communications problems sideways across the company? Do these reflect mutual distrust between groups?

Things you can do

Periodic audits of your communications system should be considered; illustrative checklists are provided on page 219. In a large organization these audits can become very complex, so that specialist advice from consultants may be helpful. You should question whether computerization has led to a loss of that personal touch which is important for people's loyalty and morale, and which is crucial for putting things right in a crisis. If there are problems in this area, find some way of re-introducing regular opportunities for direct personal contact.

Two options exist for improving sideways communications, should that be necessary. You can set up regular meetings between the different groups where people can exchange information and discuss their problems. Or, more fundamentally, you can reorganize your structure, perhaps amalgamating groups and departments so that they become the responsibility of a single manager. As pointed out in section 5.1, new technology can provide the catalyst both for reviewing your current structure and for introducing improvements.

Conflicts and trade-offs

As in other areas, you have to trade-off your need for change against the availability of resources. There is a limit to the amount of time and money which can be devoted to communication improvement.

A second conflict is less obvious. Your evaluation exercise may point to a need for simpler communication, perhaps with less dependence upon the computer. Here the trade-off is with an available set of computer functions: should you discard those costly functions in the interest of simpler communication? It is sometimes difficult to decide not to use new facilities, especially after a large investment.

Communications style and structure need to be consistent with the company's approach to centralization and bureaucracy (see sections 5.1 and 5.2). It is therefore essential to look out for possible inconsistencies in your approach across these several areas.

Questionnaire for minority use

A specialist questionnaire about organizational communications is provided on page 218.

More detailed questions for minority use

Checklists of detailed questions about communications are provided on pages 219–221.

5.4   SELECTION AND TRAINING

Importance

In evaluating organizational aspects of your computer-based technology, there is a need to examine selection and training procedures across the company. You should review skill needs and job requirements in all relevant areas. For example, are new programming and editing skills required? By whom? Who should maintain the new equipment? Your own engineers? Your

> Box 5C   Training options and the structuring of jobs
>
> In the Canon factory outside Tokyo, the engineers until recently had no training budget. But now they boast that they spend 50 per cent of their time training operators how to undertake preventive maintenance and to repair breakdowns. They are trying to make the operators as self-sufficient as possible, and they can claim considerable success. For their most advanced technical system, the engineers are now called in on average only once every two weeks. For the rest of the time the operators and supervisors solve their own problems.
>
>   This allocation of responsibilities is highly effective. Rates of output and equipment utilization are high and above budget.

operators? A combination of those? Or an outside firm of contract engineers? How will the role of your supervisors change? What new skills do they require? What will be the new demands on the local managers? Do senior managers have an adequate understanding of issues and potential developments in this area? Are they committed to the necessary personnel changes?

Only when you have thought through issues of that kind will you be able to identify whether or not you need to select staff internally or externally, and be able to determine the nature of the training that is required. The key point is that many options exist; Box 5C illustrates one possibility. Evaluating this aspect of your computer technology should make more explicit what those options are in your own company. Training issues for equipment users have been raised in section 3.1, 'Ease of learning', and in section 4.2, 'Skills required'; these should be complemented with the following broader questions.

Question you should ask

What skills are required by all the key people working with, supporting and
   managing the new technology?
Do current members of your organization have the necessary skills to work
   the system in the way that is required?
If not, can they be trained to develop these skills?
Have you examined the different types of training that are available for
   different employee groups in the application of computer technology?
Are the necessary skills available in your locality?
Can you recruit local people who can be trained in the skills you require?
Is additional education needed to raise senior management's awareness of,
   and interest in, computer technology?
Do you have capability within your organization to select people (either
   from within or from outside) to meet identified needs?

Do you have the capability within your organization to train people (either from within or from outside) to develop identified skills?

Can you buy in (for example, from external consultants) the necessary capability to help with recruitment and/or to help with training?

Things you can do

If you appear to have training problems associated with your computer-based system (or in respect of a planned system), you should first think through very carefully what new demands the technology makes (or will make) on the people involved, including the users, programmers, maintenance staff, supervisors and managers. To do this you need a clear view of how the system will be operated and supported. You should identify what specific skills are required and by whom. Those analyses will lead you into the identification of training needs and the specification of actual and required employee competences. Top management should be included in these considerations: understanding and enthusiasm at that level are essential if technology policy is to be integrated within overall business strategy.

Personnel selection can sometimes be aided through use of appropriate aptitude tests. There have been rapid developments recently in the construction of tests for selecting employees who have high potential for new technology jobs, and it would be sensible to consider whether some of these could be useful in your situation. The British Psychological Society is able to provide details of companies in the United Kingdom who are expert in this aspect of recruitment (the address is on page 238).

You also need to review very carefully whether or not your company has the capability, probably within the personnel department, to select and train staff to meet the stated objectives. Many specialist activities are involved, and, if you do not have the capability, you would be well advised to seek external help.

Conflicts and trade-offs

A systematic approach to the analysis of skill requirements takes time and money. It may be that, as a result, your implementation is delayed. However, without effective selection and training, there may be substantial long-term costs in depending upon people who lack the necessary competence or motivation. Such personnel deficiencies are undoubtedly expensive in the long run, through poor performance and/or through the need to replace or retrain unsatisfactory employees. Section 4.2, 'Skills required', suggested that around 5 per cent of an overall system budget should be allocated to training; are you achieving that figure?

Selection and training procedures in some companies are constrained by the more general industrial relations context. For example, management may feel that the best plan is to recruit some new specialists for certain jobs, but that may be difficult or impossible if some current employees are about to be made redundant.

More detailed questions for minority use

A checklist of detailed questions about selection and training is provided on page 221.

5.5   INDUSTRIAL RELATIONS

Importance

'Industrial relations' are important in all employment situations, although the term may seem strange in a small business or office. It covers the procedures whereby working conditions and levels of payment are regulated. This may involve trade unions acting on behalf of their members or, less formally, employees acting individually or in small groups. In many cases, issues of industrial relations are between management and employees, but we should also include questions of demarcation and allocation of tasks between groups of workers themselves: conflicts about 'who does what'.

It is unlikely that the introduction of a single small piece of computer equipment will have a large impact on industrial relations, but this can happen if your investment is substantial, or if the new technology has particular significance for your firm. Uncertainty and conflicting views between management and employee groups can disrupt performance or give rise to damaging disputes with extended feelings of distrust. Fears about job losses are often at the heart of these problems (these are dealt with separately in section 5.7), but other concerns may become apparent, especially in terms of shifts in the relative power of different groups. Some employees may feel threatened, because the new technology seems likely to reduce their required skills or their strategic importance and status in the organization. There may also be conflicts between different groups of employees. For example, two different trade unions may be claiming the right to maintain and repair the technology.

Questions you should ask

Has the introduction of information technology adversely affected your industrial relations? If so, why?

Have any particular groups of employees lost out as a result of this investment? If so, why?

Have demarcation disputes occurred between different groups of employees?

Are different groups competing over access to and control of the new technology?

Have those people directly affected by the new technology been adequately informed and consulted about its introduction, its method of working, and its impact on them?

Have those people indirectly affected been informed and consulted on how it will affect them and their work?

Have discussions between management and relevant representative groups been held, covering issues such as employment terms and conditions, the design of jobs and methods of working?

Has friction between groups of employees, or between different trade unions, increased as a result of the introduction of computer technology?

Things you can do

Particular attention should be paid to identifying those groups who may suffer in some way through the introduction of new technology. Conflicts associated with possible job losses are considered later (section 5.7), but major difficulties can also occur in other ways, as when one group loses relative status in the organization. This can be compounded if pay differentials change as a result of skill shortages, or if new groupings take members from one trade union into another, with resulting inter-union disputes.

Changes in relative status are in certain cases inevitable. However, it may sometimes be possible to train more people to be multi-skilled, so that earlier distinctions disappear. This can also have other benefits, for example, in terms of flexibility, lateral coordination, and the interest attaching to more varied work. However, inter-union conflicts may be temporarily increased by that type of development.

The general message is that managers, trade unions and other employee groups should develop a plan for how they will handle the industrial relations aspects of new technology, and this should attempt to embrace these contentious and emotive issues, rather than avoid them in the hope that they will 'go away'.

Many trade unions have taken a primarily reactive stance, seeking mainly to safeguard their members' health and safety and to win concessions from employers in respect of job security. This has encouraged both unions and employers to negotiate about technology only at the time of its proposed introduction. Previous and subsequent discussions about job design and opportunities for more rewarding work have thus been excluded.

Unions' reactive stance has also often led to their members viewing new technology in a similarly limited way, emphasizing only its impact on job numbers and health and safety. A broader view would be helpful for all concerned, taking in aspects of job design and the characteristics of hardware and software described in this book. We hope that trade unions, as well as managements, can use the book to assist their thinking.

Conflicts and trade-offs

The main problem that arises with a planned approach to industrial relations is that it may slow down the rate at which new technologies are implemented. Nevertheless, this can save time and expense in the longer run, since it may mean that the new systems reach a satisfactory level of performance earlier.

There can also be problems of balancing the view of established trade unions with the need for greater flexibility of working, for example in terms of multi-skilling. Both unions and management need to identify long-term needs here, recognizing that long-term goals may involve short-term difficulties as issues of conflict are worked through.

Questionnaire for minority use

A specialist questionnaire about industrial relations climate is provided on page 223.

5.6 PAY AND CAREER PROGRESSION

Importance

People soon become upset if they feel their pay has moved out of line with that of similar workers, either within the company or in other firms. They assess their contribution in terms of factors such as effort, skills, responsibilities, hours and general conditions, weighing them against the money they receive. If the balance seems wrong in comparison with other people, dissatisfaction arises, and employees are likely to seek an increase in level of pay, to reduce their efforts in the job, and/or to look for a position elsewhere.

Such considerations are especially relevant in the area of this book, since the introduction of new technology often involves changes in skill demands, responsibilities and methods of working. For example, an employee now working with computerized equipment may have lost some old machining skills and might have a job that is physically easier than before. On the other hand, he or she may have had to learn new program-editing skills, at the same time as having responsibility for a very expensive piece of equipment. Should this job be paid more than the previous work as a manual machinist? How much more?

Issues of pay at the level of the individual operator have been considered in section 4.6. Here we are concerned with assessing the situation more widely, across the company as a whole. A number of problems can occur. For example, if pay is settled on a piecemeal basis as new equipment is introduced, then relativities can soon become unbalanced, creating tensions across groups and distorting the overall pay structure.

It may also be that your old payment system becomes inappropriate once the new technology is introduced. For example, a wage system based on piecework and individual incentives will be inappropriate if an integrated computerized system is installed which requires group working and team effort. Conversely, individual performance records might now be provided through the computer, making possible individual payment for work completed. In evaluating the impact of new technology, issues of that kind should be given careful attention.

Many companies have a systematic job evaluation scheme, setting every job within a hierarchy of grades, each with an appropriate payment rate. Extending this scheme to include novel jobs of an information technology kind can sometimes present difficulties. For example, many schemes use 'points rating' methods, allotting to each job a number of points for responsibility, skills, working conditions, physical and mental requirements, and so on. The new jobs may be so different from the old ones, and their nature so unclear (comparing 'level of responsibility' can be very difficult, for example), that the total score of a new job may turn out to be unrealistic when translated into money terms.

Other problems arise in terms of policies and procedures for career progression and staff succession. Changes in the nature of jobs and in the structure of rewards can mean that previously established lines of promotion have become twisted or completely blocked. That can result in good staff leaving in frustration.

Structural distortions can also be seen when groups of people become 'bunched' for years at particular career points beyond which they cannot pass. That can lead to the organization becoming excessively set in its habitual ways of operation, and can also lead to an inability to take on new, younger staff. Without the latter possibility, the age distribution of people in a particular grade can become unbalanced, so that too few junior staff are available for later promotion.

Such problems do not arise only from new technology, but the widespread introduction of computer-based equipment can accelerate their development. Difficulties can also become greater in planning for future retirements or job changes. It is important to provide opportunities for individual employees to gain experience in different parts of the organization. However, computer technology can breed its own specialisms, and certain people can become so expert in their field that they cannot be spared for career development of that kind. As a result, they may become seemingly indispensable in their current job, but quite ignorant about other parts of the company. Transfers in both directions thus become more difficult.

Questions you should ask

Have pay relativities been affected by the information technology?

Are certain pay differentials inequitable?

Is the overall pay system appropriate to the desired method of working?

Are there sufficient grades of payment to allow for progression for valuable members of staff?

Are levels of pay for each grade about right in the current labour market?

Does the company's job evaluation scheme need revision for new-technology jobs?

Is the company well placed for staff succession, if this becomes necessary?

Is there some opportunity for career progression in jobs affected by the new technology?

Things you can do

Managers, trade union officials and other interested employees should examine the pay structure, identify areas of possible inequity or ineffectiveness,

---

Box 5D   Thinking about payment systems

Payment systems are being re-examined in many companies, and a number of quite radical alternatives have been implemented. Among these are:

profit-sharing schemes
share-option schemes
individualized payment geared to automatic logging of output
performance-related pay for managers
peer evaluation of performance as one basis of the reward package
payment for an overall number of annual hours, phased by mutual
    agreement
'cafeteria' systems, whereby individuals choose their own mixture of
    rewards (e.g. with greater or lesser proportions of income in terms of
    wages, health insurance or other fringe benefits)
harmonization of pay and conditions, with all grades of employees
    treated within a single, overall scheme
payment on a contract basis for particular items of work
a mixture of employment and self-employment, with the latter work
    under contract to the company as long as both parties find that
    beneficial.

In evaluating payment aspects of your new technology, consideration should be given to these possibilities.

---

and obtain relevant information about the local labour market. This should be done in retrospective evaluations of new technology, and also in anticipation of new purchases.

Your job evaluation scheme may also need investigation. If it does not adequately cover new-technology jobs, try to avoid the temptation to adjust the standard weighting procedures to produce a reasonable wage level irrespective of the formal calculations. Look hard both at the factors for which points are awarded and also at the basis of weighting procedures. You need to ensure consistency and appropriateness in both terms across all the jobs, the previous ones and also those which come with new technology.

Periodically, you should take an overall look at the type of pay system you have. More and more companies are finding that significant investments in new technology are increasing the interdependence between different groups and raising the need to pay for collective rather than individual output. That leads towards 'harmonization' (between blue- and white-collar conditions of service) and towards systems of measured day-work or profit-sharing, away from individualized systems of payment by results. In some other cases, separate payment is becoming possible because of the nature of the work and the fact that output is recorded automatically by the equipment. Several options in this field are illustrated in Box 5D. Specialist advice (for example, from consultants) may be helpful in examining which possibilities are most appropriate for your own company.

Conflicts and trade-offs

Discussions about wages and careers can generate considerable emotion and disruption, as well as requiring a great deal of time. Opinions about the value of jobs and individuals often differ sharply, and in general it is likely that conflict will temporarily increase. However, there is no alternative to careful discussion of the issues, and the need for organizational resources to handle such discussions and their attendant conflict should not be forgotten when technology plans are being drawn up.

   Another conflict can exist in the balance between short- and long-term goals in respect of career development and staff succession. The future effectiveness of a company may be enhanced by the provision of training and wide experience to aid staff succession. However, this may be at a short-term cost through interruption to normal working procedures, as staff are moved from jobs with which they are familiar.

Questionnaire for minority use

A specialist questionnaire to tap attitudes about pay and career opportunities is provided on page 225. See also the items about users' pay in Chapter 11 (page 206).

More detailed questions for minority use

A checklist of detailed questions about job evaluation is provided on page 226.

5.7 JOB LOSSES

Importance

A major industrial relations issue centres on the possibility of job losses and the associated feelings of insecurity which can arise as a result of investment in new technology. Expanding companies are usually untroubled by this, and even for others 'natural wastage' may be sufficient to cover changed staff requirements. Alternatively, a company might seek volunteers who are willing to leave on the basis of a lump-sum payment. This can have the disadvantage that the volunteer leavers might be highly skilled and capable, and precautions against that happening are usually desirable. Unfortunately, some companies need to shed more jobs than can be coped with voluntarily, and additional job losses may require involuntary lay-offs.

   Management of these issues requires extensive consultation and negotiation, with trade unions where appropriate, and the amount of time required, both from the company's and from the trade union's point of view, should not be underestimated. Such problems can be very complicated, particularly when several employee groups or trade unions are involved. The impact on morale and the tensions created by prolonged periods of insecurity can also be damaging, especially to the individuals concerned, but also to the organization more widely.

Questions you should ask

Will introduction of the computer-based system give rise to job losses?
Can job losses be handled by 'natural wastage'?
Can job losses be handled by growth and internal redeployment?
Can job losses be handled by voluntary redundancy?
What can the organization do to help with re-employment prospects?
Is there conflict between different unions? Or other representative groups?
How long will it take, realistically, to manage the job loss process?
Have employees been informed about what is intended?

Things you can do

There is no real alternative to careful consultation and negotiation with employees and their representatives. Opportunities should be sought for internal retraining and redeployment, voluntary redundancy, career counselling, and training for employment elsewhere. If these can be undertaken collaboratively with employee representatives, so much the better.

Initiating a programme of staff reduction is inevitably painful and difficult. However, the problems can often be greater if decisions are delayed. For example, if some compulsory redundancies are unavoidably necessary, then introducing these quickly will be stressful for the people concerned. However, deferring their introduction will be stressful for everyone, with the later additional pain for those who are required to leave when the decision is eventually taken. It is often wise to grasp the nettle at an early point if compulsory redundancies are absolutely unpreventable.

Conflicts and trade-offs

Employees' concern about possible job losses and the number of those losses will spill over into other issues raised in this chapter. Cooperation on a range of questions is likely to be reduced by disputes or uncertainty on this one issue. As long as concern about job losses persists, effective resolution of other issues may not be possible.

More detailed questions for minority use

A checklist of detailed questions about possible job losses is provided on page 227.

5.8 ORGANIZATIONAL PERFORMANCE AND MORALE

Importance

The major issue underlying all evaluation questions in this manual concerns the impact of the computer system on your organization's overall performance and financial position. In addition to the impact of a new system on the quantity, quality and price of your product or service, you will also want to consider other aspects of performance. For example, does the system make your company more or less flexible, more or less able to cope with change, more or less responsive to customer needs? Does it assist or impede you in delivering your service or product on time?

In all these cases, evaluation needs to be linked to the development of strategy and the implementation of appropriate tactics. What are the company's primary goals at present? Are new business opportunities available to which technology can contribute? In which directions does the company wish to move? What are the principal constraints and obstacles? Where should effort be concentrated? What additional resources, material and human, are needed? In what ways can specific types of equipment help? As indicated at the beginning of the chapter, the introduction of new technology can sometimes be the catalyst for change; and the need for that change derives from an assessment of current and future requirements within a more general business strategy. Similarly, assessment of costs and benefits can vary according to your stage of technological development. Wholly new installations are harder to appraise than are small additions to current technology.

A financial appraisal of costs and benefits is of course central to this part of an evaluation exercise. A surprisingly large number of companies carry out elaborate *advance* appraisals, seeking to justify an investment in financial terms, but fail to check *afterwards* how well their goals have been attained. In part, this is because the effort required in retrospective appraisals can be considerable, and because, in some cases, the system is so obviously successful or so clearly a disaster that complex calculations are not required. Nevertheless, retrospective appraisals are important if the company is to learn from its experience and if improvements are to be made.

Procedures are summarized in section 7.3 (pages 142 to 145), covering monetary costs and benefits, discounted over time, and also the less quantifiable factors which may sometimes tilt the balance one way or the other. If the rate of return is below forecast or below the level required, then you should set out to answer the evaluation questions in this and the preceding chapters.

Many companies have unrealistically optimistic expectations of their technological investments. They seek a good financial return in two or three years only. However, that is often difficult to achieve, partly because of the complex learning and adjustment that has to take place at the same time as output levels are maintained. This general problem is illustrated in the particular case of industrial robots in Box 5E.

As in Chapter 4, where the focus was upon users of the equipment, it is

---

Box 5E   Return on investment: The case of manufacturing robots

---

A recent report on robots in British industry reached the following conclusions about payback.

Installation and integration of the first robot takes on average a little over six months before it comes on-line and starts earning. Thereafter its efficiency of use improves with experience year by year, and its maximum profitability is usually not achieved until several years after introduction. Hence the two to three year payback period commonly demanded by financial controllers is inappropriate, at least for initial applications, since it ignores the cost of learning how to apply the technology and does not take indirect or qualitative benefits into account. A realistic appraisal, at least for initial robot applications, requires the longer time perspective and strategic view normally found in countries like West Germany and Japan. It also demands allowance not merely for savings in labour and other direct production costs, but also for indirect savings, for example through reduced waste and more consistently high product quality (the most frequently experienced benefit from robots), and for more intangible benefits, such as improved work conditions, better labour relations and a more modern company 'image'.

---

important to couple issues of organizational performance with those of attitudes and morale in relevant sectors of the company. This can be undertaken through the basic evaluation methods described in Chapter 6 (interviews, meetings or working parties), but more specialist questionnaires may sometimes be appropriate; these are illustrated in Chapter 11 (page 211).

Questions you should ask

Has your product or service changed? For better or worse? At lower or higher price? At lower or higher quality?

Has overall productivity improved?

Is the company more flexible in responding to change?

Is the company more responsive to customer needs?

Is the investment worthwhile in cost-benefit terms, over an appropriate pay-back period?

Have likely technological developments been surveyed, with a view to changing company strategy or tactics?

Have new business objectives been explored, which could be attained through additional computer technology?

Has labour turnover decreased?

Has absenteeism decreased?

Has morale improved?

Overall, could computer technology make a greater contribution to help the company meet its business goals?

Things you can do

If you are not achieving the performance you require from your investment, then further evaluation work is required. The nature of this will depend on the system under examination. In some cases, the focus will be on issues of equipment or usability (Chapters 2 and 3), with little senior management involvement. However, problems concerning business goals and organizational structure (in the present chapter) will always require the attention of top managers.

In order to place that evaluation on a suitable foundation, it is often sensible to create a working party which is representative of principal interest groups. That may be made up of managers alone, or extend to other staff, and it should report directly to a senior manager. The working party should have the task of examining the technology in question, reviewing its organizational and financial costs and benefits, and making suggestions about possible improvements. In carrying out its inquiries, the working party should consider the thirty issues which have been presented in the course of Chapters 2 to 5. Financial assessments illustrated in section 7.3 (page 142) should also be made.

Separate groups will no doubt wish to protect their own interests; and interpretation of evidence and final decision-making will need to recognize that fact. The chairperson (a senior manager or independent consultant) will often have a crucial role in steering discussion and decisions between the inevitable vested interests.

More detailed questions for minority use

A checklist of detailed questions about organizational performance is provided on page 228.

Questionnaires for minority use

Three specialist questionnaires about employee morale are introduced on page 230, and presented between pages 211 and 214.

6

How to carry out evaluation

The issues dealt with in this chapter are:

Managing evaluation	111
Basic methods of evaluation	114
1: Interviews	115
2: Meetings	116
3: Working parties	116
Initial diagnoses	117

In Chapter 1 (page 16) we set out the summary *principles* of evaluation. These are as follows:

(1) Look at the primary work objectives, not merely the computer-based system
(2) Don't start unless you are prepared to change things
(3) Be systematic
(4) Go beyond the immediately obvious
(5) Ask the people involved
(6) Make comparisons
(7) Do it your own way to meet your own needs (but don't forget the previous six points)

Chapters 2 to 5 presented thirty key issues to be addressed in the evaluation of new technology, but we are still left with the question: how should the principles be applied *in practice*? How do you get started and what should you actually do? We aim here to provide answers through a number of practical guidelines.

Box 6A   Summary of evaluation practice

(1) Identify purpose and scope
(2) Allocate responsibility and set limits
(3) Identify problem areas within those limits
(4) Apply the basic evaluation methods
(5) Obtain specialist help if needed
(6) Interpret findings and plan actions
(7) Manage change and review progress

MANAGING EVALUATION

Since each organization is unique, and the use of new technology varies considerably from company to company, there is no one 'correct' approach to the management of evaluation. However, the points in Box 6A cover essential actions.

These actions do not always follow each other in a fixed sequence, and different individuals and groups are likely to be involved at different points.

(1) *Identify purpose and scope*

The first *principle* of evaluation is to look at company or department goals, not merely at the technology. *In practice*, that can mean many different things. For example, the engineering factory in the case study of Chapter 1 was failing to meet business goals in terms of productivity and quality. The purpose of that evaluation was to improve manufacturing and engineering performance in those particular respects.

Other companies may wish to evaluate their new technology in more comprehensive terms, considering their overall business strategy and possible changes in product or service. Conversely, the purpose of evaluation might be very much more focused. One section of an office may be ineffective because users of the new word-processing system are making a large number of errors. Evaluation in that case could be limited to a narrow range of questions associated with a limited department goal.

As soon as you start thinking about the need for evaluation in your company, you will probably have an outline idea of the purpose it might achieve and about the scope of any exercise which should be mounted. However, you should reflect on those initial ideas before moving further. Ought the purpose to be smaller or larger? Have you considered other evaluation needs, and reviewed several options before choosing an initial purpose? Is your intended purpose achievable and realistic with the resources available? Are subsidiary objectives involved, as well as the main purpose?

Decisions about purpose and scope may be taken by managers at whatever level is appropriate for the objectives. Studies with limited purpose and narrow scope (examining single items of equipment, for example) are likely to be carried out entirely within a single department. However, evaluation inquiries in respect of broad business goals and the company as a whole can extend across several parts of a company. Senior managers are particularly likely to be directly involved in the second approach.

In all cases, two practical points need early consideration. First, is the purpose described in a way which will allow some measurement of your subsequent success? Can you define (in outline terms at this stage) criteria of performance and measurable benchmarks which can later tell you whether your purpose is being achieved?

Second, will you need to bring in specialists from outside the company? That may become clear only at a later point, but it is advisable to consider the possibility at the outset. Your company's own staff may sometimes have all the necessary technical and organizational expertise, but in other cases external consultants or computer suppliers or manufacturers might be needed if your purpose is to be achieved.

(2) *Allocate responsibility and set limits*

Evaluation, especially in the case of large systems, can be difficult; and individual and group interests can conflict with each other as possible changes are considered. It needs to be clear who has responsibility for final decisions, and who will be carrying forward the work in day-to-day terms. In the case study of Chapter 1, those responsibilities were held by the production director and a department manager respectively, and an arrangement of that kind will be quite common. However, responsibility for smaller studies of current equipment may be retained entirely within a department or section; and large inquiries encompassing business strategy and broad-ranging issues naturally involve top-level responsibility.

It is helpful to specify some limits to the evaluation, although these can of course be amended later. For example, a study of problems with word-processing in an office may be restricted to users in that department, or it could look more broadly across departments, and consider changes in the allocation of tasks to different groups.

As pointed out in Chapter 1, there are contrasting dangers: looking too widely at policy and organizational issues (losing sight of the technology), or an excessively narrow approach of examining merely equipment efficiency (missing important issues of wider goals). An explicit decision about limits is needed, often somewhere between those alternatives.

Other limits to be set at an early stage include time and resource boundaries. By when should the study be completed and recommendations for action presented? How many people and how much money may be committed to the work?

(3) *Identify problem areas within those limits*

In some cases, the purpose you have identified will already specify the problem areas to be examined. However, evaluators should avoid deciding too quickly what is the true problem. Within the scope of their inquiry (as decided above), they should initially keep an open mind about opportunities and problems, looking beyond the symptoms to identify underlying causes.

Chapters 2 to 5 have provided many suggestions about issues which might need to be examined. In small inquiries, you may not need to range very widely, since your scope has already been defined. But some consideration of all four chapters will often be appropriate.

There are occasions when an evaluator has a completely open mind about the type of problems which will come to the surface. He or she might be an external consultant, or a person moved into a separate part of the company to carry out an evaluation project. An overall initial screening process should then be undertaken, looking at all possible issues before narrowing down to the chosen degree. Brief diagnostic questionnaires can be useful in that process, and illustrations are provided later in this chapter (see page 117).

(4) *Apply the basic evaluation methods*

Chapter 1 pointed out that all evaluation work is derived from the basic methods of interviews, meetings, or working parties. These will be examined in the next section, when practical advice will be given. At this stage, the point is that evaluators must meet with individuals or groups in order to examine relevant issues and to discuss possible improvements. Select as appropriate from the 30 major issues described in Chapters 2 to 5, following these up through some combination of interviews, meetings or working parties.

It is often useful to start an evaluation with a meeting of everyone concerned; that may be managers only, or managers and other employees. Discuss the purpose and scope (as identified above), clarify responsibilities and limits, and review the basic methods. If the scope of an enquiry is quite broad, then a working party can be helpful, as in the case described in Chapter 1. Subsequent meetings of interested persons should be held to provide feedback and to consider possible actions.

The three basic evaluation methods will be adequate in most cases. However, a minority of readers may wish to look in more detail at some of the issues we have identified. Specialist skills will be required in those more detailed enquiries, and we have brought together eight 'specialist methods' which might be used. These are: questionnaires, system walk-through, formal observation, user diaries, system logging, task analysis, comparative testing, and analysis of company records.

The specialist methods are described in Chapter 8, and some are illustrated in Chapters 9 to 12. They are more difficult to apply than the basic methods, and they can produce large quantities of data which are hard to analyse. The specialist methods will therefore be used relatively rarely, and most readers can evaluate their new technology without using them. However, by glancing through Chapters 8 to 12 everyone may gain some ideas, which can be developed for their own use when applying the three basic methods.

(5) *Obtain specialist help if needed*

You may lack the expertise to examine certain issues (for example, hardware and software compatibility, section 2.2) or to predict future developments (for example, in electronic communication throughout the company, section 5.3). In those circumstances it is obviously sensible to call in additional expertise.

That may be available from another part of your own organization, but in many cases you should draw upon help from outside consultants or suppliers. This should be done sooner rather than later, since those individuals may help to direct your thinking into valuable new directions. Remember, too, that external consultants can be persuasive and powerful allies in promoting change.

National sources of expertise should also be considered. We have listed 41 such sources within the United Kingdom on page 237.

(6) *Interpret findings and plan actions*

This step covers an enormous variety of possible activities. However, we should emphasize that comparisons should be made whenever possible to help clarify the meaning of your findings. Try to obtain information about other companies, perhaps about your direct competitors. You should also make comparisons across time (are things getting better or worse?), and see if your data can be compared with published industry standards.

In the end, however, interpreting the results of an evaluation exercise is often far from straightforward. There is rarely a single index of success or failure or a single way forward. Technical and financial expertise should be used whenever possible, but ultimately the outcome must result from managerial assessments and individual judgement. You need to combine information from different sources, link together the formal and the informal, and check out your conclusions with other people.

In planning actions from among possible options, there is undoubtedly advantage in consulting as widely as possible. Once decisions have been taken, a meeting of all concerned should be held to communicate plans and reduce the possibility of misunderstanding. These points are further developed in the next chapter.

(7) *Manage change and review progress*

Principal themes in the management of change are described in Chapter 7. This covers financial aspects, conflict and commitment, and the provision of organizational support. It emphasizes that progress reviews should be seen as important elements in the cycle of decision-making and action. You should set up mechanisms to assess progress against your original goals, using the performance criteria identified from your evaluation purposes (see the first point above).

BASIC METHODS OF EVALUATION

We turn from those essential actions to look at practical aspects of the three basic methods: interviews, meetings and working parties. These are of course used in many different ways within organizations, and all readers will have had some experience of them. We aim in this section to help you build upon that experience in evaluating computer-based equipment.

One or more of the three methods should be used for those evaluative issues you wish to take up from Chapters 2 to 5. You will often need to add further questions specific to your own situation, covering aspects of your own equipment and working practices.

Basic method 1: interviews

Interviews provide an excellent way of collecting information, and they can be as focused or range as widely as is necessary. The questions listed in Chapters 2 to 5 should be used as the basis of interviews to evaluate new technology.

One difficulty is that some people feel nervous in interviews, and may not open up with their true feelings. Interviewing is thus most effective when the interviewer is seen as independent and has no particular axe to grind. For example, it may be difficult for users to criticize a system if they are interviewed by the manager responsible for purchasing it or by a member of the team which designed it.

Interviews (and the other basic methods) are mainly concerned with

---

Box 6B   Advice to interviewers

— make sure you interview a broad range of people
— limit the number of interviews you do in any single day so that you remain fresh (it is surprisingly tiring!)
— set aside plenty of time for each one, so that you need not rush
— use a quiet and private place where you will not be interrupted
— at the beginning tell the person what you are trying to find out and what will come about from the exercise
— give clear guarantees about the confidentiality of any views and opinions expressed
— prepare in advance a list of questions you plan to ask
— ask easy questions first, and harder questions (for example, involving interpretation) when the person has warmed up a bit
— ask questions in an open-ended way
— work through the questions systematically
— listen carefully to what the interviewee has to say
— make notes of answers as you go along
— look out for answers which appear to reflect what an interviewee thinks it is appropriate to say, rather than indicating what he or she really believes
— be prepared to deviate from your list of questions if a person is keen to tell you something else
— if you do not understand what someone is telling you, get him or her to explain it
— remember that the interviewee should do most of the talking
— thank the person at the end for his or her help, and summarize what will happen next with the evaluation exercise

'subjective' information, what people think and feel. But that is not the same as saying that the material gathered is wrong or invalid. The emphasis should be on obtaining *factual information*, of two kinds. First, you are seeking facts about what goes on in the department, who does what kind of work, and how the system operates. Second, you are seeking facts about people's views, beliefs and attitudes. These may concern the current situation or might relate to future possibilities, viewed as personal threats or opportunities.

In the first case, consistency between the findings from different interviews is of course desirable. If there are major discrepancies between two people's descriptions of a working procedure, then you need to make further inquiries. In the second case (views and attitudes), there may of course be differences between people. A key task for an interview programme is to map out the pattern of views held by different individuals and groups.

It is essential that interviewers do not influence the kinds of attitudes which are expressed. You should not appear to favour one kind of answer over another, and you should stress that there are no 'correct' opinions in what is an entirely confidential discussion. Interviewees must feel that they can safely express their views, even if those would be politically unacceptable in open discussion with colleagues or superiors. In some particularly difficult cases, this may only be possible if the interviewer is entirely independent, and can convince interviewees that his or her report will not permit the holder of any opinions to be identified.

Anyone who gathers information for evaluating a piece of computer-based equipment in a work setting will need to interview relevant members of staff. Some pieces of advice are listed in Box 6B.

Basic method 2: meetings

Meetings of several people have two different purposes within evaluation. On the one hand, they might serve as group interviews, providing information in response to questions. On the other hand, they may also be directed to finding solutions to problems, working out possible ways to improve the situation. Both types of meeting provide opportunities for information-gathering, but the second kind is more immediately action-oriented.

Meetings take up less time overall than the equivalent number of interviews, and they can be a very useful part of any evaluation. However, some people feel uncomfortable in public settings and may be unwilling to express their views, even when these views are firmly held. That is especially the case with opinions felt to be unpopular with colleagues or bosses. Moreover, it can be quite difficult to run meetings; it can be difficult, for example, to keep discussion to the point and to ensure that all participants get the opportunity to express their views. Some items of advice are summarized in Box 6C.

Basic method 3: working parties

A working party is one special kind of meeting, in which the members come together on several occasions to discuss problems and possible actions. The

---

Box 6C   Advice about running meetings

— make sure all relevant people are invited, but try not to have too many present
— use a room where space is adequate
— organize refreshments for a set time
— avoid interruptions from outside the meeting
— set aside plenty of time for discussion
— start the meeting on time
— agree at the outset who will record the minutes
— provide a clear statement of what the meeting is trying to achieve
— keep discussion to the point
— try and make sure everyone contributes, if necessary by asking people individually for their views
— try to make it clear where there is agreement and disagreement
— summarize any agreed actions, with particular attention to identifying the person(s) responsible for carrying them out
— set target dates for completion of each action
— agree the circulation list for the minutes
— summarize what will happen next with the evaluation exercise

---

advantage of a working party is that people can focus attention over a period of time on a set of issues, becoming thoroughly familiar with details and possible ways forward. Working parties are probably most successful when they bring together members of the company who otherwise would not get the opportunity to exchange views as a group. For example, users of the system, engineers, managers, trade union representatives, and other people affected by the system might not otherwise meet together to address joint problems.

As with the previous basic methods, the questions listed in Chapters 2 to 5 can be used to initiate the activity of a working party. But the group will usually want to develop its own themes, and it may need to gather additional information, from within the company, from suppliers, or from other users. The checklists in Chapters 9 to 12 may be helpful there. Additional advice is provided in Box 6D.

INITIAL DIAGNOSES

In some cases it is helpful to start an evaluation exercise with a wide-ranging look at some or all of the four areas covered in this book: equipment and working conditions, usability, job quality and organizational aspects. That is particularly helpful if you have not defined in advance the problems to be examined, and if you wish to learn from employees where they believe major problems lie.

Initial diagnoses can be carried out by administering a screening questionnaire to members of relevant groups. This asks people to indicate areas of

---

Box 6D   Advice about working parties

— try to make the group as representative as possible of different views, within a reasonable size limit (normally fewer than 10 people)
— agree its remit and terms of reference at the outset
— specify to whom it is responsible
— agree its method of working, its budget and an approximate time schedule
— go slowly at first, since people will probably have quite different kinds of expertise
— record and circulate the minutes of every meeting
— record who is responsible for any agreed actions, and establish target dates for their completion
— encourage the secretary of the working party to follow up agreed actions to make sure they get done
— allow discussion to roam fairly freely so that new ideas are explored, especially in the early stages
— provide the resources for working party members to attend meetings, undertake visits, consult outside experts, etc.
— try to prevent other problems, which are nothing to do with your remit, getting introduced into the working party
— ensure that the results of any other evaluation exercises are fed back to the working party
— agree how and when working party members will report back to the people they represent

---

concern, and may be extended to allow written comments about problems and their sources.

Screening questionnaires can be used in three different ways. First, anonymous replies may be gathered from a reasonably large number of people, in order to look at the overall pattern. Second, you might ask individual employees to complete a questionnaire before they are interviewed. That allows them to think before the interview about the new technology and its problems, and permits the interviewer to concentrate particularly on the topics identified on the completed questionnaire as needing attention. In this case, questionnaire completion cannot be entirely anonymous, although confidentiality within the interview process is of course essential.

The third use is rather different. Both types of questionnaire can be employed as checklists of questions for evaluators themselves. Completing the questions can permit a useful summary of an evaluator's initial thoughts, and ensures that he or she takes a wide perspective at an early stage.

Two types of screening questionnaire are illustrated here, identified as (A) and (B). The first questionnaire, in each of the four areas covered, lists a number of points, and asks whether individual employees believe those to be a problem with the technology under evaluation. Topics can be added which you consider potentially important in your own company, and you should delete any which are completely irrelevant.

In responding to questionnaire (A), people are asked to tick one of four boxes: no problems, minor problems, major problems, not sure. In using this approach in the first way described above (with a sample of people), you should work out the percentage of respondents (or simply the number, if you prefer) who have ticked each box for each item. There is no golden rule about how many ticks in a 'major problems' box are needed before a topic deserves further investigation; the choice is yours. In making that choice, respondents' comments in the second part of the questionnaire might be helpful, where they are asked to describe the problems they have in mind.

The second questionnaire for each of the four areas (identified here as '(B)') is entirely 'open-ended'. No boxes are provided for ticks; instead, respondents are asked to write down their answers to a number of questions. As with questionnaire (A), you can modify the questions to meet your own needs. In particular, you will have to indicate which system is being examined, and you may want to gather some information about the kind of job undertaken by the person completing the questionnaire.

Interpretation of replies to these open-ended questions is entirely a matter of judgement. It is rarely possible or worthwhile to aim for any form of numerical analyses. The goal is merely to provide screening information and ideas at an early stage in an evaluation. As emphasized earlier, it is important not to pre-judge which topics are important, and this screening approach can open up themes which might otherwise be overlooked.

Three other points should be made. First, you will not usually require all the screening questionnaires presented in the following pages. It is desirable in every case to consider coverage of the four areas, so that you do not miss important issues. But you are unlikely to use both type (A) and type (B) questionnaires for each area; select one to meet your needs in each area.

Second, we have defined other uses of questionnaires (apart from in this screening mode) as 'specialist' methods of evaluation. A more detailed discussion of their design and administration is provided in Chapter 8 (page 158). It may be worthwhile glancing at that section before carrying out a screening enquiry of the kind described here.

Finally, we should return to the advice introduced earlier as evaluation principle number seven: Do it your own way to meet your own needs. It would be quite wrong to start every evaluation study with a screening questionnaire. Use them only when needed. They are particularly helpful when a broad initial record is required, when an outside evaluator wishes to gain a wide picture of staff views, or when you want employees to think about issues in advance of an interview. In all cases, however, a screening questionnaire should be viewed as only a first stage; you will always need to proceed beyond it, through some form of interviews, meetings or working parties.

EQUIPMENT AND WORKING CONDITIONS: SCREENING QUESTIONNAIRE (A)

The questions below are concerned with an overall assessment of the equipment and working conditions. Please tick the box which most nearly fits your views. There are no right or wrong answers; it is your views that count. These will be helpful in assessing whether or not improvements are necessary.

In cases where you think that major problems have occurred (response column 3), please say briefly at the bottom of the questionnaire what you have in mind, indicating the question number to the left of your reply.

Your views are entirely confidential. If you are worried about this, ask the person administering the questionnaire for guarantees and assurances.

WITH THE SYSTEM, ARE THERE PROBLEMS:	No problems	Minor problems	Major problems	Not sure
1. in meeting business goals?				
2. in completing essential tasks?				
3. in coping with anticipated future needs?				
4. with under-used equipment facilities?				
5. of linking together items of equipment?				
6. of linking together different programs?				
7. of linking together different sets of data?				
8. of unreliable equipment?				
9. of software bugs?				
10. over repairs to equipment?				
11. over maintenance of equipment?				

(Contd.)

WITH THE SYSTEM, ARE THERE PROBLEMS:	No problem'	Minor problems	Major problems	Not sure
12. with equipment that is too advanced?				
13. with equipment that is out of date?				
14. over security of information within the organization?				
15. over security of information, externally?				
16. meeting legislative requirements about privacy of information?				
17. with work space layout?				
18. with the visual display unit?				
19. with the keyboard?				
20. with other poorly designed equipment?				
21. with lighting?				
22. with temperature?				
23. with humidity?				
24. with noise?				
25. with air quality?				
26. of safety?				
27. of excessive stress?				
28. of ill-health?				
29. meeting legislative requirements about health and safety?				

(Contd.)

In the case of *major problems*, please note down briefly what you have in mind:

Question number   Kind of problem

EQUIPMENT AND WORKING CONDITIONS: SCREENING QUESTIONNAIRE (B)

Please give your assessment of the equipment and working conditions by answering the following questions:

1. In getting the job done, what are the best aspects of the equipment and working conditions?

2. In getting the job done, what are the worst aspects of the equipment and working conditions?

3. To improve your effectiveness, what changes would you like to see made to the equipment or working conditions?

4. Is there anything else about the equipment or working conditions that you wish to add?

USABILITY: SCREENING QUESTIONNAIRE (A)

The questions below are concerned with an overall assessment of the usability of the system. Please tick the box which most nearly fits your views. There are no right or wrong answers; it is your views that count. These will be helpful in assessing whether or not improvements are necessary.

In cases where you think that major problems have occurred (response column 3), please say briefly at the bottom of the questionnaire what you have in mind, indicating the question number to the left of your reply.

Your views are entirely confidential. If you are worried about this, ask the person administering the questionnaire for guarantees and assurances.

WITH THE SYSTEM, ARE THERE PROBLEMS:	No problems	Minor problems	Major problems	Not sure
1. of poor documentation?				
2. of arbitrary commands which are difficult to learn?				
3. of obscure concepts which are difficult to learn?				
4. of poor on-line help facilities?				
5. of inconsistent ways of operation which are difficult to learn?				
6. of losing control of the system?				
7. of not knowing what to do next?				
8. of forgetting which mode you are in?				
9. of getting lost in a menu structure?				
10. of having to make too many difficult choices?				

(Contd.)

WITH THE SYSTEM, ARE THERE PROBLEMS:	No problems	Minor problems	Major problems	Not sure
11. of having to remember too much information while carrying out important tasks?				
12. of correcting work which has been done?				
13. of an over-complex macro-language?				
14. of response times that are too slow just when you need a quick action?				
15. of response times that are unpredictable?				
16. of incorrect priorities in a multi-user system?				
17. of delayed up-dating of databases in a multi-user system?				
18. of too much time spent entering data?				
19. of too many errors in entering data?				
20. in finding the information you need on the screen?				
21. of print-outs which are cluttered with too much information?				
22. of too many errors?				
23. of too much time spent correcting errors?				

(*Contd.*)

WITH THE SYSTEM, ARE THERE PROBLEMS:	No problems	Minor problems	Major problems	Not sure
24. of users being excessively careful, in attempts to avoid errors?				
25. of inadequate back-up storage?				
26. of occasional errors which are especially serious?				

In the case of *major problems*, please note down briefly what you have in mind:

Question number   Kind of problem

USABILITY: SCREENING QUESTIONNAIRE (B)

Please give your assessment of the usability of the computer-based system by answering the following questions:

1. In terms of ease of use, what are the best aspects of the system?

2. In terms of ease of use, what are the worst aspects of the system?

3. What parts of the system give the greatest difficulty?

(Contd.)

4. What changes would you like to see made to the system to improve its ease of use?

5. Is there anything else about the usability of the system that you wish to add?

JOB   QUALITY   AND   PERFORMANCE: SCREENING QUESTIONNAIRE (A)

The questions below are concerned with an overall assessment of system users' job quality and performance. Please tick the box which most nearly fits your views. There are no right or wrong answers; it is your views that count. These will be helpful in assessing whether or not improvements are necessary.

In cases where you think that major problems have occurred (response column 3), please say briefly at the bottom of the questionnaire what you have in mind, indicating the question number to the left of your reply.

Your views are entirely confidential. If you are worried about this, ask the person administering the questionnaire for guarantees and assurances.

WITH THE SYSTEM, ARE THERE PROBLEMS OF:	No problems	Minor problems	Major problems	Not sure
1. operators having too little influence over their job activities?				
2. operators being unable to influence the quality of the product or service?				
3. operators no longer needing to use their skills?				
4. operators lacking the skills required for the job?				
5. jobs which contain too little inherent variety?				

(Contd.)

WITH THE SYSTEM, ARE THERE PROBLEMS OF:	No problems	Minor problems	Major problems	Not sure
6. jobs which tie the operators down to one place continuously throughout every working day?				
7. work demands which are continuously at a very high level?				
8. work demands which are too low?				
9. jobs which have no sense of identity or completeness?				
10. unmet training needs?				
11. operators feeling that they need more feedback about their performance?				
12. operators being unclear about what they are required to do?				
13. operators lacking adequate understanding of the system they are using?				
14. operators feeling uncertain about their future prospects?				
15. inequitable pay levels and differentials?				
16. a wage system which contains inadequate incentive or reward for good work?				
17. an unsatisfactory job evaluation scheme?				

(Contd.)

WITH THE SYSTEM, ARE THERE PROBLEMS OF:	No problems	Minor problems	Major problems	Not sure
18. unsatisfactory *formal* communications to and from operators?				
19. unsatisfactory *informal* communications to and from operators?				
20. too few opportunities for social contact?				
21. staff complaints about physical strain and aches?				
22. a poor safety record?				
23. operators delivering an unsatisfactory product or service?				
24. low productivity?				
25. excessive labour turnover?				
26. too much absenteeism?				
27. low morale among users?				
28. operators feeling under too much job strain?				

In the case of *major problems*, please note down briefly what you have in mind:

Question number   Kind of problem

JOB QUALITY AND PERFORMANCE: SCREENING QUESTIONNAIRE (B)

Please give your assessment of system users' job quality and performance by answering the following questions:

1. What are the best parts of the job from the system users' point of view?

2. What are the worst parts of the job from the system users' point of view?

3. Which aspects of the job give people most difficulty?

4. What performance problems exist in the job?

5. What changes would you like to see made to the jobs to make them better for users of the system?

6. What changes would you like to see made to the jobs to increase the effectiveness of employees using the system?

7. Is there anything else about the job that you wish to add?

ORGANIZATIONAL ASPECTS AND EFFECTIVENESS: SCREENING QUESTIONNAIRE (A)

The questions below are concerned with an overall assessment of the organization and its effectiveness in relation to new technology. Please tick the box which most nearly fits your views. There are no right or wrong answers; it is your views that count. These will be helpful in assessing whether or not improvements are necessary.

In cases where you think that major problems have occurred (response column 3), please say briefly at the bottom of the questionnaire what you have in mind, indicating the question number to the left of your reply.

Your views are entirely confidential. If you are worried about this, ask the person administering the questionnaire for guarantees and assurances.

WITH THE NEW TECHNOLOGY, IS/ARE THERE:	No problems	Minor problems	Major problems	Not sure
1. too many levels in the organizational structure?				
2. too many different specialist groups?				
3. poor supervision and control down the hierarchy?				
4. poor co-ordination of effort across different specialist groups?				
5. too great a degree of centralization?				
6. too great a degree of decentralization?				
7. too much bureaucracy?				
8. too great a standardization of procedure?				
9. too much formality in decision-making?				

(Contd.)

WITH THE NEW TECHNOLOGY, IS/ARE THERE:	No problems	Minor problems	Major problems	Not sure
10. too much inflexibility in the face of change?				
11. ineffective internal communications?				
12. too much impersonality in internal communications?				
13. poor communication with customers and suppliers?				
14. people receiving more information than they need and can cope with?				
15. unmet needs for new staff with different skills?				
16. employees in jobs for which they are not suited?				
17. unmet needs for more training?				
18. inadequate procedures for selecting new staff?				
19. industrial relations difficulties between management and workers?				
20. disputes between employee groups and/or between trade unions?				
21. unresolved conflicts between management and employees which are preventing the solution of other problems?				

(*Contd.*)

WITH THE NEW TECHNOLOGY, IS/ARE THERE:	No problems	Minor problems	Major problems	Not sure
22. a low level of employees' trust in management?				
23. inequitable pay levels and differentials?				
24. a wage system which contains inadequate incentive or reward for good work?				
25. an unsatisfactory job evaluation scheme?				
26. problems of staff succession and career progression?				
27. unresolved questions of job losses?				
28. inter-union conflicts about job losses?				
29. a poor product or service from the company?				
30. poor overall productivity?				
31. inadequate company flexibility in the face of changing external demands?				
32. excessive labour turnover?				
33. too much absenteeism?				
34. poor staff morale?				
35. overall, poor attainment of business goals?				

(Contd.)

In the case of *major problems*, please note down briefly what you have in mind:

Question number   Kind of problem

ORGANIZATIONAL ASPECTS AND EFFECTIVENESS: SCREENING QUESTIONNAIRE (B)

Please give your assessment of the wider organizational aspects of the computer-based system (beyond merely the users and their jobs) by answering the following questions.

1. What have been the best organizational consequences of the system?

2. What have been the worst organizational consequences of the system?

3. Are there any problems of organizational ineffectiveness arising from the system? If so, what are they?

4. If problems exist (question 3), what can be done about them?

(Contd.)

ORGANIZATIONAL ASPECTS *(Contd.)*

5. Could the system better help the company to meet its business goals? If so, how?

6. Are there any other comments about organizational aspects that you wish to add?

7

Managing change

The issues dealt with in this chapter are:

7.1 Developing a strategy for change	136
7.2 Specifying your requirements	139
7.3 Assessing financial costs and benefits	142
7.4 Gaining commitment and managing conflict	146
7.5 Providing organizational support	150
7.6 Changing over from old to new	152
7.7 Reviewing progress against plans	154
Concluding advice about the management of change	154

Many people believe that recalcitrant employees and obstructive trade unions are the major forces preventing companies from introducing new technology. That is rarely the case, despite isolated dramatic examples. Employees resist technological change much less than is often believed. In a recent study of British companies using robots, 31 per cent reported that management had expected opposition from the shopfloor and trade unions; that was the second most frequently mentioned advance worry. However, looking back on difficulties actually experienced, only 2 per cent of companies reported that kind of opposition. The problem was now bottom of the list. A similar picture of willingness from junior employees is revealed in the larger study of new technology of all kinds which is summarized in Box 7A.

Nevertheless, change is not always easy. Complex problems can arise in the seven areas listed above, especially when a large investment is being considered. This chapter extends the previous discussion of evaluation procedures to present some suggestions about the management of change. It is directed to managers throughout the company, but particular emphasis is

---

Box 7A   Resistance to new technology is 'a myth'

A 1987 report from the Policy Studies Institute in London suggested that
the popular belief that trade unions and workers obstruct the introduction of new technology is a myth. The report described results from
interviews with 4000 managers and trade union shop stewards in 2000
workplaces.

Managers reported that in 75 per cent of cases of introduction of new
technology, the change was supported by manual workers. They
described 'strong' support in 37 per cent of cases. Strong resistance was
encountered in only 2 per cent of cases.

Union and worker support for change was put down to a desire to
have better equipment, more interesting jobs, and higher pay. Around 20
per cent of workers received pay increases as a result of the change to new
technology work.

---

paid to perspectives and actions which are needed at senior levels when
planning and managing significant changes.

7.1 DEVELOPING A STRATEGY FOR CHANGE

Investments in computer technology are often made through separate local
decisions, with little overall planning. However, it is desirable that senior
management in all companies should explicitly include new technology issues
within their development of a broad corporate strategy. Assessing the need for,
and the potential benefits of, computer-based equipment should be undertaken at the highest level, with priorities and investments decided in the
context of an overall strategic plan. This key theme is emphasized in Box 7B.

Box 7B   Don't be mesmerized by the glamour of advanced
manufacturing technology

The Managing Director of Ingersoll Engineers recently described his
company's world-wide experience of installing advanced manufacturing
technology (AMT) systems. In a magazine interview, he pointed out that
too many people have been 'mesmerized by the glamour' of AMT.
Instead we should 'get back to basics' by establishing first a clear
business strategy. 'New technology was irrelevant to the vast majority of
our clients, until they had got the basic logistics of their manufacturing
business sorted out.... Technology is just one tool in a company's
revival, not the be-all and end-all.... The answer is to develop a long-
term business strategy'.

Investments in particular forms of new technology can sometimes be ideal for your business; but they can also be a waste of money, failing to meet current needs. Companies often make purchases on the advice of suppliers or their own engineers and data-processing staff, yet these people are rarely in a position to identify strategic objectives. That is the job of senior management, who must ensure that investments are linked to their own strategic thinking.

One recurring theme is that computer technology should not be seen solely as a way of dealing with existing problems. That is of course important in many cases, but it may be appropriate *before computerization* to change your procedures, the company structure, or even aspects of your product or service. If prior changes are not considered, there is a danger that a costly investment might merely replace your initial problem with a bigger, automated problem. So you must think beyond merely the computerization of current tasks and structures, to examine quite new possibilities.

In developing a strategy (and solving problems more generally), it is often helpful to work through the acronym SWOT: strengths, weaknesses, opportunities and threats. That can encourage a broader view than might otherwise be taken, and avoid primarily reactive thinking.

For example, you might consider the *strengths* of the company in delivering a product or service, and examine how you can build on those strengths through technological investments. Your *weaknesses* relative to the competition and in the face of likely market changes also need to be examined: how can new technology assist in those areas? What *opportunities*, technological as well as non-technological, can you identify? How can they be grasped? Will computer-based equipment give you an advantage? Finally, you should explicitly look out for *threats* in the environment. For example, what changes in product or in manufacturing process are being developed by your competitors, especially (in this setting) computer-based changes which might undermine your position?

Analyses of that kind can be undertaken by individual senior managers, but the different perspectives of several colleagues ought to be examined as a whole. It may be helpful for senior managers first to record individually their SWOT analyses, with subsequent meetings comparing those different initial views, and building upon them to define a company strategy which purposefully embraces computer technology.

Advice from an experienced director in the manufacturing sector is summarized in Box 7C. Similar points should be included in the development of strategy in other sectors of industry and commerce.

Your initial thinking should also include a policy about how to implement and evaluate those systems which are selected within the overall strategy. We have tried to demonstrate that it is a mistake to view investments in computer technology solely in technical terms. You may have the best technology in the world but it will not perform well if you get the human and organizational factors wrong.

For example, the introduction of a flexible manufacturing system onto your shopfloor may affect the numbers of direct and indirect staff that are required, the levels and mix of skills, the type of management required, the quality of

Box 7C Elements of a good strategy for computer-based manufacturing

(1) Business objectives should be reviewed, and critical success factors identified. Possibilities include: reduction of lead times, lower costs, improved quality, increased responsiveness to market changes, enhanced product value, openness to new ideas, improved company image, better employment conditions within the company.

(2) Planning and implementation should be led by a board member with particular responsibility for new technology. Do not place computers and advanced manufacturing technology under the finance director.

(3) Design, process planning, production and ancillary functions should be reviewed and simplified.

(4) Management decision-making processes should be reviewed and simplified.

(5) Organizational structures should be reviewed and simplified. Note that the introduction of wide-ranging computer-based systems can sometimes make it difficult to change structures later, so you should aim to get them right from the outset.

(6) When planning standardization across functions in large systems, work at the level of data definition and communication possibilities, not in terms of particular hardware manufacturers or software developers.

(7) Automation should be incremental and evolutionary, following priorities based on critical success factors. Prototyping and piloting should be widely used, to test out progress, educate staff, and allow gradual specification of detailed requirements.

(8) Finance your computer technology through several different savings. Possibilities include reduced setting-up times, lower stock levels, improved materials flow, eliminated waste, reduced design costs, and smaller numbers of operating and/or managerial staff. Do not set unrealistically short periods for return on investment.

(9) Include training objectives and resources within the initial plan.

(10) Consult with suppliers and customers to develop a joint computer strategy, integrated where possible between your and their companies.

(11) Explicitly use technology as an agent for change, provoking management into a strategic mode of thinking, and speeding up profitable improvements in product design, planning, production and marketing.

jobs of the operators, the job evaluation and payment schemes, your industrial relations atmosphere and practices, and so on. That is obvious when stated at this point in the book. The problem is that issues of that kind are widely ignored in initial discussions, almost all the resources being used to tackle the technical problems. It is essential at an early stage that you debate and develop a strategic view for the non-technical issues, so that you know and can communicate the direction in which you are trying to move. Jobs and organizational structures need to be designed, as well as computers.

Most companies commit in excess of 90 per cent of their effort, time and money to the technical aspects of computer-based equipment. They get around to the 'people issues' only when it is too late. In the interview summarized in Box 7B, the managing director looked back with some misgivings: 'Where I went wrong was in overstating the importance of machines compared to people'.

7.2 SPECIFYING YOUR REQUIREMENTS

This book has introduced thirty different issues which need attention when evaluating a current or future system. It was no accident that the very first of these (in section 2.1) was 'Meeting essential requirements'. A large number of systems fail at this first hurdle, and in managing change it must receive particular attention.

How can you most effectively determine the properties you want your new system to have? As pointed out in sections 2.1 and 7.1, the initial emphasis must be on what you want to achieve and not on particular attributes of the hardware or software themselves. Specify your requirements within a business plan, and then decide what is needed in terms of equipment. Sometimes this general approach will need to be modified, as you consider whether new technological possibilities might permit you to alter your business goals and procedures.

Ask questions like these. How can we specify our current requirements? And anticipate our future ones? Who is in the best position to identify them? Are there competing views? Is additional information required? Are new technologies likely to change the nature of our business? Will the system be supporting functions that are common in organizations (accounting, word-processing, etc.) or are our requirements very specialized or even unique? Can these specialized functions be described precisely at this stage?

If the system will be supporting general tasks that have almost certainly been tackled by software developers working for other organizations, then consider looking around for packages which are already in use elsewhere. Alternatively, you might ask a consultant to identify your particular needs and recommend options in terms of off-the-shelf equipment and software configurations. These should be evaluated in the terms set out in Chapters 2 to 5.

It is often helpful to organize the introduction of large systems through processes of 'project management'. A relevant person should be designated as project manager, with responsibility for the development and implementation of the new equipment within the goals specified by senior management. This

person will usually have authority to deal with suppliers and/or manufacturers, and will make final decisions about the system specification.

In many cases, such individuals will be supported by a project team,
comprising staff with appropriate expertise and seconded to the project on a
part-time or full-time basis. It is this team which will decide about each
preferred option, how particular functions have to be traded off against
anticipated cost savings, and how the specification can best be developed in a
coordinated way.

It is desirable to involve a range of people as advisers to the project team.
That will spread participation through the company, assist in generating a
more effective system, and create more widespread commitment to the final
design and installation. (See section 7.4, on gaining commitment.) Personnel
specialists should be brought into the project team whenever possible, for
human and organizational issues need to be considered from the outset.

The project team should at an early stage identify constraints in terms of
time, money and organizational practice. Decisions by senior management
will often be required. What return on investment is required? When is the
latest date by which you are prepared to accept delivery of the system? Are
there items of equipment or software in current use which must be retained?
What organizational changes are needed before the system is implemented?
How can high job quality and performance be achieved? How much time and
money is available for training? Are there other constraints (for example,
professional or legal) on how the system should be used, and on how or where
the data should be archived?

Possible sources of error and back-up procedures should also be considered
at this stage. You should discuss the likelihood of failures in system
components (hardware and software) with the developer or supplier. They can
help you to work out the consequences of procurement decisions in terms of
system reliability. They will also be able to suggest archiving and maintenance
procedures to minimize the risk of failure, as well as manual back-up
procedures to adopt when failures occur. It is management's responsibility
however, to assess the consequences of different failures for the company, and
to decide which possible failures should be met through additional expenditure at the design stage.

A large number of detailed questions will need to be answered as the
specification is built up. In addition to technical and financial considerations,
the system developers should also be asked to review issues of the kind
examined in Chapters 2 to 5 of this book. Your developing specification
should be assessed in the light of the evaluative questions laid out there.

The final specification should be structured in a way that is readily
intelligible. Insist that the developers use easily understood diagrammatic
methods and jargon-free language. There are widely-used formatting and
diagrammatic conventions for depicting data-flows, system structure and
decision-making logic, which are easier to follow than long-winded verbal
descriptions. When verbal accounts are necessary, watch out for buzzwords
and vacuous terms. If you are in any doubt what something means, ask the
developers to be more precise.

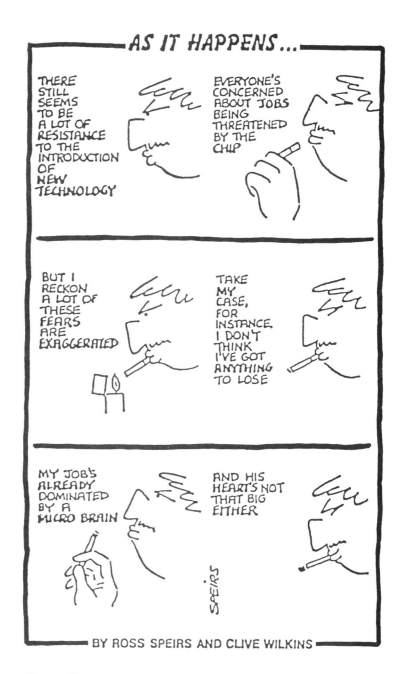

Computing

People do worry about the introduction of new technology. Sometimes these worries are due to real conflicts but more often than not they result from misunderstandings. Involving all relevant groups from the very beginning will greatly facilitate the introduction of new technology. See also section 7.4.

A good way of testing a specification is to hold a meeting in which the project team and the developers go over the proposal with a fine-tooth comb. Be prepared with a lot of 'what happens if…?' questions. These are easier to generate if you temporarily forget about the system as a technical solution and concentrate instead on what happens in the real world of your business.

Given that the system specification can determine the effectiveness of your company or a particular department for some time to come, you should not agree to it until the full implications have been worked through. This means that the person designated as project manager will need to spend a substantial amount of time on this project; he or she will have to be relieved of certain other duties if proper attention is to be paid to the task.

7.3 ASSESSING FINANCIAL COSTS AND BENEFITS

Whether you are planning a new investment in technology or evaluating the performance of an existing system, an early requirement is for a systematic assessment of financial costs and benefits. Note that the 'bottom line' of such an investment is directly related to the previous two sections. Does the system help meet your business goals? (7.1). And does it meet your requirements? (7.2). If it does not achieve both of these aims, it will not provide an acceptable return on investment.

It may appear that estimating the likely *costs* of a new investment is relatively straightforward, especially in terms of capital costs which suppliers can specify. However, capital costs are always underestimates of true costs. They exclude the costs of training (see section 5.4) and of other forms of organizational support that may be required (see section 7.5), as well as the costs of disruption to normal work during the implementation stages (see section 7.6). Remember too that maintenance and repair expenses may rise (see section 2.3), and additional costs may be incurred in operating, supervising and managing the new system. Unfortunately, as we have argued throughout this book, most organizations ignore many of these issues until very late in the day, whereas in fact they should be significant factors in any financial appraisal.

Many managers assume that achieving the lowest possible cost is the way to success. For example, they often behave as if money spent on training is a cost that should be minimized. In practice this is demonstrably wrong; training should be seen as an investment, and we have suggested elsewhere that at least 5 per cent of the capital cost of an investment should be allocated to training.

Many people also assume that minimizing labour costs, for example by using the technology to reduce staffing and skill levels, is also the best way forward. In many cases it is not. Examples are legion of systems with low direct labour costs for the above reasons, but with enormous indirect overheads because of the amount of specialist support the new system requires. Similarly, many new installations operate significantly below their anticipated levels of performance because they have tried to deskill users (see section 4.2). Counter to many people's assumptions, an investment in expensive technology should often be accompanied by investing in more highly trained people, especially when the work and the technology are complex. This is how many Japanese companies operate, and you should consider this question very carefully in your own situation.

When costing new systems, it is thus essential to look beyond the direct capital equipment figures and to consider other costs you will incur in getting the best out of the technology. In section 7.5 we will illustrate how large systems in particular require a great deal of support, sometimes in the form of an expensive infrastructure. You should never underestimate these costs in your initial financial appraisal, nor should you try to cut corners with them. If you do, then it is likely that your post-implementation evaluation will reveal lower than anticipated performance and a lower than expected return on investment.

Problems also arise in assessing financial *benefits*. With investments in old technologies this was often relatively straightforward. A new machine in the office or on the shopfloor would do the job more quickly than the old one, thereby enabling either higher levels of output, or the same level of output for less input. An accountant or the manager could in many cases easily work out the anticipated return on investment and the payback period.

However, with new technologies, especially the larger systems, such assessments are difficult. Consider a planned investment in an electronic mail system across several sites within a company. You may predict savings in mail costs and telephone bills, and reduced travel expenditure as a result of fewer meetings. But it will be much harder to obtain sensible estimates of the benefits you may anticipate of 'improved communications' between say your production staff and your sales people working in the field. Will this lead to a better service to customers? How can that be quantified in financial terms?

Difficult as they are, such formal assessments must be attempted. Without them, you are unlikely to obtain the necessary funding if you are seeking finance from outside your company; and you are equally unlikely to receive it from inside, given that most requests for capital expenditure are made within increasingly competitive environments. Such specificity also helps you plan what it is you hope to achieve with your investment; it forces you to relate it back to your goals and requirements (see sections 7.1 and 7.2) and makes you think them through in a rigorous way. Specific assessments at this stage also provide the benchmarks for monitoring progress, thereby enabling you to assess whether or not your investment has met its required financial return. That will be a useful start in any programme of planned improvement (see section 7.7, on reviewing progress).

It is useful to divide your *anticipated benefits* into three categories: those capable of quantification; those generally quantifiable but difficult to measure; and those identifiable but not quantifiable. You should place a monetary figure on the first category, and attempt conservative monetary estimates of the second. Expert advice may be helpful to achieve those estimates. In the example above of electronic mail, you could ask the sales people for an estimate of the value to the company of quick communication between sales and manufacturing in helping to meet delivery deadlines. Will electronic mail help reduce delivery failures? Will this save money, for example in sales and clerical time? How much? Will better delivery times lead to more sales? How much revenue will this generate?

Those benefits which can be identified but not quantified, the third category, should also be specified as part of the assessment procedure. For example, if you believe that investment in electronic mail will improve morale generally as a result of improved communications and accessibility, then this would be one of the benefits you list. Similarly if you expect that an investment in computer technology will contribute to your company image, then this should be included here.

It cannot be stressed too much that technology investments often involve benefits that fall into the latter two categories. Your appraisal should not be limited to the first group of benefits, those that are easily quantifiable. New technologies often bring about direct improvements which can be measured in financial terms, but they also can lead to indirect improvements and create new opportunities which are less easy to quantify as monetary costs and benefits.

For example, two of the authors worked with a manufacturing director who was keen to invest in a large and expensive flexible manufacturing system (FMS), in part for the direct quantifiable benefits of improved throughput times, enhanced quality and reduced inventory costs. But he was also determined to use the FMS to force the rest of the organization to make improvements in production scheduling, materials control, maintenance engineering, and design for manufacture. In the old manufacturing system these functions were inefficient, but the effects of their inefficiency were dissipated and hard to measure. He was using the FMS as a catalyst for more general changes that were of huge significance to the successful operation of the factory, but which he found impossible to quantify. These were at least as important to him as the planned reductions in inventory level.

We should add that not all experts in the area of financial appraisal agree with this three-way categorization. Some argue that all costs and benefits should be quantifiable, and we have heard it said that 'if you can't measure it, you don't understand it!'. Whatever your own opinion, you should examine the knock-on factors; are there potential benefits which are hard or impossible to measure? Recognizing their existence is not an excuse for sloppy thinking: you should identify and specify these factors as closely as you can. In many cases it is those benefits which carry the day, and make the whole investment worthwhile.

Currently the accepted technique for most financial appraisals is in terms of discounted cash flow (DCF). You should ask your financial expert to work out the details of this technique in your situation. It is based upon the fact that £1000 earned next year is worth less than now, because if you had the lesser amount now and invested it, it would earn you £1000 one year from now. The revenue and cost streams therefore are 'discounted' over the lifetime of the technology (in effect, the opposite of compounding), so that monetary costs and benefits are translated into present-day values. You first decide the rate at which you wish to discount the cash. Let us assume you believe an acceptable rate of alternative investment (i.e. return) is 10 per cent. You can make two calculations. First, you can work out the net present value at the end of your chosen period, say 5 years. This will be the revenue at present values minus the costs at present values, all discounted over time at 10 per cent. Alternatively, you can make the net present value equal 0, and work out the discounted rate of return that achieves this. These calculations are the same but presented in different formats. For example, the net present value for a computerized information system of $+£110,000$, discounted at 10 per cent over 5 years, might be the same as a discounted rate of return over 5 years of 11.3 per cent, given a certain pattern of expenditure and revenue across those five years. The latter format is uusually preferred bec' use it eases comparison across alternative investments.

In analysing costs and benefits in these terms, it is important to include difficult-to-measure factors of the kinds illustrated above. In that way, the first two categories will be covered in monetary terms, but the third (non-quantifiable) category requires a separate approach. Alongside the result of a discounted cash flow calculation, you should present a list of other anticipated costs and benefits. A useful technique here is to get relevant experts to make some estimate of probability that any non-quantified costs and benefits will accrue.

When you are assessing alternative investments, it is usual to compare discounted rates of return, and for most companies the higher the rate of return, the higher the priority, given limited finances. However, this may not always be appropriate, for example when some of the non-quantified benefits assume strategic importance. Again it is important to be rigorous here; if non-quantified factors are so important, you need to be confident that they have been properly identified and that the benefits can be achieved.

With major investments, especially those involving integrated systems, companies usually look for opportunities to phase their implementation over time, and many seek to spend first on those parts of the system that deliver the best return. This is clearly sensible, but not without some problems. It may be that some systems only achieve a satisfactory return when fully implemented, because the principal benefits accrue from an integrated approach, for example in the case of communications networks. You should adopt both a long-term and a short-term view. Have a long-term investment plan that meets your financial requirements, and then see if you can work towards it in a series of incremental phases.

The same assessment procedures are relevant when you are evaluating an existing system, although in many ways the analysis should be easier, since you are comparing what is actually happening against earlier predictions. Again, you should systematically identify all the costs and benefits you are actually achieving, discounted where appropriate over time. If the results are below what you require, this should provide the springboard for more detailed evaluation. Cycles of review and planning are central to the management of change (see section 7.7), and these bring in the human and organizational issues of earlier chapters as well as the financial analyses illustrated here.

7.4 GAINING COMMITMENT AND MANAGING CONFLICT

Computers need commitment. If employees do not believe that the investment in new technology will make a contribution to company or departmental effectiveness, then their doubts can become self-fulfilling. It is thus essential to strive for commitment at all levels. That requires not only a focus on technical issues but also a recognition that conflicting views are likely to exist and need to be worked through.

Explicit commitment among managers is necessary from the outset. This takes the form of investing expertise, time and money, and is most obviously needed in respect of the line managers closely involved in the changes. Visible and effective work in the areas described throughout this chapter will promote confidence and commitment. However, others should also be involved, for example from personnel, industrial relations and engineering. One crucial requirement is that someone champions the cause at the highest level in the company. Such high-level commitment can provide essential motivation and resources. This point is emphasized in Box 7D.

There is widespread reluctance in Britain to involve personnel managers in the design of information technology systems. That is not the case in many other countries, and the British approach surely needs to be changed. The importance of including personnel expertise, and also advice from full-time union officials, has been documented in several studies. When those people are involved in the introduction of new technology, wider aspects of pay, industrial relations and employee motivation are better considered, and changes are more readily accepted. If you have a project team (see section 7.2), ensure that some personnel expertise is included.

Many companies are also unwilling to provide opportunities for eventual users to participate in the specification, procurement and implementation of new systems. That is justified through several arguments: that it is costly in time, and may delay implementation; that users lack the necessary expertise to make worthwhile contributions; and that consultation increases the chance of damaging conflicts of interest.

Box 7D   The need for a champion

An influential British report about new technology described successful installations in these terms.

> Each successful company had a 'champion', usually a company executive, who spearheaded the effort and sold the idea to the people concerned. This was clearly a significant factor. In fact, we conclude that without a highly visible vocal champion constantly promoting the technology and working with the people, the chances of successful implementation are greatly reduced.

Does your company's new technology have a sufficiently powerful champion? Can you help him or her? Or should it be you?

There are certainly grounds for each of these concerns, and we shall focus later on possible conflicts. But there are also strong arguments in favour of some participation by users. In the long run, participative approaches are likely to lead to better systems, achieving effective levels of performance sooner than through traditional design methods. The end users almost certainly have some expertise and knowledge that should be harnessed; they may not be experts in computer technology, but they are experts in doing the job. Employees' commitment to new systems, along with their confidence and belief in them, can be greatly enhanced by having contributed to design and implementation.

Participative approaches can take a variety of forms. People who will manage, supervise and operate new systems may be represented on your project team (see section 7.2), or perhaps on working parties set up by that team to examine relevant issues. Briefing meetings can be used for consultation about plans and ideas, and participative problem-solving can be achieved by encouraging people to attend specially organized planning workshops.

Interim prototypes and mock-ups of early versions should be made available to future users. In the case of large systems, simulation exercises can be helpful in trying out alternative solutions and working procedures, and for identifying areas where improvement is needed. Phased development of final versions should be requested, so that potential problems can be spotted and rectified before the entire system has been completed. Except for the simplest and most urgently required systems, you should always insist on phased delivery.

Of course, participation does not magically remove conflicts; indeed, widespread discussion of possible systems and their accompanying organizational changes can raise issues about which there are differences of interest. Divergent views arise from a range of sources, but most are concerned with worries about losing out either in relative or absolute terms. Employees may be worried about adverse changes in responsibilities, workload, pay, job security, status, privacy, future career opportunities, or a number of other aspects of their work.

When there are uncertainties over the future, as is common with major investments, such fears and concerns are heightened. Managers may be as much affected as office workers or shopfloor employees. In some cases, real conflicts of interest exist, for example when one group of people see that they will lose status and power as a result of an investment. But there are also occasions where people believe they are in conflict, when in fact this is inaccurate; the conflict results from misunderstandings, because management has failed to communicate its plans clearly enough. Improved consultation and participation can have important benefits in those cases.

It sometimes happens that people *assume* a conflict of interest in the absence of information to the contrary. This is especially likely when there is no clear strategy guiding the implementation. People often suspect ulterior motives on the part of management, finding it hard to believe that no-one has a plan or can explain particular decisions. It is senior management's responsibility to provide a guiding strategy within which others can work and develop shared understandings. Consultation and other communication mechanisms are important aspects of this process.

Where genuine conflicts exist, management also has a responsibility. It is useful to work through what people will perceive as their benefits and losses, systematically identifying who is involved and in what ways. The task then is to examine whether some alternative ideas can alleviate potential conflicts, especially for groups of strategic importance. For example, engineers, who are worried that their skills in mechanical maintenance will be less important after the introduction of computer technology, may be willing to be trained to develop skills in electronic maintenance.

You should also remember that such conflicts are not simply between different levels in the hierarchy. They also exist across the organization, for example between individual managers, between groups and between trade unions. The general approach should be the same. First check whether the conflicts are real, or whether they result from misunderstandings or from lack of clarity and direction. If a conflict is unavoidable, you should identify who is involved and why, and then see if the problem can be redefined to overcome the difficulty, perhaps by looking at alternative ways of organizing the work. In such discussions you should be looking for some freedom of manoeuvre and flexibility. As in other negotiation situations, distinguish between an ideal outcome and one that is the minimum required to meet your goals. The ideal may be unattainable, but another solution may be acceptable.

Another option is to phase in the changes you seek. Avoid immediate conflicts by settling for a second-best solution in the short term, and work towards what you really want. You may be able to achieve your longer-term goals by changes and trade-offs in future negotiations.

Other tactics are also relevant. Emphasizing the benefits and positive aspects of the new technology can help persuade people. So too can money, and it is not uncommon for computerization to be accompanied by enhanced pay. However, this can cause problems if it distorts relativities and job evaluation procedures (see section 5.6). Remember too that trade union or employee representatives often have a role in persuading sub-groups of their members that change is necessary, perhaps for the more general benefit. Obviously, this is more likely to happen if people can see the wisdom of the proposed investment, and if they have confidence that the whole process is being well managed. Again, consultation and participation are likely to help.

Where conflicts are more fundamental and investments are of major strategic significance, some companies set up their new technologies on 'green-field' sites, or as separate facilities within established settings. In these cases they are usually seeking a fresh start free from the constraints of established custom and practice. Harmonized conditions of service and single-union deals are often aimed for in such contexts, in part to overcome sectional conflicts of interest.

Some conflicts can be overcome through slow and steady implementation. Experience with a new system may win some people round who were previously against it, and they may grow to appreciate the benefits it brings. However, it is still possible that a company decides to press on with an investment in the face of opposition from certain groups. If that is to happen, it is obviously important to take especial care if any disenchanted groups are of particular strategic importance.

Conflicts in these areas cannot always be resolved by participative approaches. Our own experience is that participation is neither as damaging as its critics claim, nor as wonderful as its fans would have you believe. Participative approaches can require a considerable effort, but they usually lead to better systems, higher levels of understanding and commitment, and better prospects for implementation.

Remember, too, that changes in many of these areas are of symbolic importance and involve political processes, especially as a prelude to negotiations between different groups. If you are seeking to persuade and influence people, it is worthwhile considering four kinds of related activity: gaining people's confidence; developing networks of contacts; making deals; and controlling information-flow.

The successful organizational politician works to identify the values and views of important people. He or she gains their trust and confidence by meeting their expectations, assisting them to achieve their goals, confirming them in their roles, and showing a concern for their achievements in difficult situations. He or she finds time to communicate with these important individuals, and strives to establish good working relationships with them.

The second political process, establishing networks, is similar but at the level of groups. Successful networking involves learning about the principal values held in important work or social groups, upholding those values through decisions and actions, and establishing oneself as a sound contributor and valid group member. At the same time, a person may be able to influence views within a network, building upon a previously established position. Networks provide sources of information as well as means of persuasion, allowing you to know at an early stage what is happening elsewhere in the organization.

Third, political life involves making deals, both in the short term and over a period of time. Individuals and groups may agree to support each other in respect of a current project; or they may build up credit by accepting others' proposals. This credit can be used on later occasions, calling upon assistance when needed. Of course, that reciprocal justification is not always explicit; experienced politicians are alert to the process without it being overt.

A fourth political process is the control of information-flow. People may delay making public certain facts or describing possible implications, in order to assist their allies or impede their opponents. Organizations require good information-flow, but there are undoubtedly occasions when individuals consider it wise to keep some points to themselves, at least for the time being.

These four political processes occur in all organizations, and their effective application can help in the management of conflict as new technology is introduced. Nevertheless, overt conflict may become inevitable at certain points in respect of pay and conditions, changed practices, or job losses. In those cases, a high degree of mental resilience is needed as much as political activities of the kinds described above.

In conclusion, commitment to change is a critical factor in the success of an investment in new technology. It is best promoted by good management in all the areas covered in this chapter. It is important to establish procedures for consultation with users and other staff likely to be affected and to find appropriate ways for them to participate during design and implementation. This will yield a more effective system, but in some circumstances it cannot prevent conflicts of interest, as certain groups or individuals lose out in relation to others.

7.5 PROVIDING ORGANIZATIONAL SUPPORT

Even small computer-based systems need some organizational support if they are to contribute to effectiveness and make a satisfactory return on investment. The need is much greater with larger investments—information systems, office networks or integrated manufacturing systems, for example—and here we will concentrate on those.

Organizational support for new technology is usually provided by five separate groups: senior managers, training staff, engineers, other experts, and local employees in the department concerned. Together these provide the infrastructure which makes possible effective use of computer-based equipment. Certain types of support may be temporary, in the first few months of operation for example, whereas others are required on a permanent basis.

The five groups provide, or arrange for others to provide, a wide range of supports. These are summarized in Box 7E. All have been examined in earlier parts of the book, and repetition of details would be wasteful here. The point being made is that you should consider each aspect of your company's infrastructure: are all forms of support being provided in the right place and at the right time? Two companies may have purchased very similar equipment, but the one creating a stronger infrastructure of this kind will undoubtedly meet its goals more effectively.

You should also examine the *co-ordination* of elements shown in Box 7E. It is easy to think that the infrastructure is in place, because the elements are present. However, you may still find that difficulties go unresolved, because they fall into the gaps between the parts. A senior manager should have the explicit task of designing, implementing and evaluating a support infrastructure that is appropriate for the technology in question. Without that, system performance is unlikely to meet the standards you require.

Many large investments are a disappointment, not because they fail to work at all, but because they work ineffectively. That was illustrated in the case study in Chapter 1, and is a common occurrence in all types of company. The task of the infrastructure is not merely to achieve minimum levels of performance; that is usually quite easy. The difficulty comes in shifting from moderate to excellent performance, and it is here that attention to organizational support has its major pay-off. Remember, however, that such attention requires time and money; it should be viewed as a significant part of your technological investment.

Box 7E   Elements in an infrastructure to support new technology

---

(1) *Senior managers provide:*
a strategy
a set of goals and a timetable
the necessary finance
some of their own time
leadership and
encouragement
a 'champion' to represent the
plan
an assessment of financial
costs and benefits
organizational changes to
start the process
an overview and review of
needs and achievements

(2) *Training staff provide:*
identification of training
needs
training for users and
managers of the
technology
training for maintenance staff
education about the ways in
which technology can
contribute to the company
education in wider aspects of
computer-based systems

(3) *Engineers provide:*
inputs into the design
specification
on-line help facilities
on-line training packages
usable software and
interfaces
servicing and maintenance
documentation
modifications and
enhancements
assistance in emergencies
technical experts on
secondment

(4) *Other experts provide:*
financial expertise and
monitoring
recruitment and selection
expertise
knowledge about alternative
job designs
advice about organizational
change
expertise in other personnel
matters
industrial relations expertise
advice about evaluation
procedures

(5) *The local staff provide:*
experts in the work process
information about previous
procedures and solutions
for problems
self-help groups
local documentation
support in case of difficulties
re-scheduling of work-flow to
meet temporary difficulties
local management of staff
and other resources

7.6 CHANGING OVER FROM OLD TO NEW

Many of the specific issues associated with changeover are dealt with separately throughout the book, and numerous decisions will have to be made. Who will use the new system initially? Over what period will it be phased in? What provision should there be for manual back-up? What work is involved in converting information from the old format to the new? For how long will parallel operation of the old and new systems be required? What changes need to be made to job content, to ensure high-quality jobs in the terms of Chapter 4?

You should not underestimate the amount of work that may be necessary to enter business information (e.g. customer records) into the new system. If your organization is converting from one computer system to another, the transfer of data may cause technical problems, but they should usually be solvable by a competent supplier or analyst. If you are converting from a manual to a computer system, however, there is only one way to transfer the data; a lot of typing will be needed. However, that needs to be preceded by discussions and decisions of several kinds: should we transfer all the data, or only certain parts? Should the database be re-organized in some way? What sort of needs might arise later? You can make a rough estimate of how much time is required by multiplying the number of records or documents to be transferred by the estimated average typing time. Then at least double the result, since it will certainly take much longer than the simple estimate. An example of this problem is in Box 7F.

Whether or not your system is to be delivered in phases, it is advisable to manage the early installation period as if the new system were not completely available. Keep the old system active for some of your business, and plan to institute some scheme of parallel working. What, precisely, this means depends on your organization and the penetration of the new system, but it could involve any of the following:

— only some staff use the new system initially,
— the new system is used for a limited proportion of transactions initially (e.g. customers' names beginning with the letters A to E),
— it is used for a specific range of transactions (e.g. an order and invoicing system that only deals with normal transactions, not special demands or processing of complaints),
—it is used for new transactions only (e.g. those involving new customers, or otherwise not requiring access to existing data). (This last suggestion removes the need for any extra data entry during the changeover period.)

The first form of parallel working may help the changeover, but it can cause friction between the two groups. Employees may wish all to be treated in the same manner, and can resent being split with two different ways of working. Restricting the new system's use to new transactions also has its difficulties, since it will probably cause the system to be greatly under-utilized for a long period.

Your company should have a clear arrangement with the supplier about the

---

Box 7F   Transferring medical records

A particularly promising field of computer application is in the health service. For example, many general medical practices are considering replacing their handwritten files with computerized records. That would help with rapid access to the data and greater readability and comprehensiveness of information. If suitably categorized, computerized records also permit statistical analyses and the identification of patients who might need screening or treatment for so-far-undiagnosed illnesses.

However, relatively few doctors have taken up these opportunities. The biggest obstacle is the huge amount of work involved in the initial transfer of several thousand patient records onto computer files. Once the material is on file, later additions are more straightforward. But that first hurdle seems too high for most practices.

The problem is not merely one of large typing demands. Each practice has first to develop a strategy about what kinds of patient information are to be transferred, for what purpose, and in what form. Second, there has to be agreement between the staff about procedures for summarizing the available written material, about the sequence of transfer (alphabetical order? new patients first? those attending the clinic first?) and about the pace of change. All these issues can prove difficult and expensive to resolve.

---

solution of other teething troubles. Ask about equipment maintenance and procedures for reporting software problems. Any supplier that takes the attitude that software never contains 'bugs' is deluding both of you.

Back-up copies of your data files are particularly important in the early stages of a transition. The balance between the old system and the new can gradually be shifted as the teething troubles are overcome. Initial problems that are not attributable to data entry, user unfamiliarity, or the need for new procedures, are probably due to bugs in the software. It is important to have some bug reporting and correction procedure worked out with your supplier before delivery. Most software bugs are precise and regular, and are repeated rather than occurring at random. A bug can therefore most easily be caught if you record exactly what you were doing when it occurred, and keep a written record or a computer-generated log to show the supplier.

If your organization buys a software package off the shelf, such as a word processor or spreadsheet programme, it is less likely to contain bugs. The establishment of a bug reporting procedure is here less important than adequate training for your staff. Suggestions for this have been made throughout earlier chapters, especially in sections 3.1, 4.2 and 5.4.

In all cases you should set target dates for specific achievements. These 'milestones' will allow you to check whether progress is being maintained in each important area, and permit prompt action to retrieve situations where delays are building up. Whenever possible, make it clear who has primary responsibility for the attainment of each target. so that he or she can be working towards its attainment as the changeover gets underway.

You should also remember that a new computer system will be in use for several years. In the course of that time it will change in a number of ways, some of which are unpredictable at the outset. For example, updated software or new items of equipment may become available. So an initial installation should not be regarded as the final system, and you should be prepared for later developments.

Planning for the evolution of a system is particularly important if your company is in a rapidly changing market. In general, you will preserve more options later if you choose standard equipment now, since it is those standard products for which improvements will be devised. If you are buying a tailor-made system, you can ensure some later flexibility by insisting on the use of standard programming languages, design techniques, operating systems or database management systems.

7.7 REVIEWING PROGRESS AGAINST PLANS

The theme of this section is simple to state but complex to apply. Processes of decision-making and change can be described in terms of repeated cycles: examine needs, identify options, make choices, implement changes, review consequences. Checking upon your progress is a crucial part of the management of change.

However, in practice this is not always straightforward. The necessary data may not be available, other changes may have distorted the pattern being studied, one change may have interacted with another so that a single impact cannot be identified, or you may simply lack the time and resources to carry out a systematic review. Other difficulties arise from the fact that objectives may alter and plans may be modified, so that any one retrospective review comes to embrace a sequence of decision-making cycles of the kind described above.

It is therefore sensible to avoid attempts at a single once-and-for-all review of a change programme. Preferable are frequent monitoring and adjustment decisions, taken as part of normal management tasks. At the very least, you should be examining progress against specified benchmarks.

The key point is that these reviews should be planned in advance. In setting out your plans for change, you should include some plans for reviewing that change. Objectives, milestones, target dates, specified achievement levels and other data-points should be identified at the planning stage. These points for review might be amended as you get underway, but their presence within the overall plan will provide a systematic structure for checking progress. This point is an obvious one, but it is widely ignored.

CONCLUDING ADVICE ABOUT THE MANAGEMENT OF CHANGE

Bringing together themes from this and earlier chapters, we offer the following suggestions about the management of change. You might like to use them within a checklist for action.

— ensure you have top management commitment and support
— identify how the new technology fits into the company's strategy
— state the business objectives for the new technology
— assess the financial costs and benefits of possible investments
— select the most appropriate technology
— develop a strategy for its introduction
— include in your strategy explicit consideration of the human and organizational aspects described in this book
— identify who is responsible for planning and introducing the new technology
— enlist the support of an influential 'champion' of the new technology
— specify the essential requirements to be met by the new system
— adopt an incremental approach to change
— identify how you will finance the investment
— specify a timetable for change, including key 'milestones'
— consult with suppliers of your materials or parts (if they are affected)
— consult with your customers (if they are affected)
— identify any changes (e.g. to procedures or systems) that you need to make before you implement the technology
— use your technology as a catalyst for change
— anticipate your future requirements
— anticipate how the system may evolve
— identify a role for the personnel function in managing change
— develop a plan for communicating with users and their representatives about the changes
— identify a way of involving the users in planning and implementing the new system
— identify the impact on the users
— identify the wider repercussions of the new technology
— identify any conflicts of interest which may occur
— consider how to manage the politics of conflicting interests
— decide how to incorporate the views of influential people
— identify what working practices will need to change
— work out how you will manage the changeover period
— work out the time required for, and cost of, transferring information onto the new system
— design an infrastructure to support effective use of the system
— plan for the necessary training and education
— provide the necessary documentation
— plan for the appropriate kind and level of system maintenance
— review progress against goals and plans

Introducing Chapters 8 to 12

The previous seven chapters have been intended for all readers with an interest in evaluating computer-based technology. Different sections were, no doubt, of varying relevance to different people (engineering staff versus senior management, for example), but we believe that the material is usable in a wide range of settings. Everyone can select from the thirty core issues, apply the initial questions, and pursue their chosen topics through interviews, meetings and working parties.

However, a small number of readers have additional needs. They may wish to ask more detailed questions than were provided in Chapters 2 to 5, or they might be interested in certain types of observation or specialized data-gathering. The remaining chapters are written for this limited set of readers.

Questions to supplement those given in Chapters 2 to 5 are here presented in two forms. In some cases we provide *checklists* of more detailed questions. An evaluator can use those to organize his or her thoughts, making further inquiries based upon the checklist items. For other issues we set out *questionnaires*, which are intended for administration to samples of employees; in those cases it is the employees and not the evaluators who provide initial answers to the questions.

Questionnaires are themselves one of the *specialist methods of information-gathering* which are described in Chapter 8. Other methods in that category include formal observation, system walk-through, and comparative testing. Those are powerful procedures, but they are complex and time-consuming. Most readers can carry out successful evaluation work within the previously presented framework of central issues, principal questions and basic methods.

8

Specialist methods of information-gathering

The issues dealt with in this chapter are:

1	Questionnaires	158
2	System walk-through	162
3	Formal observation	164
4	User diaries	166
5	System logging	167
6	Task analysis	168
7	Comparative testing	170
8	Company records	172
Overview		173

The specialist methods listed above are appropriate in different circumstances, depending on your company and its evaluation needs. In this chapter we illustrate the purpose and application of each method, and give advice about each one. Recall that specialist approaches should be used only rarely, in cases where you have complex and unusual requirements, and if you have the necessary additional expertise to carry out the work successfully.

SPECIALIST METHOD 1: QUESTIONNAIRES

A questionnaire is like a formal interview written down on paper. It contains a fixed set of questions, and people record their answers directly onto the page. This can provide a very effective means for summarizing a viewpoint, and data from many people can be combined to give an overall picture for the whole of a work-group, office or company.

However, the information provided by a questionnaire is restricted: unless you have asked the right questions, you will miss the important points. To get the correct focus, it is essential to precede a questionnaire study by interviews or meetings, identifying topics to be covered. In all cases you should commence a questionnaire study only when you are quite clear what you are trying to find out; otherwise, questionnaire administration can be a costly waste of time.

Questionnaires are open to some of the biases which may arise in interviews (see Chapter 6, page 115). For example, people might give only politically 'safe' responses, especially if they think they can be identified. And opinions about issues with which a person is not closely familiar can be quite temporary and influenced by views which are fashionable at the time (the 'flavour of the month' problem). Employees with a large career or personal investment in a system will tend to give rather positive opinions, even though they may have their own private reservations. So you must guarantee anonymity, and interpret the information from questionnaires (and from other methods) with considerable caution. Study the differences between groups or departments, and always look for possible rationalizations and biases in situations where separate groups have their own axe to grind.

Questions can be of two kinds: with 'closed' or 'open-ended' response alternatives. In the first case, two or more possible answers are provided by the person who drew up the questionnaire. These might be 'yes' and 'no', or 'agree' and 'disagree'. Shades of opinion can be assessed through multiple-choice questions, with alternatives like the following:

very bad, bad, neither bad nor good, good, very good;
disagree strongly, disagree slightly, neither agree nor disagree, agree slightly, agree strongly;
no problem, a slight problem, a moderate problem, a big problem, a very big problem.

Answers can then be scored, for example by counting 'very bad' as 1 and 'very good' as 5, and average scores calculated for each item. Alternatively, the percentage of the respondents giving each answer might be worked out. Those procedures allow you to look at differences between departments or between types of employee, and possibly to carry out other kinds of statistical analysis. In certain cases, multi-item scales can be formed, and scores combined across those items. These procedures are described in Chapter 11 (page 200).

The second type of question is 'open-ended', in the sense that no response alternatives are suggested. You might ask people to 'describe the main problem you have experienced with the computer in the past week', leaving a space for them to write directly onto the questionnaire page. This has the advantage of providing more freedom of expression, and may reveal issues which would otherwise have been missed. The disadvantage is that numerical scoring is less feasible, so it may be difficult to combine answers into an overall picture.

Questionnaires with both types of item are often more interesting to fill in than those restricted to a single format, and the mixed types can often cover a domain more effectively. (Examples, in the form of screening questionnaires

---

Box 8A   Advice about questionnaire design

—ensure you have good coverage of the issues you are investigating

—avoid asking double questions (e.g. 'is your job demanding and tiring?')

—avoid asking leading questions (e.g. 'why is the equipment a problem?')

—copy the kinds of format used in Chapters 6, 11 and 12

—consider putting in both types of question, open-ended as well as closed

—give clear instructions about how to answer each question

—decide in advance who will receive for discussion a report about the responses; consult those groups about questionnaire content at an early stage of the project

—try out the first version of your questionnaire on an informal basis, to see if people think it makes sense and to identify possible improvements

—decide in advance how you will analyse responses, and make sure that the questionnaire construction is suitable for your chosen analyses

—ensure that the questionnaire is not too long, so that respondents' interest can be retained

—consider including space at the end of the questionnaire for 'Comments: Please write here any other points you would like to make.'

---

for initial diagnoses, have been provided at the end of Chapter 6.) In all cases, it is essential to make it clear how people are expected to reply (for example, 'place a tick in one of these five boxes'); and it is, of course, crucial that the items in your questionnaire cover those issues which are central to the goals of your evaluation. Questionnaires have a tendency to get longer and longer in the design process, and you may need to be ruthless in cutting out the less important items.

You should always try out (or 'pilot') a questionnaire on a small number of people before using it in a substantial study. The pilot respondents should be asked to describe any difficulties they experienced in completing the questionnaire and to identify any ambiguities they noticed. It may also be sensible to ask them to suggest additional or alternative questions. Amendments can then be made before administering the final version. A summary of suggestions is provided in Box 8A.

Responses are usually anonymous, with no names indicated on the forms. However, some information about a person's job and department might be requested, to assist in grouping responses and interpreting patterns. Completed questionnaires can be returned through a special mail-box in the company, preferably in sealed envelopes to maintain confidentiality. It is very desirable to allow people to fill in their answers during working time, perhaps in an office or meeting room provided for the purpose. Other advice on administration is given in Box 8B.

Box 8B   Advice about questionnaire administration

— decide in advance which groups of employees will be studied or compared with each other
— administer the questionnaire to a broad range of people, appropriate for the chosen comparisons
— arrange for completion during working time
— guarantee individual confidentiality
— ensure that your sample is representative of the people in question
— if individuals are to complete the questionnaire in their own work-places, arrange for this to be done before a specified time and date
— if groups of employees are to complete the questionnaire together, arrange for them to be freed from work at pre-arranged times
— use a room that is big enough for people to sit in comfort
— ensure that respondents will be free of interruptions
— ensure that people have long enough to think about the questions you ask
— let people know why you are asking them to fill in a questionnaire and what will happen to the results

---

You may choose to obtain questionnaire responses from all users of the system or from an entire department; these are usually the best procedures. However, if you need to select a sample from the full group, take care that this is not biased in terms of age, job, likely attitudes, etc. The best way to prevent that kind of bias is to draw every (say) third name from an alphabetical list.

Questionnaires can give rise to a large amount of information. For example, a quite brief questionnaire (say, 30 items) administered to a fairly small sample (of, say, 40 people) will obviously yield over 1000 responses. In many cases, a questionnaire study will be much more extensive than that, yielding 10 000 items at least. Unless you feel competent to handle those large amounts of information, you should use only the simplest and shortest of questionnaires.

In all cases, interpretation of data must be subjective, being a matter of judgement for the evaluation team. There is no golden rule that an average score of, say, 2.2 on a particular five-point scale is the minimum acceptable figure. Many average scores fall into a region on the response scale which is quite difficult to interpret, and decisions about action should be taken only if questionnaire responses clearly suggest a definite problem. For example, you may find a strong pattern, where one group of people scores systematically lower than others on certain items; or within a group there may be some questions where average scores are substantially lower than in the rest of the questionnaire. However, single questions alone will rarely provide enough evidence for recommending changes.

In fact, decisions about change should not usually be taken on the basis of questionnaire responses on their own; the data will often prompt other inquiries, the results of which may, or may not, support the need for action. In defence of questionnaires, the same limitations apply to *any* method of information-gathering. In all cases, it is essential that an evaluator assesses the information obtained, weighs it against other data, obtains additional facts when needed, and finally decides how to judge the pattern of information as a whole. This complex process is inherent in any evaluation work, and an evaluator's skill in combining and interpreting different kinds of data can make the difference between a successful or an unsuccessful exercise.

Recall also that the evaluation methods are interconnected; you will rarely use one method on its own. Questionnaires are particularly valuable if results can be fed back to a meeting or working party for interpretation and discussion. Participants in the meeting could be the people who completed the questionnaire, and they might be invited to discuss the pattern of average responses or the nature of observed differences between groups. Feed-back to respondents is, in any case, desirable in its own right, since they have a direct interest in the material.

In other circumstances, questionnaire findings might be presented to a meeting of senior managers or to an evaluation working party. If that is planned, you should at an early stage make available the draft questionnaire to likely subsequent discussants. They may wish to recommend additional questions, or to modify suggested wording; and obtaining their commitment at the outset will sustain their interest later, and increase the prospect of successful innovation.

SPECIALIST METHOD 2: SYSTEM WALK-THROUGH

This second specialist method focuses more directly upon the actual performance of work tasks. An evaluator himself or herself works on the system, carrying out selected job tasks, and seeking to view hardware and software from the perspective of users. This is particularly appropriate in the case of new or prototype systems, when a company by definition has no users with direct experience. However, there may also be occasions when a current system is examined in this way, providing 'hands-on' information for an evaluator.

In either case, a system walk-through will only be effective if the evaluator has adequate knowledge and operational skill, and if he or she is able to make appropriate inferences about the users. It is also essential that the evaluator has identified in advance the specific issues about which information is required.

The five steps of a system walk-through are summarized in Box 8C. First, you must define the user population and identify key characteristics of likely users. When evaluating a prototype or a new system for possible purchase, you will need to make some assumptions, for example based upon current staff. Points to consider include the following. How much general experience of computer technology will users have? What systems do they use at the moment? Do those systems involve similar work? How much do they know about this software? How skilled are possible users with the keyboard or other input devices? How do they approach situations that require problem-

---

Box 8C   Steps in a system walk-through

Step 1
Define the population of people who use or who are likely to use the system. Characterize this population in terms outlined in the text, with particular reference to likely differences between the evaluator and probable users.

Step 2
Define the key tasks, which will form the basis for system evaluation.

Step 3
Devise a set of test activities which embody those key tasks. Identify criteria of success and failure for each task. Consider whether a checklist should be drawn up to cover the points to be examined.

Step 4
Work through the tasks yourself, asking what problems a typical user might have with regard to each, and whether the success criteria would be met. If you have prepared a checklist, apply that systematically during or after the tasks.

Step 5
Form your conclusions about this part of the evaluation. In the case of current systems, check how users' opinions agree or disagree with your view.

---

solving? What vocabulary do they use to describe the tasks to be undertaken? How much do possible users differ among themselves in abilities and experience relevant to the above? More generally, an evaluator has, throughout, to consider how he or she differs in these respects from the users in question.

The second step is to define the key tasks to be studied. In some cases you might wish to carry out a detailed task analysis (see 'Specialist method 6', below), especially when developing large new systems for a particular organization. However, smaller computer applications can often be studied adequately on the basis of a task definition derived from less formal observation of users at work.

The minimum requirement is to collect detailed information about key tasks and their objectives. You might record a list of actions to be undertaken, or collect transcripts of instructions given to users. Or you could obtain copies of finished documents or other products, in order to pin-point key elements. It is sometimes helpful in the case of current systems to ask users to describe core activities to you, in their own words and illustrating the sequence they follow.

By whatever means, the evaluator should obtain a clear idea of the key tasks which are to be studied.

The third step is to generate a set of test activities, embodying the key tasks which an evaluator will 'walk-through'. These must be very specific, and known from the previous step to be important. For example, in editing a machine-tool program or printing a document with a desktop publishing system, you might examine particular issues from Chapter 2 or 3, dealing with specific aspects of equipment requirements or usability. In some cases it may be useful to prepare questions in the form of a checklist; an evaluator can then answer each one, either during or after the walk-through. Such checklists are helpful in systematically covering a range of detailed questions; examples are provided in Chapters 9 and 10.

Fourth is the actual walk-through itself, in which the evaluator carries out the test activities. Whereas other methods of information-gathering rely on actual users to operate the system, it is the evaluator who here obtains data directly. He or she is employing prior expertise to infer from task activities how well or poorly the system undertakes key tasks in everyday use. The checklist (if there is one) should be applied either during or immediately after the walk-through.

Finally, you will be able to reach conclusions about the effectiveness of the system on the defined tasks when operated by the target population of users. With a possible purchase or prototypes of a system under commission, it may be sensible to make comparisons between two or more alternatives; see 'Specialist method 7', below. In cases where a current system is being evaluated, it is important at this stage to compare your interpretation with the opinions of actual users. The latter should not necessarily be accepted, but if there is a marked divergence of views it may be sensible to gather some more information, for example through one of the other specialist methods.

System walk-through is a practical and powerful procedure, especially appropriate for new or prototype systems. It has the limitation that an evaluator standing in for an actual user might bring different skills or attitudes to the task. In the case of current systems, it is therefore usually desirable also to observe or interview users themselves. As in all types of evaluation study, the final assessment depends on a balanced judgement about evidence of several kinds.

SPECIALIST METHOD 3: FORMAL OBSERVATION

This method involves systematic observation of users at work. It is similar to the walk-through procedure, in that key tasks have to be defined and examined. Observations are normally summarized by an evaluator on an appropriate record form, but in some cases it may be sensible to consider video-recording procedures.

Particular attention should be given to the selection of people to take part in an observation study. In smaller installations you may be able to observe each of the users, but elsewhere a sample might have to be drawn. That should aim to cover typical employees, so that results can be generalized. It is in all cases essential to gain the commitment of users, and you need to be explicit that it is the system, and not the person, which is being evaluated. The purpose of the information-gathering (to improve working effectiveness) must be made very clear. As with other methods, you should check your conclusions and interpretations against the opinions of users themselves.

In order to get some idea of what a person is thinking, you can ask him or her to 'think aloud', describing objectives and decisions at each stage, and identifying particular memory or other cognitive demands. Such 'verbal protocols' are usually tape-recorded and then transcribed for analysis. A more natural technique may be to get two users to solve a problem together. In explaining to each other what is to be done, they can provide insights into the way they view the task.

Formal observations can be very time-consuming, and you need to be sure that you require this degree of detail before starting out. Gathering data is only a small part of the process; analysis and interpretation often take three or four times as long again. That is particularly the case with video-recording, where continuous records over long periods of work are likely to yield rather more information than is useful. It is therefore essential that a focus is provided in

---

Box 8D   Steps in a formal observation study

Step 1
Define the population of users. Decide whether all are to be observed, or whether a sample is to be drawn. If the latter, select a typical group of people.

Step 2
Define the key tasks, which will form the basis for system evaluation.

Step 3
Carry out preliminary observations of those tasks, to acquire more detailed understanding of key tasks (step 2) and to develop effective recording procedures (for step 4).

Step 4
Observe the selected users' performance of the key tasks, recording details about issues as previously decided. Make a number of repeated observations, being sure to pick different times of the day. Work through any checklists, usually after each period of observation.

Step 5
Examine the data you have collected, and form your conclusions about this part of the evaluation. Check how users' opinions agree or disagree with your view.

advance of observation, picking out critical incidents for example, or examining certain difficult periods in a day.

A two-stage approach is usually advisable. The early observations should be broad and exploratory, identifying key issues which can form the focus of the second stage. At that later point you should have a definite plan, recording only certain events or covering only selected periods of the day. A stop-watch can be useful, and you might prepare some special record-forms.

It may also be sensible at that point to devise a checklist of questions covering themes central to the issue, which an evaluator can answer in the course of observation. Checklists of that kind have an important role in focusing thinking and ensuring that nothing is omitted. Several illustrations will be provided in Chapters 9 and 10.

The steps involved in formal observation are summarized in Box 8D. As with other methods, these should be modified in appropriate ways to meet your own needs; and final assessments require judgement on the part of the evaluator.

SPECIALIST METHOD 4: USER DIARIES

Observational studies of the kind described above are necessarily limited, and can rarely extend beyond a few hours of system use. Yet some important problems will not come to light in that way, since they might be quite rare or since a pattern may emerge only over a longer period of time. It is therefore sometimes desirable to ask the users, in effect, to observe themselves, recording in a diary certain pre-specified events.

Diary records can cover anything of interest in your setting: occurrences of a single problem, bugs in the system, descriptions of any task which the user found particularly difficult, details of waiting time or periods of breakdown, errors of particular kinds, cases where the user had to ask for help, problems which remained unsolved, and so on. However, the issues must be defined in advance of the study.

By obtaining information from several different users over, say, a fortnight or some other appropriate period, you not only identify key problems, but you might also be able to see some patterns, pointing beyond the surface symptoms to more fundamental general issues. The same procedure can be adopted with people who are not directly operating the system but who are in contact with it. Diaries kept by associated workers can often point to possible improvements in the way jobs are carried out and the way work is organized.

User diaries can take any shape which seems suitable. You may simply employ a sheet of paper, with users or associated workers writing a note of problems as they occur. Or you might design a more structured form, asking specific questions or requiring information to be recorded in boxes. In all cases, details should be gathered of what tasks were being undertaken at the time of an entry, and the time itself should be recorded. However, it is essential that operators are not overloaded by the diary procedure itself; keep it simple. It is also important that people filling in the diaries see the point of what they are doing, and that they know that the purpose is to evaluate the system and not themselves.

Box 8E   Steps in a user diary study

Step 1
Define the population to be studied. Decide whether all are to complete diaries, or whether a sample is to be drawn. If the latter, select a typical group.

Step 2
Decide on the issues which will form the basis for system evaluation.

Step 3
Carry out a preliminary diary study of those issues, asking users to record comprehensive information. The aim is to acquire more detailed understanding of key issues (step 2) and to develop economical recording procedures (for step 4).

Step 4
Ask the users to make diary entries as specified for an extended period of time.

Step 5
Examine the data you have collected, and form your conclusions about this part of the evaluation. Check how users' opinions agree or disagree with your own.

A two-stage procedure is again often appropriate. You should aim (by the second stage) to have a data-gathering form which requires minimal effort from users, and which interferes as little as possible with their routine work. This form will ask specific questions and require very simple responses (ticks in boxes, for example). But a previous stage will often be required, as you ask more open-ended questions to gather information about possible issues and potential problems. In that first stage, users should be asked to report in greater detail, and some interruption to their work will be inevitable. However, without this exploratory stage, important themes are liable to be missed.

User diary studies may be viewed in terms of five main steps, as summarized in Box 8E. These parallel the steps of formal observation (Box 8D), but differ in that the user now records the key information, without the need for an observer to be present.

SPECIALIST METHOD 5: SYSTEM LOGGING

A system log (sometimes known as a 'journal') is a record of what the user has done, which has been taken automatically by the system itself. Logs can be of several different kinds. For example, you might obtain a record of what the user typed and how the system responded. With more advanced systems which have pointing devices such as mice, the log might be a record that can be 'played back', so that you can see how the screen changed throughout a recorded session, rather as if you had video-recorded the screen. Obtaining these sort of records can be a difficult technical feat, and they are not always possible with standard equipment.

The advantage of a system log as a source of information for evaluation is that the recording is unobtrusive and objective, unlike user diaries or formal observation. The main disadvantage is the same as for any other detailed record: there is a lot of information to store and to analyse. This can only be managed if you are very clear about the purpose of the evaluation, knowing exactly what issues you need to examine, and if you have the necessary software and other resources for analysis and interpretation. System logging provides a detailed record of what has happened, but an evaluator has to look for and identify patterns in the data and infer from those patterns some explanation in terms of cause and effect. That is often difficult.

Another common use of a system log is to measure the hour-by-hour and overall throughput of a system. In this case also you will need additional software to abstract the information from the logs. Specially written software will also be required if you need to search for occurrences of particular types of error or particular sequences of commands. In general, it is a good idea to check out these possibilities at the time of purchase; suppliers or manufacturers can sometimes provide these additional logging facilities from the outset.

SPECIALIST METHOD 6: TASK ANALYSIS

The previous four specialist methods depend upon an investigator having some idea about particular tasks performed when working with the computer-based system. This knowledge about tasks may sometimes be quite straightforward, in terms simply of 'saving a file', 'correcting errors' or 'setting up the printer', but it is occasionally desirable to carry out a more sophisticated analysis to identify the main elements of a job. The results of such a task analysis can provide a framework for detailed information-gathering, for example through system walk-through or formal observation, or they might be useful for quite different purposes, such as identifying training needs.

The general aim of task analysis is to split any work activity into its basic elements, each identified as being directed to a particular goal. You start with the overall activity, break that down into principal tasks, and then break down each of those tasks into sub-tasks. That process can in principle continue through many levels, but in practice you need continue to split down the tasks only as far as will be useful for what you are doing.

In all cases, you should set out to identify units of behaviour which are defined in relation to a specific goal. In this way one might point to elements such as 'assess current stock of item x, in order to check whether customer order y can be met', or 'edit CNC tape t, in order to make modification m'. Each element can in principle be re-described in terms of smaller elements (each with its own goal), so that one can produce a *hierarchy* of task elements.

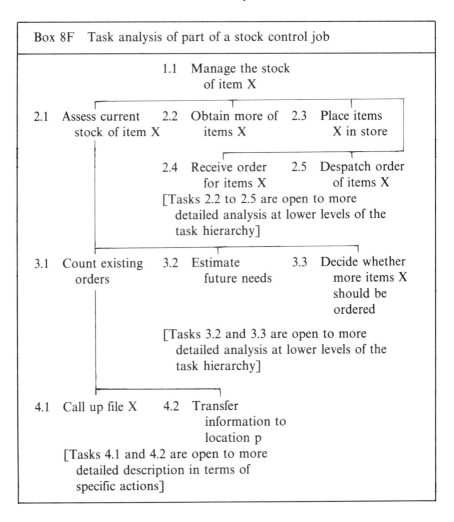

Box 8F   Task analysis of part of a stock control job

1.1   Manage the stock
       of item X

2.1   Assess current   2.2   Obtain more of   2.3   Place items
       stock of item X   items X   X in store

                           2.4   Receive order   2.5   Despatch order
                                  for items X   of items X
                           [Tasks 2.2 to 2.5 are open to more
                                  detailed analysis at lower levels of the
                                  task hierarchy]

3.1   Count existing   3.2   Estimate   3.3   Decide whether
       orders   future needs   more items X
                                                           should be
                                                           ordered

                           [Tasks 3.2 and 3.3 are open to more
                                  detailed analysis at lower levels of the
                                  task hierarchy]

4.1   Call up file X   4.2   Transfer
                                  information to
                                  location p
                           [Tasks 4.1 and 4.2 are open to more
                                  detailed description in terms of
                                  specific actions]

The overall unit of behaviour forms the top of the hierarchy, with increasingly detailed elements forming lower levels of the structure. A partial example is shown in Box 8F.

The top-level activity may be divided into any number of tasks, but for practical reasons it is best to aim for between four and eight second-level elements. You need also to identify the 'plans' which link sub-tasks together, usually in a fixed sequence. In addition, you should spotlight any important or difficult tasks, and record any factors which strongly affect success or failure.

Complicated activities usually have 'if... then...' links between sub-tasks, so that a multi-option account will sometimes be needed. Care should be taken in identifying procedures of that kind. You should also look carefully at alternative ways of doing the work: different people may in practice undertake different tasks in achieving the same goal. In all cases, check your analysis with the employees involved, to learn whether any points have been missed.

Different sources of information should be used, comparing between them

---

Box 8G   Questions to ask at each stage of task analysis

---

(1) *What* is the person doing?
(2) *Why* is he or she doing that?
(3) *How* is it being done?
(4) What was the *previous* activity?
(5) Are any activities undertaken *in parallel*? If so, how is priority decided?

---

in the search for accuracy. For example, you might examine relevant documents, such as operating manuals, company procedures, job descriptions, etc. Each of these is helpful up to a point, but can sometimes bear only a little resemblance to what actually happens. So you will also need to consult employees such as managers and supervisors, and of course users themselves. Members of the last group are particularly important, but problems can arise from the fact that even very skilled people may not be able clearly to put into words what they are doing. As with other methods in this chapter, you should try to identify in advance the right questions to ask, so that staff are helped in describing complex activities.

In drawing up a task analysis you should always aim to observe the work being done. Some tasks have a high degree of physical activity, and different behaviours can easily be recorded. Other tasks are more a question of perceiving, thinking, remembering and deciding, where outwardly little can be observed. In those cases it is of course essential to obtain some description of the work from employees themselves.

As pointed out above, it is not enough to record merely what someone is doing; you need to understand the goal of activity at each level of the analysis. A five-point framework for inquiry is summarized in Box 8G, and this should be applied at every stage.

The description from your task analysis should be used to focus attention when applying one of the other information-gathering methods. Concentrate on the key sub-tasks you have identified, examining those through one or more of the specialist methods of system walk-through, formal observation, user diaries, system logging, or comparative testing.

SPECIALIST METHOD 7: COMPARATIVE TESTING

A small number of readers might occasionally find it useful to set up special 'experiments', testing alternative systems on a series of criterion tasks. Detailed comparisons of these kinds are also valuable in the development of new hardware or software, carrying out interim evaluations as part of the design process. In that setting, designers might create a 'prototype', and assess its performance in comparison with others. On the basis of those tests, improvements would be made, and the revised prototype assessed in the same way.

However, broad-ranging, unfocused comparisons are a waste of time and money. It is important first to undertake some form of task analysis (see the previous section), to identify key themes for comparison between the systems or prototypes. That will permit specific questions to be asked in your comparison.

Measurements in a comparative test will usually be based on one of the specialist methods 2, 3, 4 or 5: system walk-through, formal observation, user diaries or system logging. Particularly useful information can often be obtained by timing how long it takes to complete each task or sub-task and by recording any problems experienced by the user. A stop-watch might be helpful here, but (as noted above) some systems can be programmed to record actions and their timing and to print out a full record of events. Those records permit you to compare times between different systems, and identify exactly where users made mistakes or used inefficient procedures.

It is essential to obtain data from more than a single user. Ideally, you should aim for up to six different users per test, but three people for any one version is a good general target. Always try to employ your company's current users. In the case of new prototypes, or if you do not have enough staff in your own company, it might be sensible to hire some temporary staff through a local employment agency. The problem then remains that those temporary users know little about your company's work tasks. Other suggestions are summarized in Box 8H.

A series of questions to users should follow each test. Issues of equipment and usability (covered in Chapters 2 and 3) are particularly open to comparative testing, and questions based upon those can be supplemented by

---

Box 8H   Advice about comparative testing

— carry out a task analysis to identify tasks of importance to your company
— set up some experimental conditions to examine key aspects of performance, comparing alternative versions on each task
— use one or more of these methods: system walk-through, formal observation, user diaries or system logging
— for the last three methods, select users who are typical of staff operating the system and ensure that users know you are evaluating the system rather than them
— start off with some straightforward tasks and progress to more difficult ones
— try to carry out experiments in everyday working conditions, with typical levels of noise, interruptions etc.
— obtain users' opinions about each version
— only carry out experimental tests if you are certain that they are worth the substantial costs involved

open-ended questions along these lines:

— what was the best thing about this system?
— what was the most annoying/frustrating thing about it?
— where are improvements needed?
— how can these needed improvements be made?

When you have finished your programme of tests, you should have some detailed comparative results covering times, errors and user attitudes. In choosing between systems or prototypes on the basis of this information, you will almost certainly be involved in trade-off decisions. For example, model X may be much the best at tasks 1, 4 and 5, but unable to do task 6, which is important to you. On the other hand, model Y may be able to perform all the tasks but at a slow pace, except that it is excellent at task 7, which is not of great concern to you. The choice here is likely in part to depend on other considerations within the framework of your overall evaluation, such as whether or not a system is likely to meet future needs.

SPECIALIST METHOD 8: COMPANY RECORDS

This final procedure makes use of the kind of information which is routinely collected within a company, seeking to apply it to your evaluation needs. For example, financial records are widely kept, and most companies gather data about reported injuries, absenteeism and labour turnover. Many firms, particularly those in manufacturing, also collect systematic data about machine performance, breakdowns and utilization. All of these can have some role in evaluating existing computer systems, although in most cases they can only provide background information, pointing to the presence of symptoms, rather than giving details of their underlying causes.

For example, evidence of high staff absence or labour turnover rates may be linked to problems with particular pieces of technology, but there are many other possible causes. Furthermore, low rates of accidents, absence and staff turnover do not necessarily indicate that all is well. For these reasons, most forms of company record can only be used as the broadest of indicators of system performance.

Even with seemingly direct indices, care must be taken, since several interpretations may be possible. For example, manufacturing companies usually keep records of machine breakdowns, machine efficiencies and machine utilization. Poor utilization figures for, say, computer-controlled machine tools are certainly a problem, but causes can vary from situation to situation. You will therefore need to supplement the evidence from company records with information gathered by one or more of the basic or specialist methods.

In some circumstances, it may be desirable to amend the current record-keeping procedures to help with your evaluation. For example, data may not be held separately for the section or department which particularly concerns you. Or more specific material could be gathered, with direct reference to the computer-based equipment in question. These amendments are likely to be particularly helpful in the case of prospective evaluation, when you are deciding between purchase options and following up the choice after it has been made. However, even in retrospective cases, looking back on equipment in operation, it may prove possible to re-examine the aggregate records to obtain data which bear more directly on the system being evaluated.

OVERVIEW

We stressed earlier that these specialist methods of information-gathering should not be seen as alternatives. They are complementary means of gathering different kinds of evidence, and they will always need to be linked to the basic approaches of interviews, meetings or working parties. For example, a meeting of users and other people may identify the major issues for follow-up investigation. Interviews may then be designed to explore these issues and identify potential causes. A short questionnaire, along with a system walk-through to examine one particular theme, may provide more detailed information. Or a system logging exercise could be linked to a user diary study to obtain complementary types of data. And a working party might be set up to manage the evaluation, gathering and analysing of the information, and the planning of a course of action.

You may find it necessary to seek information and advice from outside experts. The thrust of this book is that systematic evaluation should, wherever possible, be carried out by using a company's own resources and motivation. We have outlined procedures which make that possible, but carrying out some of the evaluation procedures and interpreting data from them may need additional expertise, provided by specialists from outside the company.

In all cases, interpretation of the information depends upon judgements made by the people involved. Evaluation data might be in precise quantitative form (for example, a certain number of user errors of a particular type, an average processing speed of a certain magnitude, or an average score on a questionnaire response scale), but that numerical value is usually open to more than one interpretation. In other cases, the information might be qualitative and impressionistic, perhaps based on a series of comments made during interviews. Both types of data are important, and both require careful judgement. That will often involve bringing together facts from different sources: are different kinds of evidence consistent in suggesting a particular interpretation? Evaluation data should be varied, and as precise and reliable as possible, but ultimately personal judgement and interpretation are essential.

Finally, we should again stress that few readers will need to employ the specialist methods described here. In the majority of cases, examining the thirty key issues from Chapters 2 to 5 through the basic methods of information-gathering will be sufficient. The specialist methods are needed only on unusual occasions, by companies which have special needs and also the additional resources required for the large amount of work which is involved. In general, the greater the financial investment and/or the cost of failure, the greater will be the need for more detailed inquiries.

9

More detailed questions about equipment and working conditions

This chapter provides assistance for readers who wish to gather more detailed information about certain of the issues examined in Chapter 2. At that point we introduced several sets of questions for the initial evaluation of computer-based equipment and the conditions in which it is used. We now provide more detailed questions for two of those issues: system security and working conditions.

These questions are in the form of checklists and questionnaires. As pointed out previously, *checklists* are helpful for organizing your inquiries in almost any setting. They can be used to supplement the questions being addressed through the basic methods of information-gathering (interviews, meetings and working parties; see Chapter 6), or they can be applied within specialist methods such as system walk-through or formal observation (see Chapter 8).

Questionnaires (see page 158) are for administration to employees themselves. In later chapters, examples will be provided which might be completed widely throughout a company. However, the focus here is upon users of the technology themselves, and as examples we provide two short questionnaires for VDU and keyboard users. Following the advice in Chapter 8, readers with other types of equipment might wish to develop similar questionnaires for users in their own setting.

A CHECKLIST ABOUT SYSTEM SECURITY (2.5)

In assessing the security of a system, the following detailed questions may be helpful. They should be asked in conjunction with the initial questions listed in Chapter 2 (page 35).

1. Which types of fraud is the company open to: disclosure of information to rivals, changes to files, deletion of data?
2. Is there recent evidence of fraud of any of those kinds?
3. Are there problems within the organization of staff gaining inappropriate access to restricted or confidential information about other employees?
4. Has anything changed lately, inside or outside the company, to increase any of those risks?
5. Have knowledgeable members of staff recently moved to rival companies?
6. Are some employees or ex-employees likely to feel alienated to the extent that they might corrupt data or otherwise sabotage the system?
7. Have the different risks in all different parts of the company been examined (e.g. the data-processing department, each local network, free-standing and interlinked personal computers)?
8. Which parts of the computer system are most vulnerable to unauthorized entry? How can they be made more secure?
9. Who has responsibility for information security, overall and within departments? Are changes in responsibility needed? Should the post of data-security manager be created, or is it preferable to assign responsibility to individual managers?
10. Should an explicit security policy be drawn up and applied?
11. Have you considered cards or other procedures to allow access to individuals according to their need and security status?
12. Is confidential data transmitted through an electronic mail system? If so, can other people gain access to that data?
13. If you send confidential data down public telephone lines, is it worth introducing coding procedures?
14. Do employees' contracts of employment, or other written agreements, adequately cover the requirements of information security?
15. Is communication about security requirements between the data-processing department and other parts of the company so restricted that security provisions fail to spread beyond d-p staff?
16. Are printouts, disks and other items outside the computer treated in a secure manner in all parts of the company?
17. Have staff been involved in discussions and decisions about security procedures and training provisions?
18. What about security against fire? Are back-up files stored in a separate location?

FOUR CHECKLISTS ABOUT WORKING CONDITIONS (2.6)

Chapter 2 covered three aspects of working conditions: the environment, the equipment and its siting, and physical hazards. Advice was given about each of those, and initial evaluation questions were presented.

Four more detailed sets of questions are given here, in the form of checklists. These mainly cover office systems, and you may wish to amend and extend the lists to meet other needs in, say, manufacturing settings. The emphasis in section 2.6 was on hardware rather than software, and that is maintained here. Detailed questions about software and interfaces are presented in the next chapter.

The checklists are longer than will normally be required. We have opted for over-inclusiveness rather than the converse, so that individual readers can omit items as they choose. A 'yes' response is generally desirable, but in some cases you may need to use the 'not applicable' response (the 'N/A' box as laid out below). A small number of items require technical knowledge before they can be answered, so that staff with a background in engineering or ergonomics may sometimes be required.

(a) *Checklist on the working environment*

	Yes	No	N/A
1. From the operator's position, is the room lighting acceptable?			
2. Is the operator's field of vision free of direct reflections from the display screen, keyboard, desk, papers, etc.?			
3. Is the operator's field of vision free of glare sources (lights, windows, etc.)?			
4. If necessary, are the luminaires equipped with prismatic or grid-type glare shields?			
5. Are the VDU workplaces positioned such that the operator's line of vision is			
parallel to luminaires?			
parallel to windows?			
6. If needed, are the windows fitted with blinds or curtains?			
7. Can the room temperature be maintained between 19 and 23 °C?			
8. Can the relative humidity be maintained between 40% and 60%?			

	Yes	No	N/A
9. If needed, are the operators and other staff protected against			
thermal radiation?			
warm air flow?			
10 If needed, have adequate steps been taken to avoid local hot spots in corners, etc.?			
11. Is the working environment free of draughts?			
12. Is the noise level acceptable, that is: less than 55 dB(A) in task areas requiring a high level of concentration?			
less than 65 dB(A) in routine task areas?			
13. Is the noise environment free from high frequency tones?			
14. Is the workroom reasonably free from external noises (e.g. from neighbouring rooms, the outside world)?			
15. Is the workroom free of disturbing noises from other equipment (e.g. printers, teletypes)?			

(b) *Checklist on VDU, keyboard, and speech communication*

	Yes	No	N/A
1. Can both upper- and lower-case characters be displayed?			
2. Do the descenders of lower-case characters project below the base line of the text?			
3. Are the ascenders and descenders of lower-case characters on adjacent lines well separated?			
4. Can the following letters and numbers be easily distinguished? X and K; O and Q; T and Y; S and 5; B and 8; I and L; U and V; I and 1; O and zero. If problems are present, list them here:			

	Yes	No	N/A
5. Can an adequate amount of text be viewed on the screen?			
6. Does the screen have a display capacity (i.e. number of available character spaces) that is sufficient for the task?			
7. If the display capacity is less than the maximum capacity required by the task, is there sufficient display memory?			
8. Is the set of characters sufficient for the task?			
9. Is the character height greater than or equal to 3 mm?			
10. Do the character height and viewing distance ensure a visual angle of at least 16′ (minutes of arc), preferably 20′?			
11. Is the character width between 70% and 80% of the upper case character height?			
12. Is the space between the characters between 20% and 50% of the character height?			
13. Is it possible to swivel the screen or the VDU about its vertical axis?			
14. If desirable, is it possible to tilt the screen about its horizontal axis?			
15. If the screen is fixed, is it approximately vertical?			
16. Is the upper edge of the screen at or below eye height?			
17. Where appropriate, does the visual display format correspond to the format which is used on documents, such as order forms?			
18. Is the use of colour, for coding purposes, kept to a minimum?			
19. Is it possible easily to distinguish the cursor from other symbols on the display?			

	Yes	No	N/A
20. If desirable, can the cursor be suppressed?			
21. If desirable, is it possible to generate graphic symbols via the keyboard?			
22. If desirable, is it possible to blink selected parts of the display?			
23. If desirable, is it possible to display characters of differing sizes?			
24. If desirable, is it possible to display characters of differing styles?			
25. Are all displayed characters unambiguous?			
26. If screen filters are used, are the characters in the display sharply defined?			
27. If desirable, can forms be generated with protected fields?			
28. For negative contrast displays (with light characters on a dark background), is the character luminance			
greater than 45 cd/m²? (this is the minimum acceptable)			
between 80 and 160 cd/m²? (this is preferred)			
29. For negative contrast displays (with light characters on a dark background), is the character luminance (brightness) adjustable to appropriate levels without blurring the characters?			
30. Do the character images remain sharply defined at desired character luminance (brightness)?			
31. Is it possible easily to distinguish between the different luminance (brightness) levels at the desired setting?			
32. Is the display background luminance between 15 and 20 cd/m² under the appropriate office lighting conditions?			

	Yes	No	N/A
33. Is the contrast between characters and background acceptable?			
34. Are the displayed character images free from flicker or other movement?			
35. Is the display background flicker-free and without after-images?			
36. Are the colours comfortable to look at?			
37. Is the level of glare from the screen acceptable?			
38. From the operator's position, is the display free of unwanted reflections?			
39. If necessary, has an anti-glare treatment been fitted to the screen?			
40. Overall, does the display produce clear, sharp and stable characters?			
41. Does the surround of the display consist of matt material with a low reflectance?			
42. Is the keyboard detachable from the display screen?			
43. Is the weight of the keyboard sufficient to ensure stability against unintentional movement?			
44. Is the thickness of the keyboard (i.e. base to the home row of keys): less than 50 mm? (acceptable) 30 mm? (preferred)			
45. Is the distance between the underside of the desk frame and the home row of keys on the keyboard less than 60 mm?			
46. Is the angle of the keyboard in the range between 5 and 15 degrees?			
47. Is the surface of the keyboard surround matt finished?			

	Yes	No	N/A
48. Is there at least a 50 mm deep space provided on either the keyboard or the desk for resting the palms of the hands?			
49. For square keys, is the keytop size between 12 and 15 mm square?			
50. Is the centre spacing between adjacent keys between 18 and 20 mm?			
51. Are the key legends resistant to wear, through the legends being moulded into the keytop?			
52. Are the keytop surfaces concave, so as to improve accuracy of keying?			
53. Are the keytop surfaces such that reflections are kept to a minimum?			
54. Is the activation of each key accompanied by a feedback signal such as an audible click or a snap action?			
55. Is the key action always effective?			
56 Does the layout of the alphabet keys correspond to the conventional typewriter keyboard layout?			
57. Does the layout of the numeric keys (above the alphabet keys) correspond to the conventional typewriter keyboard layout?			
58. If an auxiliary numeric keyset is provided, are the keys arranged in a familiar way, for example, as in the calculator layout (7, 8, 9 along the top row) or as in the telephone layout (1, 2, 3 along the top row)?			
59. Is the space bar at the bottom of the keyboard?			
60. Does the number and type of function keys correspond to the requirements of the task?			
61. Are all keys for which unintentional or accidental operation may have serious consequences especially secure by their position, a higher required key pressure, a key lock, or two-key chord operation?			

	Yes	No	N/A
62. Is the colour of the alphanumeric keys neutral (e.g. beige, grey), rather than black, white, red, yellow, green or blue?			
63. Are the different function key blocks distinct from the other keys by colour, shape, position,or spacing?			
64. Are the most important function keys colour-coded?			
65. Do the function key labels and symbols correspond to the same function on other keyboards used in the same workplace, e.g. typwriters or other VDUs?			
66. If desirable, are user-programmable function keys provided?			
67. Are areas of the keyboard with different functions easily distinguished?			
68. Are the key legends clear and unambiguous?			
69. From the operator's position, is the keyboard free of unwanted reflections?			
70. Is the VDU resistant to knocks and vibration?			
71. Are the operators and cleaning staff aware of which cleaning materials may be used without causing damage to the screen, housing and other components of the VDU?			
72. Is there sufficient space for maintenance access to both the VDU and VDU workplace?			
73. If desirable, are there any user-serviceable repairs (e.g. fuse changes) that can be easily carried out by the operator?			
74. Is the operator provided with an audible or visible warning signal in the event of system or VDU malfunction?			

	Yes	No	N/A
75. Is the operator provided with a warning in the event that the VDU is no longer able to register keystrokes, e.g. when the memory storage is filled?			
76. Is operational status (e.g. if the terminal is in send, receive or queue mode) made known to the operator in a clear fashion?			
77. If several terminals share a common transmission line to the computer, can each terminal transmit and receive information independently of the status of the other terminals on the line?			
78. If speech input is used, is that effective without too great an emphasis in enunciation?			
79. If speech input is used, does the system exclude other voices nearby?			
80. If speech input is used, can the user switch conveniently between speech and keyboard input (e.g. voice for text input, keys for cursor movement)?			
81. If speech output is used, is its quality acceptable in normal conditions?			
82. If speech output is used, can this be adjusted for			
volume?			
speed?			
tone?			
83. If speech output is used, can this be switched off and replaced by visual information only?			
84. If speech output is used, and headphones would be desirable for the user, are these available?			

(c) *Checklist on workstation design*

	Yes	No	N/A
1. Are sufficient number of work surfaces provided?			
2. Are the working surfaces of sufficient size?			
3. Are all items of equipment and job aids within arm reach without requiring excessive movement of the body?			
4. Is the desk height between 660 and 680 mm?			
5. If the desk height is adjustable, is the range offered between 600 and 770 mm?			
6. Is the height of the keyboard above floor level between 680 and 720 mm?			
7. Is the surface of the desk matt finished?			
8. Is the reflectance of the desk surface:			
0.4? (optimum)			
0.5? (acceptable)			
0.6? (maximum)			
9. Is the height of the leg area sufficient?			
10. Is the leg area free from obstructions, such as desk frame spars?			
11. Is the leg area at least 800 mm wide to permit unobstructed turning?			
12. Is the leg area at least 700 mm deep?			
13. If necessary, is the leg area shielded against heat?			
14. Can small items of equipment be stored when not in use?			

	Yes	No	N/A
15. Is adequate space provided for storage of copies, handbooks, documents, personal belongings, etc.?			
16. Is it possible for the operator to easily re-arrange the workplace, e.g. by changing the positions of the VDU and other items of equipment?			
17. If footrests are used, are they adjustable			
in height?			
in inclination?			
in location?			
18. If footrests are used, do they cover the entire leg area?			
19. If footrests are used, are they stable?			
20. If footrests are used, does their surface permit comfortable movement of the feet without slipping?			
21. Does the design of the chair satisfy the requirements of national standards?			
22. Is the chair stable, i.e. safe from tipping over?			
23. If the chair is provided with castors, are they self-locking?			
24. Does the chair swivel, to facilitate access?			
25. Is the seating height easily adjustable?			
26. Is the seat angle adjustable?			
27. Is the front edge of the seat rounded to avoid cutting into the thighs?			
28. Is the seat surface padded?			

	Yes	No	N/A
29. Is the height of the backrest adjustable?			
30. Can the backrest be adjusted forwards and backwards?			
31. Can adjustments be made easily and safely from the seated position?			
32. Does the backrest provide good lumbar support?			
33. Are all seat adjustment mechanisms safe against unintentional release?			
34. Are the documents that are necessary for the task satisfactory with regard to:			
character formation?			
contrast between characters and background?			
35. Are all paper surfaces matt?			
36. Can all of the information which is relevant to the task, including documents, be easily read?			
37. Are the source documents free from reflections?			
38. Are the source documents positioned at an appropriate angle and field of view?			
39. If desirable, is a document holder provided?			
40. Are all items of equipment and jobs aids (such as documents) so positioned that—apart from short-term considerations—the operator may assume an optimum working posture according to the following criteria?			
head inclined forward at an angle of about 20 degrees			
spine slightly arched and forward leaning when seen from the side			
upper arms vertical			

	Yes	No	N/A
no twisting of the head and trunk			
thighs approximately horizontal			
lower part of the leg approximately vertical			
sufficient leg room both in height and depth			
frequent changes of visual object accommodated within an angle of 15 to 30 degrees relative to the normal viewing direction			

(d) *Checklist on physical hazards*

	Yes	No	N/A
1. Is the operator secure against electrical accident, even when tampering with the equipment?			
2. Does the equipment satisfy the requirements of all national and local safety standards?			
3. Are the electrical supply cables and other services to the equipment adequately secured and concealed?			
4. Is there adequate space for movement between items of equipment?			

TWO QUESTIONNAIRES ABOUT EQUIPMENT (2.6)

As described in Chapter 8 (page 158), there is sometimes a need to obtain information about aspects of equipment through a questionnaire administered to the users. Two examples are provided below, referring separately to visual display units and to keyboards.

Note that negative responses do not necessarily indicate failings in the equipment. They may arise from faulty job design (such as insufficient task variety), or they can point to staff issues which need consideration. For example, are spectacles (or different spectacles) now needed by some people? Would training assist in keyboard use? Are particularly small or large users being asked to work in standard work-spaces?

(a) *VDU questionnaire*

PLEASE INDICATE BELOW THE DEGREE OF DISCOMFORT YOU EXPERIENCE IN USING YOUR VISUAL DISPLAY UNIT. FOR EACH ITEM, PLACE A TICK IN THE BOX WHICH MOST CLOSELY DESCRIBES YOUR VIEW. THERE ARE NO RIGHT OR WRONG ANSWERS.

Characteristic	Degree of discomfort		
Discomfort to eyes	None	☐☐☐☐☐	Severe
Dryness in eyes	None	☐☐☐☐☐	Severe
Irritation in eyelids	None	☐☐☐☐☐	Severe
Difficulty in focusing	None	☐☐☐☐☐	Severe
Headache	None	☐☐☐☐☐	Severe
Backache	None	☐☐☐☐☐	Severe
Ache in neck or shoulder	None	☐☐☐☐☐	Severe
Other problems (please specify, below)	None	☐☐☐☐☐	Severe

(b) *Keyboard questionnaire*

PLEASE INDICATE BELOW YOUR OPINIONS ABOUT THE KEYBOARD. FOR EACH ITEM, PLACE A TICK IN THE BOX WHICH MOST CLOSELY DESCRIBES YOUR VIEW. THERE ARE NO RIGHT OR WRONG ANSWERS.

Characteristic	Your judgement		
Feel of the keyboard in use	Like very much	☐☐☐☐☐	Dislike very much
Keying rhythm	Like very much	☐☐☐☐☐	Dislike very much
Effort required for keying	Low	☐☐☐☐☐	High
Aches caused by keying	None	☐☐☐☐☐	Severe
Tiredness from keying	None	☐☐☐☐☐	Severe
Posture required for keying	Very comfortable	☐☐☐☐☐	Very uncomfortable
Overall ease or awkwardness of use	Easy to use	☐☐☐☐☐	Awkward to use

Comments

Please write below any other relevant points about the keyboard:

10

More detailed questions about usability

This chapter provides seven checklists of questions. As in Chapter 9, these may be used to supplement the basic evaluation questions provided earlier; or they might be included within applications of the specialist methods of system walk-through, formal observation or comparative testing (see Chapter 8). Also as previously, a 'yes' response is usually the desirable answer.

Aspects of usability overlap with each other, so that assessment of one feature often brings in questions about others. Although particular methods or checklists may be applied separately to some individual issues, it will frequently be sensible to look at several topics within a single investigation. For example, you might link together the questions listed in Chapter 3 for, say, 'Being in control' and 'Degree of effort', and explore them as a whole through interviews or group discussions; or the specialist method of formal observation might be applied in a single study of, say, both 'Ease of learning' and 'Getting information in and out'.

THREE CHECKLISTS ABOUT EASE OF LEARNING (3.1)

In Chapter 3 we suggested that ease of learning could be viewed in terms of three features: commands employed (both single-key and sequences of instructions), core concepts and documentary support. The initial questions listed in section 3.1 can be supplemented through the following checklists about those features. These lists overlap to some extent with other questions later in the chapter, since systems which are easier to learn are typically also easier to use.

(a) *Checklist on system commands*

	Yes	No	N/A
1. Is a suitable prompt provided to make it clear what kind of response is required of the user at all times?			
2. Are commands grouped sensibly on the display and/or keyboard?			
3. Do commands and menu items correspond to the vocabulary with which users describe the task?			
4. Is the sequence in which the commands have to be invoked appropriate to the way users think about the task?			
5. Are menu items grouped sensibly on the display?			
6. Where special function keys are used to invoke commands, are these keys sensibly grouped?			
7. Can commands be learned piecemeal, so that users do not have to learn a lot before they can do something useful?			
8. Is it possible easily to reverse the effect of any mistaken action or command?			

(b) *Checklist on core concepts*

	Yes	No	N/A
1. Are the core concepts easy to learn?			
2. Is it easy for a learner to discover what the core concepts are (e.g. from clear graphics, documents, or on-line help)?			
3. Are the core concepts consistent with how the users view the task and the operations?			
4. Are the core concepts consistently applied throughout all work with the system?			

	Yes	No	N/A
5. If changes in core concepts are made, is each switch made explicit to the user?			
6. Does the system operate in the same sequence as the user normally thinks?			
7. Do changes in mode (points when different command sets become available) occur at natural points in the task?			

(c) *Checklist on documentation*

	Yes	No	N/A
1. Can the user easily find relevant parts of the manual or other documents:			
when getting started?			
when there is an error?			
2. After an appropriate section has been found, is it easily comprehensible:			
when getting started?			
when there is an error?			
3. Are the indexes and contents pages clear?			
4. Are there sufficient cross-references?			
5. Is the material comprehensible to novice users?			
6. Does the vocabulary correspond to that of the users?			
7. Are there sufficient diagrams and pictures?			
8. Are later sections based upon a level of understanding of earlier sections which is reasonable?			

	Yes	No	N/A
9. Is the manual consistent in terminology and layout in all its sections?			
10. Are there useful summaries of complex information?			
11. If appropriate, are locally prepared documents available to suplement the manual?			
12. Is the documentation consistent in its terminology with the system?			

A CHECKLIST ABOUT BEING IN CONTROL (3.2)

	Yes	No	N/A
1. Does the system always behave in an expected manner?			
2. Does the system respond to every command by indicating its appropriateness or otherwise?			
3. Are changes in system modes clearly indicated?			
4. Are the menu options easily understandable, both in wording and layout?			
5. Is the process of selecting menu options clearly explained?			
6. Is the process of selection menu options consistent across menus?			
7. Are menu structures clear, so that users do not get lost?			
8. If users make a wrong choice, is it easy to get back to the previous stage?			
9. Is it possible easily to step forward in a menu structure, if that is desired?			

	Yes	No	N/A
10. Is the on-line 'help' facility adequate?			
11. Is it clear how to get into or out of the 'help' facility?			
12. Is 'help' information presented clearly without interfering with users' work?			
13. Does the help facility use language suitable for a novice user?			
14. Is help offered at different levels of complexity, to reflect differences in expertise?			
15. Do the 'help' items closely map onto problems met in everyday work?			
16. Can information held in the 'help' facility easily be updated to keep pace with system changes?			
17. Is it possible for novice users to work in a safe, limited part of the system, without needing to move into areas which are too difficult for them?			
18. Generally, is it easy to move backwards in the system to regain control?			

A CHECKLIST ABOUT DEGREE OF EFFORT (3.3)

The following questions may be used to supplement the initial points raised in section 3.3. For this checklist, the desirable answer is always 'no'.

Does the operation of the computer-based technology involve users in:	Yes	No	N/A
1. extensive heavy lifting or carrying?			
2. standing for long periods?			
3. a lot of stretching or bending?			
4. working in awkward positions?			

	Yes	No	N/A
5. data-entry work for long periods?			
6. excessive amounts of key-stroke work?			
7. reading from a screen for long periods?			
8. sustained concentration for long periods?			
9. using a very complex macro-language?			
10. memorizing pieces of information that are hidden between operations?			
11. thinking through the knock-on effects of frequent actions?			
12. having to make extensive changes as a result of single modifications?			
13. making too many decisions about how the system should be set up and operated?			
14. making very difficult choices between options?			
15. coping with particularly complex methods of operation?			

A CHECKLIST ABOUT GETTING INFORMATION IN AND OUT (3.5)

In the following checklist, 'yes' is the desirable answer, except for questions 1, 2, 3, 4, 5 and 8.

	Yes	No	N/A
1. Are certain aspects of data-entry unnecessarily complex?			
2. Could lengthy inputs be abbreviated, by shortening or omitting words, or through a macro-language?			

	Yes	No	N/A
3. Does the system request information in a sequence or format incompatible with the user's source of information?			
4. Are there too many errors in data-entry?			
5. Could additional visual templates be designed to assist with the entry of data?			
6. When entering data into a form, are the maximum lengths of data fields clearly indicated?			
7. Is there a clear distinction between mandatory fields (which must be completed) and non-mandatory fields (which may be left blank)?			
8. Would different input devices (character readers, mice, touch screens, voice input, etc.) be helpful?			
9. Is all the necessary information available on each display?			
10. Is the amount of non-relevant information always kept within reasonable limits?			
11. Does the display avoid unnecessary clutter?			
12. Do items on the display appear in logical groups or sequences?			
13. Is the use of upper-case (capital) text kept within reasonable limits?			
14. Are all abbreviations and codes easily understandable?			
15. Are different colours used in a helpful way?			
16. Is the number of different colours about right?			

	Yes	No	N/A
17. Are highlighting techniques used in a helpful way (underlining, reversing, blinking, italicizing, etc.)?			
18. Is clear information available about previous steps and possible future actions?			
19. Is the user informed where to find the information which is needed next?			
20. When associated with each other, are screen displays always consistent?			
21. Are screen layouts consistent with the layout of source documents?			
22. Are all questions from the system clear?			
23. Are all questions from the system necessary?			
24. Are system messages kept sufficiently short for easy comprehension?			
25. Do all icons have a clear meaning for novice as well as experienced users?			
26 Do all icons have a clear meaning for users of varying cultural background?			
27. Can users obtain verbal information about the meaning of icons, if they are unsure?			
28. Are icons sufficiently distinct from each other?			
29. Is the number of different icons kept within reasonable limits?			

A CHECKLIST ABOUT ERRORS AND ERROR CORRECTION (3.6)

The desirable answer below is 'yes', except for questions 1 and 2.

	Yes	No	N/A
1. Are certain errors repeated frequently?			
2. Are experienced users prone to:			
confusion errors?			
errors in switching between modes?			
errors from memory requirements which are too great?			
errors arising from inconsistencies in system use?			
errors arising from ambiguous instructions?			
capture errors?			
errors arising from setting-up routines?			
3. Does the system help to prevent errors by:			
requiring confirmation of inputs with a high error cost?			
avoiding frequent changes between upper and lower case, excessive punctuation, or inputs which may be unnatural to the user?			
4. Are error messages easily understood?			
5. Are error mesages specific to the task in hand?			
6. Are error messages informative and helpful in practical terms?			
7. Do error messages appear in a consistent manner and location?			
8. Is it possible to call for 'help' to supplement an error message?			

	Yes	No	N/A
9. Are errors easily corrected, for example by:			
an 'undo' key, allowing the user to return to a previous position?			
easy re-entering and editing of commands?			
the cursor returning to the error position?			
10. Is there a clear distinction between error messages requiring action and warning messages that do not require action?			

11

More detailed questions about job quality and performance

This chapter contains thirteen questionnaires and one checklist for more detailed examination of the issues covered in Chapter 4. The focus is upon the users of computer-based equipment, their opinions, attitudes and performance.

As pointed out in Chapter 8, questionnaires can produce a large amount of information, so they should be used only rarely. They are most valuable when relatively large samples can be drawn for comparison, or when changes can be monitored across time. Advice about construction, administration and interpretation has been given in pages 158 to 162.

The initial questions provided throughout Chapter 4 will be sufficient for most readers. These can be asked and followed up through the basic evaluation methods: interviews, meetings or working parties. The more detailed items which are presented here cover all the issues of Chapter 4, and are unlikely to be required in their entirety. Select only those which meet your needs; conversely, you should add new questions if you wish.

The items presented in many of the following sections refer to 'the job', and this sometimes needs to be qualified when you are evaluating specific items of new technology. No difficulties arise if a person is using the same computer-based equipment throughout the entire working day; in these cases 'the job' is 'the computer-based job'. However, in some situations an employee may be a user of the system for only part of the time. Questions about, say, 'the speed at which you work' or about 'variety in the tasks you do' might then be ambiguous. Some employees might answer in respect of the job as a whole, whereas an evaluation project may be seeking information in relation to the new-technology work on its own. If so, this should be made clear in the initial instructions and explanations.

In some investigations you may choose to summarize data from a questionnaire in terms of the number, or proportion, of respondents who have given each answer. That is helpful in providing information about particular questions. However, it is sometimes desirable to calculate an overall score for a multi-item scale. In these cases, you should score each response numerically from 1 to 5 from left to right (or up to 4 or 6 where those numbers of alternatives are provided). Scores for each question can then be added together or averaged, providing all items are worded in the same direction. If a question is worded in the opposite direction, scoring should be reversed, to ensure that a higher figure always indicates the same kind of answer. In those cases you should count in the opposite direction: from 1 to 5 from right to left. The need for reverse-scoring is usually clear from the meaning of items, but you are reminded of the requirement above each questionnaire when that is relevant.

In producing overall scores for all items in a questionnaire, it is usually better to calculate an *average across items* rather than merely the total. (That is, you should divide the total score by the number of items involved.) The average score (two decimal places are recommended) can then be interpreted in terms of the wording of response alternatives used on the questionnaire.

In most cases, a higher average score indicates a more desirable response for the scale as a whole. However, several of the questionnaires used in this chapter have 'about right' as their middle point, with 'too little' or 'too much' on either side of that (see, for example, the questionnaire immediately below). The desirable average value here is 3 (the mid-point), with shifts towards 1 or 5 (the end-points) both representing undesirable patterns.

With large investigations, you will probably use a computer for data-processing, so that the calculation of average scores will present no difficulties. You might also choose in that case to score 'about right' as 0, with -1 and -2 representing degrees of 'too little' and $+1$ and $+2$ indicating 'too much'. (Scores would thus be -2, -1, 0, $+1$, $+2$; instead of 1, 2, 3, 4, 5.) An average scale score of, say, -0.95 is then quickly interpretable as 'too little' of the feature in question.

If you plan to use all the items in a questionnaire as printed here, you may wish to photocopy directly from the book. There are no copyright restrictions on the questionnaires themselves.

QUESTIONNAIRE ABOUT USERS' CONTROL OVER THEIR WORK (4.1)

The following items cover aspects of users' personal discretion. If you plan to calculate overall scale scores, items 9, 10 and 11 should be reverse-scored.

TO WHAT EXTENT DO YOU:	Much too little	Too little	About right	Too much	Much too much
1. have control over the order in which tasks are done?					
2. have control over the speed at which you work?					
3. have control over the methods to be used?					
4. have control over preparatory aspects of the job?					
5. have control over output targets?					
6. have control over output levels?					
7. have control over quality standards?					
8. have control over quality levels?					
9. feel controlled by the technology?					
10. feel controlled by outside experts?					
11. have to cope with unwanted interruptions from other people?					

A QUESTIONNAIRE ABOUT SKILLS REQUIRED (4.2)

If you plan to calculate overall scale scores, item 4 should be reverse-scored.

TO WHAT EXTENT DO YOU:	Much too little	Too little	About right	Too much	Much too much
1. have to use manual skills in your work?					
2. have to use mental skills in your work?					
3. have the opportunity to learn new skills?					
4. have to do 'left-over' tasks, ones the equipment can't do?					
5. feel challenged by your work?					
6. feel your abilities are being put to good use?					

A QUESTIONNAIRE ABOUT VARIETY IN THE JOB (4.3)

In calculating overall scale scores, all these items can be scored in the same direction.

TO WHAT EXTENT DO YOU:	Much too little	Too little	About right	Too much	Much too much
1. have variety in the tasks you do?					
2. have variety in the speed at which you work?					
3. have variety in the difficulty of your task?					
4. have variety in the concentration demanded?					

TO WHAT EXTENT DO YOU:	Much too little	Too little	About right	Too much	Much too much
5. have variety in the skills you use?					
6. have variety in where you work?					
7. have variety in who you work with?					

A QUESTIONNAIRE ABOUT WORK DEMANDS (4.4)

If you plan to calculate overall scale scores, item 12 should be reverse-scored. Item 13 should be omitted from the total, since it already covers an overall response. It is also recommended that items 14 and 15 be combined separately, since these cover a distinct aspect of demands.

TO WHAT EXTENT:	Much too little	Too little	About right	Too much	Much too much
1. does the job require you to concentrate for long periods?					
2. does the job require you to think carefully?					
3. does the job require you to make detailed plans?					
4. does the job require you to make decisions?					
5. is the job physically demanding?					
6. is the job mentally demanding?					

TO WHAT EXTENT:	Much too little	Too little	About right	Too much	Much too much
7. does the job require heavy lifting?					
8. does the job require you to stand for long periods of time?					
9. does the job require you to work in awkward positions?					
10. does the job involve physical discomfort from noise?					
11. does the job require fast movements?					
12. does the job allow rest pauses?					
13. is the overall job demanding?					
14. is the job a 'complete' one?					
15. does the job have a clear beginning and end?					

A QUESTIONNAIRE ABOUT UNCERTAINTY (4.5)

In calculating overall scale scores, all these items can be scored in the same direction.

TO WHAT EXTENT DO YOU AGREE OR DISAGREE WITH THE FOLLOWING STATEMENTS?	Strongly disagree	Disagree	Neither disagree nor agree	Agree	Strongly agree
1. I have clear work targets to pursue					
2. I get feedback from the job about my performance					
3. I get feedback from my boss about my performance					
4. I know to whom I am responsible					
5. I know what is required of me in my job					
6. I know what my boss thinks about my work performance					
7. I understand the computer-based system					
8. I understand where my job fits into the work of the department					
9. I know how my career will develop					
10. I know about future prospects for the company					

A QUESTIONNAIRE ABOUT PAY (4.6)

In calculating overall scale scores, all these items can be scored in the same direction. Item 4 should be excluded from the overall value, since it covers a separate, though related, theme.

HOW DO YOU FEEL ABOUT:	Very bad	Bad	About right	Good	Very good
1. your pay in comparison with other people in the company?					
2. your pay in comparison with people in other companies?					
3. the degree to which the pay system provides an incentive for good performance?					
4. the quality of the company's job evaluation scheme?					
5. the degree to which people can understand how their pay is calculated?					
6. the share you get of the financial benefits achieved by the technology?					

A QUESTIONNAIRE ABOUT COMMUNICATIONS AND SOCIAL CONTACT (4.7)

In calculating overall scale scores, all these items can be scored in the same direction.

HOW GOOD OR BAD ARE:	Very bad	Bad	About right	Good	Very good
1. communications between yourself and your immediate boss?					
2. communications about work issues with colleagues in the department?					
3. communications about work issues with colleagues in other departments?					
4. your opportunities to learn what is happening elsewhere in the company?					
5. your opportunities for informal contact with colleagues?					
6. communications with customers or clients? (if relevant)					
7. the *amount* of information you receive via the computer system?					
8. the *quality* of information you receive via the computer system?					
9. the amount of face-to-face contact you have with other people?					

THREE QUESTIONNAIRES ABOUT HEALTH AND SAFETY (4.8)

In scoring the following three sets of items 1 to 4 from left to right, remember that a higher score represents a bigger problem.

TO WHAT EXTENT IS EACH OF THE FOLLOWING A PROBLEM TO YOU?	No problem	A slight problem	A moderate problem	A big problem
1. feeling that your job is harming your health				
2. working under a great deal of tension				
3. feeling anxious as a result of your job				
4. feeling irritable as a result of your job				
5. being kept awake at night because of problems associated with your job				
6. feeling worried that something at work is going to go wrong				
7. feeling that your job is interfering with your family life				

TO WHAT EXTENT IS EACH OF THE FOLLOWING A PROBLEM TO YOU IN YOUR JOB?	No problem	A slight problem	A moderate problem	A big problem
1. headache				
2. eye-strain				
3. backache				
4. aches in your hands or wrists				
5. aches in your neck				
6. any other physical symptom—please write in the type of symptom which is a problem:				

TO WHAT EXTENT IS EACH OF THE FOLLOWING A PROBLEM IN YOUR JOB?	No problem	A slight problem	A moderate problem	A big problem
1. the risk of accidents				
2. lack of protection from moving equipment				
3. poor safety procedures				
4. poor safety training				
5. people's failure to follow safety procedures				

A CHECKLIST ABOUT USERS' PERFORMANCE (4.9)

The following checklist items can be considered by anyone evaluating the performance of system users. It may be helpful sometimes to obtain answers from a number of people who then discuss points of agreement or disagreement between their answers. [Recall that *checklists* differ from *questionnaires* such as those presented previously in the chapter: checklists are for completion by evaluators themselves, whereas questionnaires are for administration to job holders.]

In considering these questions, focus particularly on the users themselves. Broader organizational issues are raised in Chapter 12.

WITH THE SYSTEM, ARE YOU SATISFIED:	Yes	No	Not applicable
1. that the system meets its objectives?			
2. that the system is cost-effective?			
3. that the system is providing an acceptable return on investment?			
4. with the quantity of work produced?			
5. with the quality of the work produced?			
6. with the productivity of the system?			
7. with its overall level of performance?			
8. that customers are getting a better product or service?			
9. that you can identify direct benefits from using the system?			
10. that you can identify indirect benefits from using the system?			
11. that the users are adequately trained?			
12. that the users are highly motivated?			
13. that the users are able to anticipate problems and take remedial action?			

WITH THE SYSTEM, ARE YOU SATISFIED:	Yes	No	Not applicable
14. that users are getting the best out of the system?			
15. that the system is helping get the best out of its users?			
16. that the users' jobs are designed to achieve optimal levels of performance?			
17. that you are aware of any problems which exist with the system?			
18. that you can resolve these problems?			

THREE QUESTIONNAIRES ABOUT USERS' ATTITUDES (4.9)

In considering users' attitudes toward their jobs, it will sometimes be appropriate to administer questionnaires. Three examples are provided here, covering job satisfaction, job-related feelings and intention to leave.

(a) *Job satisfaction*

If you plan to calculate overall scale scores, item 18 should be excluded, since it is already an 'overall' item.

EACH ITEM BELOW NAMES ONE ASPECT OF YOUR JOB. PLEASE INDICATE HOW SATISFIED OR DISSATISFIED YOU ARE WITH IT BY PLACING A TICK IN ONE OF THE BOXES.	Very dis-satisfied	Moderately dis-satisfied	Neither satisfied nor dis-satisfied	Moderately satisfied	Very satisfied
1. the physical work conditions					
2. the freedom to choose your own method of working					
3. your fellow workers					

EACH ITEM BELOW NAMES ONE ASPECT OF YOUR JOB. PLEASE INDICATE HOW SATISFIED OR DISSATISFIED YOU ARE WITH IT BY PLACING A TICK IN ONE OF THE BOXES.	Very dis-satisfied	Moderately dis-satisfied	Neither satisfied nor dis-satisfied	Moderately satisfied	Very satisfied
4. the recognition you get for good work					
5. your immediate boss					
6. the amount of responsibility you are given					
7. your rate of pay					
8. your opportunity to use your abilities					
9. relations between management and workers in your firm					
10. your chance of promotion					
11. the way your firm is managed					
12 the attention paid to suggestions you make					
13. your hours of work					
14. the amount of variety in your job					
15. your job security					
16. the training you have received					
17. the computer system on which you work					
18. Overall, taking everything into consideration, how satisfied are you with your job?					

(b) *Job-related feelings*

The satisfaction items in the previous questionnaire can provide useful information based upon the job aspects included in the list. However, there are occasions when a more detailed look at different kinds of feelings is required.

For that purpose it is helpful to think in terms of two separate dimensions of feelings. One dimension runs from *anxious* to *calm*, and the other from *tired* to *alert*; and we can examine how much a job makes people feel anxious or calm, and also how much it makes them feel tired or alert. (The anxious–calm dimension has also been considered in the first questionnaire about health and safety, above; see page 208.)

Six items are included here for each of the two main dimensions. Scoring of responses should be from 1 to 6, as laid out below. If you wish to calculate an overall score for each dimension, half of the items need to be reserved-scored. These are identified in brackets, such that a higher score always represents more desirable feelings ('calm' and 'alert' respectively). The items are:

anxious to calm: (1) tense; (4) relaxed; (5) worried; (8) calm; (9) uneasy; (12) contented. (Reverse-score items (1), (5) and (9))

tired to alert: (2) lively; (3) tired; (6) alert; (7) fatigued; (10) full of energy; (11) lifeless. (Reverse-score items (3), (7) and (11))

It should again be emphasized that this kind of questionnaire yields a large amount of data. Questionnaire approaches are recommended only for that minority of readers who have special interests and resources.

THINKING OF THE PAST FEW WEEKS, HOW MUCH OF THE TIME HAS *YOUR JOB* MADE YOU FEEL EACH OF THE FOLLOWING?	Never	Occa-sionally	Some of the time	Much of the time	Most of the time	All of the time
(1) tense						
(2) lively						
(3) tired						
(4) relaxed						
(5) worried						
(6) alert						
(7) fatigued						
(8) calm						
(9) uneasy						
(10) full of energy						
(11) lifeless						
(12) contented						

(c) *Intention to leave*

A more extreme form of negative job reaction is in terms of voluntary staff turnover. Intention to leave can be assessed through items of the following kind. Note that, if your scoring is 1, 2, 3 from left to right, a higher score is in this case more undesirable.

DO YOU AGREE WITH THE FOLLOWING STATEMENTS?	No	I'm not sure	Yes
1. I often think of leaving this job			
2. I will probably look for a new job in the next few months			
3. I would prefer to work for another company			
4. If I could find another job with the same rate of pay, I would be happy to move			

12

More detailed questions about organizational aspects and overall effectiveness

In this chapter we return to the wider organizational issues that were introduced in Chapter 5. To examine those, information is required from people in several different parts of the company, mainly through the basic evaluation methods of interviews, meetings and working parties. However, in a minority of cases, there may be a need for more detailed investigation, and questionnaires and checklists are provided here for that purpose.

Whereas the questionnaires in Chapter 11 were primarily for new-technology users themselves, the present examples are for more widespread completion throughout the company. General advice about questionnaire design, administration and interpretation may be found in Chapter 8 (pages 158 to 162).

The questionnaires described below will be used only infrequently, and they will be of value mainly within larger companies. Individual scores have limited meaning on their own, and results can best be interpreted through comparisons between the average responses of different groups. How similar or different are questionnaire results from managers and shopfloor employees? What differences are present between plants, between departments, or between different staff groups?

In comparing responses in those ways, you will need to attach numerical scores to each answer. As in the last chapter, we recommend values of 1 to 5, from left to right in the alternatives provided. Overall scale scores can sometimes be useful. As pointed out in Chapter 11 (page 200), their calculation requires the reverse-scoring of certain items. That need arises here in only one questionnaire (concerning section 5.5), and it is indicated above the items.

If you plan to use all the items in a questionnaire as printed, you may wish to photocopy directly from the book. There are no copyright restrictions on the questionnaires themselves.

Checklists differ from questionnaires in that they are for completion by evaluators themselves. As in previous chapters, we have brought together questions which may be helpful in shaping an evaluator's thinking. He or she should work through the checklists where appropriate, perhaps discussing the issues with knowledgeable colleagues. As in other cases, items should be deleted or added to meet your own needs.

A QUESTIONNAIRE ABOUT ORGANIZATIONAL STRUCTURE (5.1)

Aspects of structural differentiation and integration may be examined through questions of the following kind. In scoring answers 1 to 5 from left to right below, remember that a higher score represents a more negative attitude.

TO WHAT EXTENT DO YOU AGREE OR DISAGREE WITH THE FOLLOWING STATEMENTS:	Strongly disagree	Disagree	Neither disagree nor agree	Agree	Strongly agree
1. There are too many levels in the hierarchy					
2. We have problems co-ordinating the work of groups at different levels in the hierarchy					
3. There are too many specialist groups in the company					
4. We have problems of lateral co-ordination between sections and departments					
5. People lower down the organization have to refer upwards for any important decisions					
6. Decision-making is too centralized					
7. Communications are too much controlled from the centre					
8. Services (finance, distribution, etc.) are too much controlled from the centre					
9. All the specialist staff are employed centrally					

TO WHAT EXTENT DO YOU AGREE OR DISAGREE WITH THE FOLLOWING STATEMENTS:	Strongly disagree	Disagree	Neither disagree nor agree	Agree	Strongly agree
10. Our specialist staff are out of touch with day-to-day operations					
11. We need to be more flexible in trying out different kinds of organizational structure					
12. Senior managers ought to work out a new policy for the structure of the company					

A QUESTIONNAIRE ABOUT BUREAUCRACY AND DECISION-MAKING (5.2)

The following items can be used to tap employees' views about high levels of bureaucracy; a higher score indicates a belief that bureaucracy in the company is too great. If you plan to calculate overall scale scores, item 10 should be excluded, since it is already an 'overall' item.

TO WHAT EXTENT DO YOU AGREE OR DISAGREE WITH THE FOLLOWING STATEMENTS:	Strongly disagree	Disagree	Neither disagree nor agree	Agree	Strongly agree
1. Procedures in the company are excessively standardized					
2. Communication is too tightly controlled					
3. Decision-making processes are too formalized					
4. There is too much demarcation of responsibility between individual jobs					
5. There is too much demarcation of responsibility between different levels					
6. The company is too inflexible in responding to change					

TO WHAT EXTENT DO YOU AGREE OR DISAGREE WITH THE FOLLOWING STATEMENTS:	Strongly disagree	Disagree	Neither disagree nor agree	Agree	Strongly agree
7. People feel that many procedures are inappropriate					
8. Company rules of procedure are too rigid					
9. Computers have made the company too bureaucratic					
10. Overall, we need to reduce the level of bureaucracy					

A QUESTIONNAIRE ABOUT COMMUNICATIONS (5.3)

The following items cover broader aspects of communication than were tapped by the similar questionnaire for system users in Chapter 11 (page 207).

TO WHAT EXTENT DO YOU AGREE OR DISAGREE WITH THE FOLLOWING STATEMENTS:	Strongly disagree	Disagree	Neither disagree nor agree	Agree	Strongly agree
1. It is very hard to get the information you need in this company					
2. Most employees need to know more about what is happening elsewhere in the company					
3. Communication with customers/clients could be a lot better					
4. Communication with suppliers could be a lot better					
5. Downward communication in the company could be a lot better					
6. Upward communication in the company could be a lot better					
7. Lateral communication between departments is not good enough					

TO WHAT EXTENT DO YOU AGREE OR DISAGREE WITH THE FOLLOWING STATEMENTS:	Strongly disagree	Disagree	Neither disagree nor agree	Agree	Strongly agree
8. Users of new technology are inadequately supported by specialist departments					
9. Computers make too much information available, more than people can use					
10. Middle managers are made less effective because they are by-passed by computer-generated information					
11. Technical specialists have too much control over communications in the company					

TWO CHECKLISTS ABOUT COMMUNICATIONS (5.3)

Two checklists are presented next, for use by evaluators carrying out a communications audit. The first list will help you pinpoint specific blockages, and the second focuses upon the computer system itself.

In using these checklists, you need to consider in turn each major employee group (sales representatives, designers, production supervisors, etc.). There is clearly a limit to the number of groups you can examine, so start with those which appear from initial evaluation work to be particularly likely to have communication problems.

DOES THE GROUP RECEIVE THE RIGHT INFORMATION, IN THE RIGHT DEGREE OF DETAIL, AT THE RIGHT TIME:	Yes	No	N/A
from senior management?			
from their local manager?			
from their immediate superior?			
from other directly related departments?			
from technical specialists?			

DOES THE GROUP RECEIVE THE RIGHT INFORMATION, IN THE RIGHT DEGREE OF DETAIL, AT THE RIGHT TIME:	Yes	No	N/A
from their subordinates?			
from the computer system itself?			
from customers or clients?			
from suppliers?			
about how the company is performing?			
about the company's plans and prospects?			
about what is happening elsewhere in the company?			
about customers or clients?			
about suppliers?			
about plans and prospects in their own work area?			
about matters directly affecting their own work?			
about their targets and goals?			
about their own performance?			

FOR THIS GROUP, HAS THE COMPUTER-BASED SYSTEM LED TO PROBLEMS:	Yes	No	N/A
of too much information?			
of information in the wrong format?			
of information to the wrong people?			
of information that is too late?			

FOR THIS GROUP, HAS THE COMPUTER-BASED SYSTEM LED TO PROBLEMS:	Yes	No	N/A
of information that cannot be understood?			
of information that is not used?			
of information that is inaccurate?			
of information that people do not trust?			
of communication that is too formal?			
of communication that is too impersonal?			
of communication that by-passes some individuals or groups?			
of communication that has made some groups too powerful?			

A CHECKLIST ABOUT SELECTION AND TRAINING (5.4)

In cases where a company intends to install a new computer-based system, careful thought about selection and training of staff is essential. Personnel or line managers charged with these tasks should consider the questions below. Initially, 'yes' or 'no' answers will suffice, but, in the latter case, work is of course required to bring together the necessary information. In complex cases, you should consider employing selection and training consultants.

AT THE PRESENT TIME, CAN YOU:	Yes	No	N/A
1. describe in detail how the system will work, and who will do what?			
2. list the knowledge, skills and attitudes required by all relevant people (including users, occasional users, engineers, supervisors and managers)?			

AT THE PRESENT TIME, CAN YOU:	Yes	No	N/A
3. say how you will identify within the company who has these skills, or the capability of developing them? (For example, will you use interviews, selection tests, the manager's opinion, or what?)			
4. identify the gaps you have, and specify what skills may be required through external recruitment?			
5. specify how you will attract new staff? (For example, will you use advertisements in newspapers or trade magazines, or what?)			
6. detail how you will identify people from outside the company who have the required skills or the capability to acquire them? (For example, will you use interviews, selection tests, references, or what?)			
7. say what changes are required to make your selection procedures more effective?			
8. describe the training that will be required and who will provide it both for existing employees and for new staff? (For example, will you tailor-make your own course, or buy into an existing course? Will you train internally or externally? Will you use the suppliers of the equipment? How much training can be done on the job? Are other operators able to act as trainers?)			
9. say who will be responsible for each part of the training? (For example, what will be the job of the personnel department, and what will line management be responsible for?)			

AT THE PRESENT TIME, CAN YOU:	Yes	No	N/A
10. specify a realistic timetable for each form of training?			
11. say what changes are required to make your training procedures more effective?			
12. say how much you are constrained by local agreements? (for example, concerning whether or not you can recruit from outside)			

A QUESTIONNAIRE ABOUT INDUSTRIAL RELATIONS (5.5)

If you are concerned about the impact of the technology on levels of trust in your organization, and on your industrial relations climate more generally, the following questionnaire might be administered to a range of employees.

Questions 1 to 7 focus on the levels of trust and confidence that people have in management, while questions 8 to 13 concern views about industrial relations more generally. If you plan to combine responses to the first set of items, scores for questions 2 and 7 should be reversed. In the second set of items, scores for questions 8, 12 and 13 need reversing if you are calculating overall scale scores.

TO WHAT EXTENT DO YOU AGREE OR DISAGREE WITH THE FOLLOWING STATEMENTS:	Strongly disagree	Disagree	Neither disagree nor agree	Agree	Strongly agree
1. The management is sincere in its attempts to meet the employees' point of view about new technology					
2. Our firm has a poor future unless it can attract managers with a more positive approach to new technology					
3. The management can be trusted to make sensible decisions about investing in new technology					

TO WHAT EXTENT DO YOU AGREE OR DISAGREE WITH THE FOLLOWING STATEMENTS:	Strongly disagree	Disagree	Neither disagree nor agree	Agree	Strongly agree
4. The management introduces computer equipment in a way which takes account of employees' needs.					
5. The management is effective in running the technology					
6. I feel quite confident that the firm will always treat me fairly					
7. The management would be quite prepared to gain advantage by deceiving the workforce					
8. There is so much tension here about new technology, you feel things could blow up at any moment					
9. The management here approach new technology issues in a spirit of trust and good faith					
10. The unions here (or other representative groups) approach new technology issues in a spirit of trust and good faith					
11. There is a family atmosphere here in which people work together to solve common problems about new technology					
12. There is a widespread feeling here of 'them' and 'us'					
13. The employees here have many grievances about new technology					

A QUESTIONNAIRE ABOUT PAY AND CAREER PROGRESSION (5.6)

Attitudes to pay and career opportunities can be assessed through the following questionnaire. As emphasized in the introduction to the chapter, particular attention should be paid to comparisons between different employee groups. For example, in what ways do the opinions of new-technology users differ from those in similar grades who are still using non-computerized equipment? (See also the items about pay in Chapter 11, page 206.)

FOR EACH ITEM BELOW PLEASE INDICATE HOW SATISFIED OR DISSATISFIED YOU ARE, BY PLACING A TICK IN ONE OF THE BOXES:	Very dis-satis-fied	Moder-ately dis-satis-fied	Neither satis-fied nor dis-satis-fied	Moder-ately satis-fied	Very satis-fied
1. your rate of pay, relative to others in your organization					
2. your rate of pay in comparison with others doing similar work in other organizations					
3. your opportunities for overtime, relative to others in your organization					
4. the job evaluation scheme in your organization (if there is one)					
5. the incentives offered for good performance (e.g. bonuses, profits, shares)					
6. your overall pay scheme (piecework, added value, profit-sharing, etc.)					
7. your opportunities to get promotion					
8. your opportunities to develop your career generally (e.g. by learning new skills)					

A CHECKLIST ABOUT JOB EVALUATION (5.6)

Managers concerned with job evaluation and payment systems should consider the following questions. Some will be irrelevant in any one situation, but others may serve as reminders about issues which might otherwise be overlooked. Causes and implications of any problematic answers can be followed up by more detailed investigations.

---

1. Are there signs that your current methods of job evaluation are failing to cope with the new-technology jobs?
   Is there difficulty in evaluating previous jobs which have been affected by new technology?
   Is there difficulty in evaluating new jobs introduced as a result of new technology?
   Is 'red circling' increasing because of new technology? (This is the procedure whereby current employees retain their previous wage level, even though their job has been re-evaluated as deserving less money.)
   Are existing factors and grade definitions in the schemes still appropriate?
   Do existing factors and grade definitions need re-defining; in what directions?
   Are existing job descriptions available and accurate?
   Are there problems with job titles, in defining jobs?
   Has the number of appeals increased in jobs affected by new technology?
   Is it taking longer to clear appeals on jobs affected by new technology?
   Do jobs now cut across the boundaries of existing job evaluation schemes, because of changing technology and new forms of work organization?
   Is the system becoming too rigid in its application?

2. Are additional factors or new grade definitions needed?
   How can they be identified?
   Can any existing factors in current schemes be eliminated because work has changed?

3. Is the weighting of factors still valid?
   Which factors need re-weighting, and in what way?
   What weighting should be given to any new factors introduced?

4. Can methods of job evaluation currently in use be adapted to cope with the effects of new technology, by amending factors, grade descriptions, factor weightings, etc?
   What would be the effect of amendments on jobs which had been earlier evaluated?

5. Are new job evaluation schemes needed?
   What criteria need to be taken into account in deciding what kind they would be?
   Are there any constraints of time, resources, expertise, if a new scheme is to be introduced?

6. Does the new technology require some job redesign or changes in work organization?

What impact would this have on factors, grade definitions and factor weightings?

7. Will the existing process of job evaluation be affected by the new technology in any way?

Is the composition of evaluation committees still appropriate to retain effective representation?

Are additional representatives needed from new-technology jobs?

Is a different approach to writing job descriptions needed?

Are existing means for dealing with appeals effective?

Are benchmark jobs still appropriate?

8. Is the existing method of maintaining the effectiveness of the job evaluation scheme adequate?

Will increased attention need to be paid to maintenance of the scheme at a time of rapid technical change?

Who will be responsible?

In what ways will the effects of any technical change on jobs be recorded, and to whom communicated?

Is the method of communicating information on job evaluation matters to those involved effective?

Should your previous job evaluation manual now be revised?

9. Is the job evaluation scheme free of sex, or any other, bias?

10. Is it time to consider an overall review of the scheme, perhaps leading to radical changes?

A CHECKLIST ABOUT JOB LOSSES (5.7)

In cases where a company intends to install a new computer-based system, personnel and/or line managers should consider the questions below. If the initial answer to any item is 'no', further work is needed.

AT THE PRESENT TIME, CAN YOU:	Yes	No	N/A
1. specify how many and what type of job losses will result?			
2. say how many job losses will be absorbed by natural wastage?			
3. say how many will be absorbed by internal redeployment and retraining?			

AT THE PRESENT TIME, CAN YOU:	Yes	No	N/A
4. specify how many voluntary redundancies will occur?			
5. specify the numbers and types of involuntary redundancies?			
6. specify how the process will be managed (timing, resourcing, setting up alternative plans, etc.)?			
7. describe your plans for consultation and negotiation, both with employees and their representatives?			
8. describe your plans to help employees find jobs elsewhere (for example, through counselling and training)?			
9. identify where particularly difficult conflicts may occur?			

A CHECKLIST ABOUT ORGANIZATIONAL PERFORMANCE (5.8)

Here we are concerned with the impact of computer technology on wide-ranging aspects of performance, rather than focusing on performance in particular jobs. (That was covered at the end of the previous chapter.) This section will only be relevant if you have made a substantial investment in new technology, and in many cases the initial questions listed in section 5.8 (page 108) will be sufficient to initiate inquiries.

The following checklist can be considered by anyone undertaking an evaluation of organizational impacts. It may sometimes be helpful to obtain answers from a range of evaluators, who then discuss points of agreement or disagreement.

ARE YOU SATISFIED:	Yes	No	N/A
1. that the new system links into your business plan?			
2. that the system is helping you meet your business goals?			

ARE YOU SATISFIED:	Yes	No	N/A
3. that the system meets its objectives?			
4. with the financial return on your investment?			
5. with the overall effectiveness of the system?			
6. with the quality of work produced?			
7. with the quantity of work produced?			
8. with the impact of the system on your organization more broadly?			
9. with the impact on your market share?			
10. with the impact on your customer service?			
11. with the impact on your company image?			
12. with the impact on your competitive edge?			
13. with the impact on your information use?			
14. that the system gives you better control of your business?			
15. with the impact on lead times?			
16. with the impact on stock levels?			
17. with the pace of implementation?			
18. that the implementation is being well managed?			
19. with the impact on staffing levels?			
20. with the cost of system support?			

ARE YOU SATISFIED:	Yes	No	N/A
21. with the cost of maintenance?			
22. with the cost of upgrading other equipment?			
23. with the cost of implementation?			
24. with your investment in training?			
25. with changes made to working practices?			
26. that employees are in favour of the system?			
27. that you can sustain your commitment to new technology over the next two or three years?			
28. that your organization is learning from its experience?			
29. that your organization is getting the best out of the system?			
30. that your system helps get the best out of your organization?			
31. that you are aware of any organizational problems which exist because of the system?			
32. that you can resolve those problems?			

QUESTIONNAIRES ABOUT EMPLOYEE MORALE (5.8)

In assessing morale and work attitudes, the concern of this chapter is with groups across the organization as a whole. Chapter 11 (pages 211 to 214) included three attitude questionnaires for completion by new-technology users, and these can of course be applied more widely in the company. As with other issues in this chapter, attention should be directed less at an overall average response (for the company as a whole) and more specifically at similarities or differences between particular groups.

Additional reading

CHAPTERS 2 and 9: EQUIPMENT AND WORKING CONDITIONS

Recommended books

Dainoff, M.J. and Dainoff, M.H. *A Manager's Guide to Ergonomics in the Electronic Office*. Wiley, 1987.
Basic introduction to ergonomics: seating, vision, physical environment, 'software ergonomics' (usability—see also chapters 3 and 8), quality of life in the electronic office, and likely future directions. A useful section on designing simple studies to investigate usability, another on how to put together a VDT workstation. No specialist knowledge required.

Grandjean, E. *Ergonomics in Computerized Offices*. Taylor and Francis, 1987.
Explains how to avoid or, where necessary, to remove, ergonomic problems arising from the use of computer-based equipment in offices. No previous understanding of the area is assumed.

Oborne, D. *Computers at Work*. Wiley, 1985.
Another broad-based review of research findings. After a discussion of social aspects of computers in the workplace there are chapters on the usability of different types of input and output hardware, the working environment, and how to display information effectively; then short discussions of computers in the office, in medicine and in education. Also includes a bibliography.

Further reading

Bailey, R. W. *Human Performance Engineering: A Guide for Systems Designers*. Prentice-Hall, 1982.

Health and Safety Executive. *Visual Display Units.* Her Majesty's Stationery Office, 1983.

Lewis, C. *Managing with Micros.* Blackwell, 1983.

Pearce, B. *Health Hazards of VDTs?* Wiley, 1984.

CHAPTERS 3 and 10: USABILITY

Recommended books

Nickerson, R.S. *Using Computers: Human Factors in Information Systems.* MIT Press, 1986.
A review of a broad field of research with bibliographic entries leading to the original papers; quite detailed, yet clearly and comprehensibly written. Covers how information systems are used, the nature of different types of interaction, the growth of artificial intelligence and expert systems, a brief look at effects on the quality of life, and other topics.

Shneiderman, B. *Designing the User Interface: Strategies for Effective Human–Computer Interaction.* Addison–Wesley, 1986.
Describes and illustrates selected research findings about the usability of many different styles of interface, including menu selection systems, command languages, direct manipulation systems, and different types of device, including lightpens, mice, trackballs, etc.; also has section on system response time and system messages. An easy-to-read account.

Further reading

Briefs, U., Ciborra, C., and Schneider, C. (eds.). *Systems Design for, with, and by Users.* North-Holland, 1983.

Christie, B. (ed.). *Human Factors of Information Technology in the Office.* Wiley, 1985.

Gaines, B.R. and Shaw, M.L.G. *The Art of Computer Conversation.* Prentice-Hall, 1984.

Monk, A.F. (ed.). *Fundamentals of Human–Computer Interaction.* Academic Press, 1984.

Rasmussen, J., Duncan, K., and Leplat, J. *New Technology and Human Error.* Wiley, 1987.

Rubenstein, R. and Hersh, H.M. *The Human Factor: Designing Computer Systems for People.* Digital Press, 1984.

Sime, M.E. and Coombs, M.J. (eds.). *Designing for Human–Computer Interaction.* Academic Press, 1983.

CHAPTERS 4 and 11: JOB QUALITY AND OPERATOR PERFORMANCE

Recommended books

Otway, H.J. and Peltu, M. *New Office Technology: Human and Organizational Effects.* Frances Pinter, 1983.

Provides a practical guide to the impact of IT on many facets of the office working environment and the people working in it. Covers the planning and evaluation of new systems, systems design, the changing roles of secretaries, clerks and managers, as well as ergonomic, software and training requirements.

Wall, T.D., Clegg, C.W., and Kemp, N.J. (eds.). *The Human Side of Advanced Manufacturing Technology.* Wiley, 1987.
Concentrates on the manufacturing sector, and includes the choices which companies can make in the design of operator jobs. Also discusses the role of supervisors and approaches to selection and training.

Warr, P.B. *Work, Unemployment, and Mental Health.* Oxford University Press, 1987.
Considers nine principal features of jobs, similar to those in Chapter 4 of this book, and draws out the implications of each for the mental health of job holders.

Further reading

Bailey, J. *Job Design and Work Organization.* Prentice-Hall, 1983.
Cook, J.D., Hepworth, S.J., Wall, T.D., and Warr, P.B. *The Experience of Work: A Compendium and Review of 249 Measures and their Use.* Academic Press, 1981.
Fletcher, C. and Williams, R. *Performance Appraisal and Career Development.* Institute of Personnel Management, 1985.
McLean, A. *High-tech Survival Kit: Managing your Stress.* Wiley, 1986.
Toplis, J., Dulewicz, V., and Fletcher, C. *Psychological Testing: A Practical Guide.* Institute of Personnel Management, 1987.
Wainwright, J. and Francis, A. *Office Automation, Organizations, and the Nature of Work.* Gower Press, 1984.
Warr, P.B. (ed.). *Psychology at Work* (third edition). Penguin, 1987.

CHAPTERS 5 and 12: THE WIDER ORGANIZATION AND OVERALL EFFECTIVENESS

Recommended books

Buchanan, D. and Boddy, D. *Organizations in the Computer Age.* Gower Press, 1983.
Uses seven case studies drawn from a variety of business environments and IT applications to examine the impact of information technology on organizational structure, management control, and overall performance.

Handy, C.B. *Understanding Organizations* (third edition). Penguin, 1985.
Introduces topics such as motivation, roles, leadership, politics and culture; and applies those in practical examples to illustrate the factors influencing organizational effectiveness.

Mintzberg, H. *Structure in Fives: Designing Effective Organizations.* Prentice-Hall, 1983.

Divides organizations into five basic parts, and introduces five processes of coordination. Applies those ideas to identify five principal forms of organization.

Further reading

Child, J. *Organizations: A Guide to Problems and Practice* (second edition). Harper and Row, 1984.

Hirschheim, R. *Office Automation: A Social and Organizational Perspective.* Wiley, 1985.

Lawler, E.E. *Pay and Organization Development.* Addison-Wesley, 1986.

Robbins, S. *Organization Theory.* Prentice-Hall, 1983.

Somogyi, E. and Galliers, R. *Towards Strategic Information Systems.* Abacus Press, 1987.

Sorge, A., Hartmann, G., Warner, M., and Nicholas, I. *Micro-electronics and Manpower in Manufacturing.* Gower Press, 1983.

Wilkinson, B. *The Shop-floor Politics of New Technology.* Heinemann, 1983.

CHAPTERS 6 and 8: EVALUATION AND INFORMATION-GATHERING

Recommended books

Boddy, D. and Buchanan, D.A. *The Technical Change Audit: Action for Results.* Manpower Services Commission, 1987.
The audit presents a management guide to the effective implementation and use of new computing technologies and information systems. It is organized in five modules and it aims to help clarify problems, identify solutions and give confidence and authority to decisions and actions. Much of the audit is concerned with evaluation.

Central Computer and Telecommunications Agency (CCTA). *Method for Evaluating the Impact of New Office Technology Systems.* Her Majesty's Stationery Office, 1984.
Presents a structured approach for evaluating and reporting on the impact of new technology systems. It describes a wide range of evaluation methods and information-gathering techniques, as well as how to use the results of such exercises.

Fink, A. and Kosecoff, J. *How to Conduct Surveys: A Step-by-Step Guide.* Sage, 1985.
Covers many aspects of designing, administering and analysing both questionnaires and interviews, as well as advising on how to present the results. The book aims to provide readers with the skills to conduct their own meaningful surveys and to evaluate others'.

Meister, D. *Human Factors Testing and Evaluation.* Elsevier, 1986.
Covers different types of testing and evaluation procedures. It describes how to

administer a wide range of evaluation methods, including walk-throughs, performance testing, observations, task analysis and rating methods.

Further reading

Carnall, C.A. *The Evaluation of Organizational Change.* Gower, 1982.
Cook, T.D. and Reichardt, C.S. (eds.). *Qualitative and Quantitative Methods in Evaluation Research.* Sage, 1979.
Easterby-Smith, M. *Evaluation of Management Education, Training and Development.* Gower, 1986.
Legge, K. *Evaluating Planned Organizational Change.* Academic Press, 1984.
Maynard-Smith, J. *Interviewing.* Routledge & Kegan Paul, 1982.
Patton, M.Q. *Creative Evaluation.* Sage, 1981.
Silvey, J. *Deciphering Data.* Longman, 1975.
Webb, E.J., Campbell, D.T., Schwartz, R.D., and Sechrest, L. *Unobtrusive Measures: Nonreactive Research in the Social Sciences.* Rand McNally, 1966.

CHAPTER 7: MANAGING CHANGE

Recommended books

Huse, E.F. and Cummings, T.C. *Organizational Development and Change.* West, 1985.
A general text which covers the field of organizational development without specific attention to new technology.

Boddy, D. and Buchanan, D.A. *Managing New Technology.* Blackwell, 1986. Presents a systematic approach to the use of computer-based technology in manufacturing and office settings. The aim is to expand the range of options considered when introducing change.

Lippitt, P., Langseth, P., and Mossop, J. *Implementing Organizational Change.* Jossey-Bass, 1985.
A general account of practical approaches to the introduction of change in work organizations.

Further reading

Huczynski, A. *Encyclopaedia of Organizational Change Methods.* Gower Press, 1987.
Institute of Personnel Management. *How to Introduce New Technology: A Practical Guide for Managers.* Institute of Personnel Management, 1983.
Lupton, T. and Tanner, I. *Achieving Change: A Systematic Approach.* Gower Press, 1987.
Plant, R. *Managing Change and Making it Stick.* Fontana, 1987.
Price, S. *Managing Computer Projects.* Wiley, 1986.

GENERAL REFERENCES TO PEOPLE AND COMPUTERS

Bessant, J., Guy, K., Miles, I., and Rush, H. *I.T. Futures*. UK National Economic Development Office, 1985.

Blackler, F. and Oborne, D. (eds.). *Information Technology and People*. British Psychological Society, 1987.

Eaton, J. and Smithers, J. *This is IT: A Manager's Guide to Information Technology*. Philip Alan, 1982.

Forester, T. (ed.). *The Information Technology Revolution*. Blackwell, 1985.

Francis, A. *New Technology at Work*. Oxford University Press, 1986.

Handy, C.B. *The Future of Work*. Blackwell, 1984.

Marstrand, P. (ed.). *New Technology and the Future of Work and Skills*. Frances Pinter, 1984.

Meadows, A.J., Gordon, M., Singleton, A., and Feeny, M. *Dictionary of Computing and Information Technology*. Kogan Page, 1987.

Picrcy, N. (ed.). *The Management Implications of New Information Technology*. Croom Helm, 1984.

Salvendy, G. (ed.). *Handbook of Human Factors*. Wiley, 1987.

Senker, P. (ed.). *Planning for Micro-electronics in the Work-place*. Gower Press, 1985.

Zorkoczy, P. *Information Technology: An Introduction* (second edition). Pitman, 1987.

Some sources of information

In this section are listed details of organizations which might be able to assist you with technical, human or organizational aspects of computer-based technology. In addition to the sources identified here, many universities, polytechnics and colleges have centres of expertise which might meet your requirements on a local level. Reputable commercial consultancy firms should also be approached when appropriate.

Two lists are provided, of organizations within the United Kingdom and in the United States. Telephone numbers are included in brackets. Other countries do, of course, have comparable sources of information.

SOURCES WITHIN THE UNITED KINGDOM

Advanced Manufacturing Technology Centre (AMTEC), Hulley Road, Macclesfield, Cheshire, SK10 2NE. (0625–26189)

Advisory, Conciliation and Arbitration Service/Work Research Unit, 27 Wilton Street, London, SW1X 7AZ.

Association for the Instrumentation, Control and Automation Industry in the UK (GAMBICA), Leicester House, 8 Leicester Street, London, WC2H 7BN. (01–437–0678)

BACIE (British Association for Commercial and Industrial Education), 16 Park Crescent, London, W1N 4AP. (01–636–5351)

British Computer Society, 13 Mansfield Street, London, W1M OBP. (01–637–0471)

British Institute of Management, Management Information Centre, Management House, Cottingham Road, Corby, Northants, NN17 1TT. (0536–204222)

British Psychological Society, St. Andrews House, 48 Princess Road East, Leicester, LE1 7DR. (0533–549568)

British Robot Association, Aston Science Park, Love Lane, Aston Triangle, Birmingham, B7 4BJ. (021–359–0981)

British Standards Institution (BSI), 2 Park Street, London, W1A 2BS. (01–629–9000)

— Technical Information, BSI, Linford Wood, Milton Keynes, MK14 6LE. (0908–221166)

Business Equipment and Information Technology Association (BEITA), 8 Southampton Place, London, WC1A 2EF. (01–405–6233)

CADCAM Centre, P.O. Box 222, Riverside Park, Middlesborough, Cleveland, TS2 1RJ. (0642–226211)

CAD–CAM Data Exchange Technical Centre, 177 Woodhouse Lane, Leeds, LS2 3AR. (0532–334455)

Central Computer and Telecommunications Agency, HM Treasury, Riverwalk House; 157–161 Millbank, London, SW1P 4RT. (01–217–3350)

Confederation of British Industry, Centre Point, 103 New Oxford Street, London, WC1A 1DU. (01–379–7400)

Department of Trade and Industry, The Department for Enterprise. (Freephone 0800–500–200)

— Information Engineering Division, Kingsgate House, 66–74 Victoria Street, London, SW1A 6SW. (01–215–8333)

— Information Technology Division. (01–215–2622)

— Manufacturing Technology & Markets Division, Ashdown House, 123 Victoria Street, SW1E 6RB. (Towards Integration, the DTI Institute for Competitive Manufacturing.) (01–212–0155)

Economic and Social Research Council, Cherry Orchard East, Kemberey Park, Sweden SN2 64Q. (0793–513838)

Employment Relations Resource Centre, Compass House, 80 Newmarket Road, Cambridge, CB5 8DZ. (0223–315944)

Engineering Industries Association, 16 Dartmouth Street, London, SW1H 9BL. (01–222–2367)

Engineering Employers' Federation, Broadway House, Tothill Street, London, SW1H 9NQ. (01–222–7777)

Ergonomics Society, c/o Department of Human Sciences, University of Technology, Loughborough University, Loughborough, LE11 3TU. (0509–234904)

Health and Safety Executive, Public Enquiry Point, Baynard's House, 1 Chepstow Place, Westbourne Grove, London, W2 4TF (01–229–3456)

Industrial Participation Association, 85 Tooley Street, London, SE1 2QZ. (01–403–6108)

Industrial Society, Peter Runge House, 3 Carlton House Terrace, London, SW1Y 5DG. (01–839–4300)

Institute of Management Services, 1 Cecil Court, London Road, Enfield, Middlesex, EN2 6DD. (01–363–7452)

Institute of Manpower Studies, Mantell Building, University of Sussex Falmer, Brighton, BN1 9RF. (0273–686751)

Institute of Measurement and Control, 87 Gower Street, London, WC1E 6AA. (01–387–4949)

Institute of Personnel Management, IPM House, 35 Camp Road, Wimbledon Common, London, SW19 4UW. (01–946–9100)

Institute of Quality Assurance, 10 Grosvenor Gardens, London, SW1W 0DQ. (01–730–7154)

Institution of Electrical Engineers, Savoy Place, London, WC2R 0BL. (01–240–1871)

Institution of Mechanical Engineers, 1 Birdcage Walk, London, SW1H 9JJ. (01–222–7899)

Institution of Production Engineers, Rochester House, 66 Little Ealing Lane, London, W5 4XX. (01–579–9411)

Manpower Services Commission, Moorfoot, Sheffield, S1 4PQ. (0742–703338)

—Open Learning Branch (Open Learning Directory) (0742–753275)

Medical Research Council, 20 Park Crescent, London, W1N 4AL. (01–636–5422)

National Centre of Systems Reliability, UK Atomic Energy Authority, Wigshaw Lane, Culcheth, Warrington, WA3 4NE. (0925–31244, Ext. 4214)

National Computing Centre, Oxford Road, Manchester, M1 7ED. (061–228–6333)

National Engineering Laboratory, East Kilbride, Glasgow, G75 0QU. (03552–20222)

PERA, Melton Mowbray, Leicestershire, LE13 0PB. (0664–501 501)

Science and Engineering Research Council, Polaris House, North Star Avenue, Swindon, SN2 1ET. (0793–26222)

Trades Union Congress, Congress House, Great Russell Street, London, WC1B 3LS. (01–636–4030)

Training Commission. Previously Manpower Services Commission: see above.

United Kingdom Automatic Control Council, 87 Gower Street, London, WC1E 6AA. (01–387–4949)

Work Research Unit, 27, Wilton Street, London, SW1X 7AZ.

SOURCES WITHIN THE UNITED STATES

American Management Association, 135 West 50th Street, New York, NY 10020, USA. (212–586–8100)

American Psychological Association, 1200 17th Street NW, Washington, DC 20036, USA. (202–955–7600)

American Society of Heating, Refrigeration and Air Conditioning Engineers (ASHRAE), 1791 Tullie Circle NE, Atlanta, Georgia 30329, USA. (404–636–8400)

Association for Computing Machinery (ACM), 11 West 42nd Street, New York, NY 10036, USA. (212–869–7440)

Bureau of Labor-Management Relations, Room N5419, US Department of Labor, 200 Constitution Avenue NW, Washington, DC 20210, USA.

Computer Professionals for Social Responsibility, P.O. Box 717, Palo Alto, CA 94301, USA. (415–322–3778)

Data Processing Management Association, 505 Busse Highway, Park Ridge, IL 60068, USA. (312–825–8124)

Human Factors Society, Box 1369, Santa Monica, California 90406, USA (213–394–1811)

Illuminating Engineering Society of North America (IESNA), 345 East 47th Street, New York, NY 10017, USA.

Institute for Electrical and Electronics Engineering (IEEE) Computer Society, 10662 Los Vaqueros Circle, Los Alamitos, California 90720–9970, USA.

International Labour Organization, 1750 New York Avenue NW, Washington, DC 20036, USA.

National Computer Association (Users' Association), 1485 East Fremont Circle, S. Littleton, CO 80122, USA. (303–797–3559)

National Institute for Occupational Safety and Health (NIOSH), Robert A. Taft Laboratories, 4676 Columbia Parkway, Cincinnati, Ohio 45226, USA. (513–533–8326) (For technical inquiries within USA: 1–800–35–NIOSH)

Office Automation Management Association, 111E. Ave., Norwalk, CT06851, USA. (203–866–9637)

Public Interest Computer Association, 1025 Connecticut Ave., NW, Suite 1015, Washington, DC 20036, USA. (202–775–1588)

Society for Computer-Aided Engineering, 7811 N. Alpine Road, Rockford, IL 61111, USA. (815–654–1902)

Society for Computer Simulation Internationa, 4838 Ronson Court, Suite L, San Diego, California 92111, USA. (619–277–3888)

Society for Computer Applications in Engineering, Planning and Architecture (CEPA), 5 Park Avenue, Gaithersburg, Maryland 20877, USA. (301–926–7070)

Society for Information Display, 8055 West Manchester Avenue, Suite 615, Playa Del Rey, California 90293, USA. (213–305–1502)

Index

absence, 5, 108, 172
accidents, 83, 84, 172
air quality, 37, 38, 39, 83
aptitude tests, 99
attitudes, (*see also* commitment, morale,
    satisfaction), 39, 64, 66, 69, 84–86, 105,
    108, 116, 161, 164, 172, 199
    questionnaires about, 211–214, 230
automatic guided vehicles, 83
automation, 71, 138

backache, 83
back-up, 8, 11, 29, 30, 62, 63, 152, 153
benchmarks, 14, 112, 143
benefits, 20, 25, 31, 32, 66, 107, 108, 109,
    135, 136, 142–145, 148, 151, 155
breakdowns, 3, 5, 8, 29, 30, 66, 98, 166, 172
bugs, 28, 29, 30, 32, 153, 166
bureaucracy (*see also* decision-making), 8,
    9, 82, 87, 92, 97
    questionnaire about, 217-218
business opportunities, 27, 108, 112, 137,
    144

capital expenditure, 3
capital errors, 59–60, 61
career counselling, 106
career progression (*see also* pay), 11, 70, 78,
    80, 102–105, 147
    questionnaire about, 225
cash-flow, 33
centralization/decentralization, 89–92, 97
champions, 146, 151, 155
change, 20, 25, 88, 97, 107, 110, 111, 114,
    135–155, 161
    resistance to, 135, 136
changing over from old to new, 135,
    152–154, 155
checklists,
    about:
        being in control (of software), 192–193
        commands, 190

communications, 219–221
core concepts, 190–191
documentation, 191–192
ease of learning, 189–192
effort, 193–194
errors and error correction, 197–198
getting information in and out, 194–196
hazards, physical, 187
job evaluation, 226–227
job losses, 227–228
performance, organizational, 228–230
performance, users', 210–211
selection and training, 221–223
system security, 174–175
VDU, keyboard and speech
    communication, 177–183
working conditions, 175–188
working environment, 176–177
workstation design, 184–187
use of, 118, 157, 163, 164, 165, 166, 174,
    216
choice, 70, 88, 90, 93, 94
cohesiveness, 47, 81
colour coding, 58
commands, 42, 43, 46, 48, 49, 50, 54, 57, 60,
    61, 168
    checklist about, 190
commercial risks, 34
commitment (*see also* conflict), 26, 47, 64,
    71, 81, 84, 85, 114, 135, 140, 146–150,
    155, 162
communications , (*see also* social contact),
    8, 9, 11, 64, 65, 78, 81–83, 87, 89, 90, 92,
    93, 94–97, 143, 144
    checklists about, 219–221
    questionnaires about, 207, 218–219
company records, 5, 113, 158, 172–173
comparative testing, 26, 48, 54, 113, 157,
    158, 170–172, 189
compatibility, 8, 10, 11, 21, 25, 26–28, 34,
    56, 57, 92, 113
competitiveness, 32, 33, 72
computer-aided design, 37, 53
computer-based process-control system, 44
computer-controlled machine tools, 42

computerized information and control systems, 22, 94, 150
computerized medical records, 153
concepts, 42, 43, 44, 47, 58
    checklist about, 190–191
confidentiality, 115, 116, 118, 161
conflict (*see also* commitment), 20, 100, 101, 105, 106, 112, 114, 135, 141, 146–150, 152, 155
confusion errors, 42, 59
consultants, 1, 24, 90, 96, 99, 105, 109, 112, 113, 114, 139
consultation, 100, 105, 106, 147, 148, 150
control, of software, 9, 10, 41, 43, 48–50, 54
    checklist about, 192–193
control, user's, 5, 9, 26, 31, 64, 65–69, 71, 74, 84
    questionnaire about, 200–201
co-ordination, 91, 94, 101, 150
costs, 3, 20, 25, 27, 28, 29, 31, 32, 33, 66, 72, 75, 79, 84, 99, 107, 108, 109, 135, 138, 142–145, 151, 155, 171
cost effectiveness, 23, 27, 32
customization, 51
cryptographic techniques, 35

Data Protection Act, 1984, 34–35
data-bases, 23, 49, 51, 54, 55, 56, 67, 152, 154
data-entry programs, 49
data-processing departments, 34, 137
decision-making (*see also* bureaucracy), 82, 87, 89, 90, 91, 92–94, 96, 138, 154
    questionnaire about, 217–218
defects, 3,5
delays, 29, 56, 146, 154
demands, work, 8, 9, 11, 39, 40, 51, 64, 65, 68, 71, 74, 75–77, 81, 84, 99, 102, 147, 165
    questionnaire about, 203–204
demarcation, of work, 69, 78, 92, 93, 94, 100
depreciation, 33
deskilling, *see* skill
desktop publishing systems, 53, 164
diagnosis, *see* screening questionnaires
differentiation, organizational, 88, 89, 90, 96, 148
    questionnaire about, 216–217
discounted cash flow (DCF), 144–145
discretion, 8, 65, 66, 67, 68, 69, 84
displays and controls, 37, 57
documentation, 42, 44, 45, 47, 50, 54, 60, 61, 151, 155
    checklist about, 191–192
downtime, 29, 30, 72

education, *see* training
effectiveness, 1, 2, 3, 5, 8, 12, 28, 29, 31, 34, 41, 47, 48, 50, 67, 69, 74, 84, 85, 92, 103, 105, 111, 140, 147, 150, 164, 165

efficiency, 12, 112, 114, 172
effort, degree of, 11, 41, 51–54, 55
    checklist about, 193–194
electrical shock/electrocution, 37, 83
electronic mail, 52, 82, 95, 143, 144
employee representatives, 80, 106, 148, 155
enhancements, *see* upgrading of equipment
equipmental conditions, 36, 83
    checklist about, 176–177
errors and error correction, 8, 10, 11, 15, 28, 29, 30, 34, 41, 50, 58, 59–62, 65, 66, 72, 84, 111, 140, 166, 168, 172, 173
    checklist about, 197–198
errors, serious, 8, 9, 10, 41, 59, 62–63
evolution,
    managing, 110–114, 173
    basic methods of, 111, 113, 114–117
    specialist methods of, 113, 119, 157, 158–173
    principles of, 12–15, 110
eye strain, 37, 38, 74, 83, 84

Fair Labor Standards Act, 1938, 37
faults, 29, 31, 72
fault-tolerant, 29, 62
feedback, 9, 32, 44, 55, 65, 77, 78, 113, 162
    questionnaires about, 205
feelings, job-related,
    questionnaires about, 213
financial appraisal/assessment, 25, 33, 107, 108, 109, 135, 142–145, 151, 155
financial incentives, *see* pay
financial investment, 31, 33, 138, 144–145, 155, 173
financial return, 1, 25, 79, 145
flexibility, 42, 67, 72, 80, 85, 92, 93, 94, 101, 107, 108, 154
flexibile manufacturing systems, 89, 137, 144
formal observation, 54, 62, 113, 157, 158, 163, 164–166, 167, 168, 170, 171, 174, 189
formatting, 28
fraud, 34, 35
functionality, 23, 25, 26, 97
furniture, 38, 39

goals/objectives, 1, 3, 6, 12, 14, 15, 21–26, 27, 28, 32, 56, 72, 85, 86, 88, 90, 107–109, 110, 111, 114, 137–139, 142, 143, 148, 151, 154, 155
go back, 49, 60
graphics-based system, 46
greenfield sites, 148

harmonization of pay and conditions, 104, 148
hazards, physical, 37
    checklist about, 187
headache, 74, 83

health (*see also* safety, working conditions), 2, 9, 11 , 38, 39, 64, 65, 74, 83–84, 85, 101
 questionnaires about, 208–209
Health and Safety at Work Act, 1975, 37
Health and Safety Executive, UK, 37
hierarchy, 91, 92, 93, 94, 95, 148
home-working, 81
humidity, *see* air quality

icons, 44, 46
image, of company, 3, 138, 144
industrial relations, 9, 79, 87, 99, 100–102, 105, 139, 146, 151
 questionnaire about, 223–224
information, getting in and out, 8, 10, 11, 41, 57–59
 checklist about, 194–196
information-sharing, 27, 78, 82
infrastructure, *see* support, organizational
input devices, 58, 162
integration, organizational, 88, 89, 90
 questionnaires about, 216–217
intention to leave, 214
interactive computer systems, 72
interviews, 5, 19, 23, 41, 108, 110, 113, 114, 115–116, 118, 157, 158, 159, 164, 173, 174, 189, 199, 215

Japan, 71, 92, 98, 143
job evaluation (*see also* pay), 79, 80, 102, 103, 104, 105, 139, 148
 checklist about, 226–227
job identity/completeness, 74, 76
job loss, 9, 11, 77, 87, 99, 100, 101, 105–106, 149
 checklist about, 227–228
job redesign, 64, 82
 autonomous work groups, 68, 71
 job enrichment, 68, 71, 74, 77
 job rotation, 68, 74, 75, 77
job security, 101, 105, 106, 147
jump-ahead facilities, 43, 44
junk-mail, 95

keyboards, 22, 37, 38, 40, 57, 58, 74, 162
 checklist about, 177–183
 questionnaire about, 188
keystrokes, 51, 53
knock-on effects, 36, 51, 53, 54, 55, 56, 80, 81, 96, 144

learning, ease of, 7, 8, 9, 11, 41–48, 49, 60, 71, 98
 checklists about, 189–192
leasing, 33
left-over tasks, 70
lighting, 37, 38

machine-minders, 3, 4, 5, 6, 65
machine downtime, 3, 4, 5
macro-language, 51, 53, 54, 61
mainframe system, 22, 34
malfunction, 28
management, senior, 14, 21, 69, 82, 87, 98, 99, 109, 111, 112, 136, 137, 138, 139, 140, 146, 147, 150, 151, 157, 162
manuals, *see* documentation
manufacturing technology, 2, 3, 8, 42, 44, 63, 67, 72, 75, 83, 136, 150, 168, 172
maturity and obsolescence, 11, 21, 31–34
meetings, 19, 23, 41, 81, 82, 94, 97, 108, 110, 113, 114, 116, 157, 159, 162, 173, 174, 199, 215
memory load, 10, 51, 52, 54, 56, 59, 75
menus, 42, 44, 49, 50, 54
micro-computers, 28, 50, 95
milestones, 153, 154, 155
mock-ups, *see* prototypes
modes, 48, 49, 50, 59
morale, 4, 6, 9, 29, 48, 70, 76, 81, 87, 96, 106, 107–109, 144
 questionnaires about, 211–214, 230
motivation, 7, 42, 66, 71, 72, 73, 76, 77, 79, 85, 92, 99, 146
multi-skilling, 6, 101
multi-user systems, 34, 54, 56, 57, 62
muscular problems, 13, 37, 38, 73

negotiation, 101, 105, 106, 148, 149
net present value, *see* discounted cash flow
networks, 34, 93, 150
noise, 37, 38, 171

obsolescence, 21, 31–34
Occupational Safety and Health Act, 1970, 37
office automation, 26, 70, 75, 83
Offices, Shops and Railway Premises Act, 1963, 37
on-line help, 47, 49, 151
on-line training programs, 44, 47, 151
organizational culture, 68, 90
organizational structure, 8, 11, 73, 82, 87, 88–92, 97, 109, 137, 138, 139
 questionnaire about, 217–217
organizational style, 68
output, 5, 64, 65, 66, 77, 79, 85, 98, 143

pace, pacing, 67, 75, 76, 84
participation, 13, 14, 67, 140, 146–149, 150, 155, 162
password, 35, 36
pay (*see also* career progression), 9, 11, 64, 65, 72, 79–81, 84, 87, 100, 102–105, 139, 146, 147, 148, 149
 differentials, 79, 80, 101, 102, 148, questionnaires about, 206, 225

pay-back periods, 72, 107, 108, 138, 143, 145
performance, 1, 3, 4, 5, 6, 7, 15, 28, 31, 34,
    36, 64, 67, 68, 72, 76, 77, 78, 81, 84–86,
    87, 99, 100, 101, 107–109, 111, 112, 114,
    140, 143, 150, 162, 170, 171, 172, 199
  checklists about, 210–211, 228–230
personal computers, 22, 34
personnel function, 71, 73, 77, 98, 99, 140,
    146, 155
politics and political processes, 149, 155
power, 28, 69, 95, 96, 100, 147
pregnancies, 37
printers, 39, 57, 168
privacy, 34, 147
Privacy Act, 1974, 35
productivity, 2, 3, 4, 5, 6, 7, 8, 15, 66, 71,
    77, 79, 84, 85, 108, 111
profit-sharing, 104
progress review, 114, 135, 143, 145, 151,
    154, 155
project management, 139–142, 146, 147
promotion, 103
prototypes, 50, 59, 138, 147, 162, 164, 170,
    171, 172

quality, 2, 3, 4, 5, 6, 8, 27, 64, 65, 66, 67, 72,
    76, 77, 84, 85, 107, 108, 111, 138
quality control, 4, 5, 67, 68
questionnaires (*see also* screening
    questionnaires),
  about:
    attitudes, 211–214
    bureaucracy and decision-making,
        217–218
    communications, 218–219
    communications and social contact, 207
    control, users', 200–201
    demands, work, 203–204
    equipment, 187–188
    health and safety, 208–209
    intention to leave, 214
    job satisfaction, 211–212
    feelings, job-related, 213
    keyboards, 188
    morale, 211–214, 230
    organizational structure, 216–217
    pay, 206
    pay and career progression, 225
    skills, 202
    uncertainty, 205
    variety, 202–203
    VDUs, 188
  administration, 161
  design, 160
  interpretation, 161–162
  pilots, 160
  sampling, 161
  use of, 5, 113, 157, 158–162, 173, 174,
      199–200, 215

radiation, 37, 38
recruitment, 3, 6, 8, 68, 85, 98, 99, 151
redundancy, *see* job loss
reliability, 8, 9, 21, 28–31, 32, 34, 63, 69,
    140, 142
renting, 33
repairs, *see* reliability
repetition strain injury, 74
repetitive tasks, 73, 74, 75
replacement equipment, 29, 32, 33
requirements, 8, 10, 11, 20, 21–26, 27, 28,
    32, 85, 94, 135, 139–142, 143, 146, 151,
    155
response times, 54, 55, 56
responsibility, 2, 5, 6, 9, 65–69, 70, 102, 147
responsiveness, 138
return on investment, 3, 6, 15, 107, 140,
    143, 144–145, 150
Right to Financial Privacy Act, 1978, 35
robots, 30, 31, 107, 108, 135

safety (*see also* health, working conditions),
    9, 11, 37, 38, 39, 64, 65, 74, 83–84, 101
  questionnaires about, 208–209
satisfaction, job, 5, 7, 11, 64, 66, 70, 71, 76,
    79, 84, 95, 102
  questionnaire about, 211–212
screening questionnaires, (*see also*
    questionnaires),
  about:
    equipment and working conditions,
        120–122
    job quality and performance, 126–129
    organizational aspects and effectiveness,
        130–134
    usability, 123–126
  use of, 113, 117, 118, 119, 159
security, system, 10, 19, 21, 34–36
  checklist about, 174–175
selection (*see also* training), 9, 10, 11, 15,
    46, 68, 71, 73, 76, 87, 97–100, 151
  checklist about, 221–223
setting up, 5, 60, 61, 168
shift-working, 79, 80
shop stewards, 6, 136
simulation, 147
skill, 2, 4, 5, 6, 9, 10, 30, 31, 42, 45, 47, 48,
    64, 65, 66, 67, 68, 69–73, 74, 75, 78, 79,
    81, 85, 96, 97, 98, 99, 100, 101, 102, 137,
    142, 148, 162, 164
  questionnaire about, 202
social contact (*see also* communications),
    40, 64, 65, 81–83, 94
  questionnaire about, 207
sources of information,
    within the United Kingdom, 237–239
    within the United States, 239–240
specialization, 91, 103
speech communication,
    checklist, about, 177–183
speed, system, 8, 10, 22, 41, 54–57

spreadsheets, 43, 45, 51, 57, 153
staffing levels, 78, 142
standardization, 92, 93, 94, 138, 154
static electricity, 29, 38, 39
status, organizational, 101, 147
strategy, 12, 14, 20, 25, 27, 73, 86, 87, 90,
    107, 108, 111, 112, 135, 136–139, 147,
    148, 151, 153, 155
stress, 75, 76, 77, 83, 84, 106
suggestions scheme, 31
supervisors/supervision, 2, 4, 8, 22, 69, 78,
    89, 91, 98, 99, 170
supplies, 1, 3, 22, 25, 27, 30, 32, 33, 56, 112,
    114, 117, 137, 138, 140, 142, 152, 153,
    155, 168
support, organizational, 8, 20, 29, 30, 46,
    68, 69, 71, 73, 1 14, 135, 142, 143,
    150–151, 155
SWOT, 137
system logging, 31, 50, 54, 62, 113, 153, 158,
    167–168, 170, 171, 173
system walk-through, 26, 48, 50, 54, 59, 113,
    157, 162–164, 168, 170, 171, 173, 174,
    189

task analysis, 26, 48, 54, 59, 113, 158, 163,
    168–170, 171
technological determinism, 67
tele-sales, 54
temperature, 36, 37, 38, 83
throughput, 2, 3, 4, 5, 8, 67, 70, 168
trade union(s), 3, 4, 5, 6, 69, 80, 100, 101,
    103, 105, 106, 117, 135, 136, 146, 148
training (*see also* selection), 3, 5, 6, 8, 9, 10,
    11, 15, 30, 35, 38, 42, 44, 45, 46, 47, 48,
    61, 62, 70, 71, 73, 75, 76, 77, 78, 87, 92,
    96, 97–100, 105, 106, 138, 140, 142, 150,
    151, 153, 155, 168
    checklist about, 221–223
translators, 28
turnover, 2, 9, 84–85, 102, 108, 172
    questionnaire about, 214

uncertainty, 64, 77–78, 106, 147
    questionnaire about, 205
understanding, 77, 78, 149
undo, 49, 60
updated versions, 32, 33, 34
upgrading of equipment, 2, 11, 27, 151
upward compatibility, 32
user diaries, 5, 31, 54, 57, 63, 113, 158,
    166–167, 168, 170, 171, 173
user involvement, *see* participation
utilization, of machine/system, 5, 42, 66, 98,
    152, 172

variety, 9, 11, 13, 39, 64, 65, 68, 73–75, 81,
    84
    questionnaire about, 202–203
verbal protocols, 165
visual display unit (VDU), 27, 37, 38, 39,
    40, 44, 58, 74, 79, 81, 83
    checklist about, 177–183
    questionnaire about, 188

word processing, 7, 13, 28, 42, 43, 48, 53,
    111, 112, 139, 153
working conditions (*see also* health, safety),
    7, 8, 9, 11, 21, 36, 74, 83, 100, 102
    checklists about:
    hazards, physical, 187
    VDU, keyboard and speech
      communication, 177–183
    working environment, 176–177
    workstation design, 184–187
    questionnaires about:
    keyboards, 188
    VDUs, 188
working parties, 4, 5, 19, 23, 41, 85, 108,
    109, 110, 113, 114, 116–117, 118, 147,
    157, 162, 173, 174, 199, 215
workstation design, 38
    checklist about, 184–187